TRACEE DUNBLAZIER

TRANSFORMATIVE
GRIEF

An Ancient Ritual of Healing
for Modern Times

REDFeather™
MIND | BODY | SPIRIT

4880 Lower Valley Road, Atglen, PA 19310

Cover design by Brenda McCallum
Type set in New Hero/ Minion

Yin Yang Symbol Sticker Image © by rawpixel.com on Freepik
Native American Sun symbol vector icon in simple outline style © DizTiknonov. Courtesy of www.bigstockphoto.com
WU XING China 5 elements of nature circle icon sign © beginos. Courtesy of www.bigstockphoto.com
Illustration of woman falling underwater © fran_kie. Courtesy of www.shutterstock.com

ISBN: 978-0-7643-6631-4
Printed in China

Published by REDFeather Mind, Body, Spirit
An imprint of Schiffer Publishing, Ltd.
4880 Lower Valley Road
Atglen, PA 19310
Phone: (610) 593-1777; Fax: (610) 593-2002
E-mail: Info@redfeathermbs.com
Web: www.redfeathermbs.com

For our complete selection of fine books on this and related subjects, please visit our website at www.redfeathermbs.com. You may also write for a free catalog.

REDFeather Mind, Body, Spirit's titles are available at special discounts for bulk purchases for sales promotions or premiums. Special editions, including personalized covers, corporate imprints, and excerpts, can be created in large quantities for special needs. For more information, contact the publisher.

We are always looking for people to write books on new and related subjects. If you have an idea for a book, please contact us at proposals@schifferbooks.com.

FSC
www.fsc.org
MIX
Paper
FSC® C017606

...

"Tracee Dunblazier GC-C with the American Academy of Grief Counseling has presented to the grieving world both personal and academic an excellent and thorough text on grieving....Ultimately, Dunblazier looks to unlock the mystery of grief and help individuals properly face grief and loss in a healthy way. Understanding that grief, loss and dying and death are parts of life itself in an imperfect world is a critical element of her work."

—Mark Moran, MA, GC-C Assistant Executive Director AIHCP

...

Tracee Dunblazier's marvelous book *Transformative Grief: An Ancient Ritual of Healing for Modern Times* ... is poignant, educational, and uplifting. I happened to be dealing with the death of my father while I read it, and I thought she was there in the house with us. She detailed exactly what I was going through, as well as what I perceived my father was, too. Her description of the process of grief and dying matched up with our experience completely, and it helped me manage my feelings before, during, and after my father's passing. The personal stories and first-person accounts she quotes are stunning in their beauty and powerful in their honesty. Truly, this is a book I'll be referring to for years to come: to help me process my feelings around death and to allow those feelings to move me forward into a higher spiritual healing place. If you are mourning the death of a family member or friend from either an expected or unexpected death, or if you're just grieving for the state of the world and the trying times we live in, this is the book for you. Allow it to transform those feelings into an unforeseen state of grace and peace.

—Stephen J. Miller, bestselling author of *Keepers of Mana 'an*

...

...

Tracee Dunblazier has written a must-read primer for anyone involved in the process of grief…Read this book—and learn from one of the best. In this personal book, Ms. Dunblazier writes to outfit you with a new way of seeing and experiencing the journey of loss. Her book, *Transformative Grief: An Ancient Ritual of Healing for Modern Times*, tells us that there is a gift of magic that grief brings. I recommend you read the book to find out why.

—Debbi Dachinger, award-winning *Dare to Dream* podcast host,
    4x international bestselling author

...

I absolutely believe that grief is a teacher that can help us live fuller lives, and this book illustrates all of this and so much more. For anyone wrestling with grief, or if you know someone who is going through the depths of suffering from loss, this powerful book will bring peace and healing. Highly recommended!

—Stephanie Chandler, CEO Nonfiction Authors Association and
    Writers Conference

...

Grief is so often ignored or avoided in modern society, to everyone's detriment. Tracee gently yet courageously faces it head-on and leads the reader through their trauma, loss, and grieving to the empowerment and understanding that awaits them on the other side. This isn't surface level; this book takes you right down to the root. *Transformative Grief: An Ancient Ritual of Healing for Modern Times* is full of anecdotes and personality, as well as hands-on work, that every person can benefit from in their life. This book is a must-read for any counselor or spiritual advisor and should be in every practitioner's toolkit!

—Alex Fernandez, spiritual Practitioner and owner of Hearthside
    Candles & Curios

...

•••

I'll tell you what I deeply appreciate about *Transformative Grief: An Ancient Ritual of Healing for Modern Times*: I believe the author. I, like everyone, have dealt with a lot of grief over the years, and many of the people who write about it and what to do with it give me a form of the creeps—but not this author. When others speak about this subject and related ones, I sometimes feel like they are just adding to the voices trying to tell me to "get over it" but dressing that up in spiritual language. Tracee Dunblazier gets the difference between "processing" and "denial."

My work as a writer tends to deal with other fields: music; mythology; classics—but there's a no-nonsense foundation to Tracee's work that makes me see the commonalities between all these fields. She acknowledges that this stuff is not easy, and you can't solve the gut-wrench just by waving stones in the air. Some confrontation will be necessary—but ultimately liberating. And the suggested actions for working toward that do not feel like denial at all. In fact, she even says things that remind me of one of my greatest mentors, the philosopher and classicist Norman O. Brown. He said at the end of *Life Against Death*—that the whole point of the journey he had laid out was so people in the future might be able to see what not even Freud could see: in the old Enemy, a Friend. The transformation Tracee works with is beyond personal… it is a transformation of grief itself.

—William Berger, radio commentator for the Metropolitan Opera
and author of *Seeking the Sublime Cache: Opera Articles Selected and Written by William Berger*

•••

•••

This book is a grief game changer.

Just. Wow. A book which truly offers what its big title claims. This is Tracee Dunblazier's, *Transformative Grief*.

In the Mind, Body, Spirit and Health and Wellness worlds of publishing, books about grief are a dime a dozen. The sales buzz words are always highlighted on the cover— "it's easy," "3 small steps to…," or "this proven method…." These books are designed to sell, sell, sell rather than heal and transform. And then there's Tracee's book, *Transformative Grief: An Ancient Ritual of Healing for Modern Times*.

A more comprehensive tome on the topic of healing and grief you'd be hard-pressed to find. Her book is clearly meant to help people think differently about grief and healing, no matter what type of heartache they are experiencing. Whether in yourself or someone else, you'll discover aspects to grief included that you may not have recognized as grief.

Also clear, is how personally committed Tracee is to helping others through the most difficult and painful times of their life. She presents a wide variety of exercises and rituals for using grief to transform ourselves through the renewed perspective and decision making that comes through grieving—guiding us into a state of peace, grace, and love.

Transformative Grief is a grief game changer. It's the book I wish I'd had when my mom was killed. But I have it now and twenty-five years after mom's death Tracee's book is transforming me. I'm betting it can do the same for you.

—Bernadette King, author of *The Ark Animal Tarot & Oracle Deck*

•••

...

Author and spiritual empath Tracee Dunblazier's *Transformative Grief: An Ancient Ritual of Healing for Modern Times* is an eloquent, straight-forward lighthouse for anyone lost in the deep waters of grief. Sourcing from her professional and personal experience, she illuminates the inward decent of grief as an opportunity for deeper self-awareness and personal empathy. Through poignant exercises and introspective guidelines, the reader is guided toward navigating the depths of their grief and emerging a more conscious and heart-open soul. A master guidebook for anyone going through extraordinary change.

—Austyn Wells, author of *Soul Conversations: A Medium Reveals How to Cultivate Your Intuition, Heal Your Heart, and Connect with the Divine*

...

"Transformative Grief is an extraordinary book full of healing light, important insights, ancient wisdom and spiritual guidance to help each of us to compassionately transform our entire being and to improve our life path. Tracee Dunblazier is an expert that truly guides the reader to a path of emotional and spiritual wellbeing – leading us back to our heart center in the most authentic and natural way. A must read for anyone wanting to heal from deep seated grief, emotional turmoil, unconscious guilt and shame; yet also as a sacred way to truly transform our consciousness to let in more light, truth and awareness. A very necessary book at this exact moment in time to uplift, bless, and serve humanity for the good of all and for evolution of the soul."

—Joanne Brocas, Author of Clear Spirit: The Life-Changing Power of Energy Clearing

...

CONTENTS

NINE

TEN

I DEDICATE THIS BOOK TO THE GREAT OCEANS OF PLANET EARTH AND THE AFRICAN ORISHA: OLOKUN. Olokun governs the bottom of the ocean, from whom all things are created and to whom all things will find their home again in the loving arms of the ocean floor.

Like grief, the ocean is an unfathomable abyss of which only a small percentage has been discovered. It carries the secrets of our history, our sustenance, and our future. It shares the depth of our burdens, the bounty of our fruitfulness, and the weight of our human folly. Like grief, with ruthless compassion, time-and-again it offers us second chances to make pristine choices and emerge anew from the rubble of our old ways. Ache'

WHAT IS TRANSFORMATIVE GRIEF?

Transformative grief is the mechanism we use to cause real change on all levels in our selves—it transforms our energy patterns and habits, it causes healing to the physical body, it releases emotion and memory, it inspires new beliefs and ideals, and it cultivates our relationship to wisdom and the Divine. I know you're thinking, "Well why didn't you just say that? I've been suffering all this time." Our suffering (grief) is the way the body culls what is necessary for its survival, and releases what is not. That release must take place in every layer of our energy body (aura) and physical body, to cause the Divine body to connect and awaken the new information we carry in each of our organs. This awakening shifts the old information and causes the healing, transformation, and integration everyone will experience in their human development.

Now, I know you may have heard the first stages of grief are shock and denial (cooking/eating, cleaning obsessively, fixing every little broken thing in your home, or other controlling behaviors), but an individual will have their own unique response to a loss based on the circumstances and gravity the loss has in their lives—the process ultimately ending in tears. Traditionally, we think of grief as the emotional crying we do in response to loss, but in fact it is the selection process we use to let go of any outdated information we have and prepare ourselves for the inevitable new awakening that will take its place. Grief has many forms and will occur, in part or in whole, during every transition we experience. It is surely a friend, not foe.

The act of crying for ten minutes or more, not only changes neurons in the brain, but it awakens our sacred imprints and information when we are most ready for them, at different intervals in our lives. It is why babies cry so much when they are born and for the first year, and why mother's cry so often during pregnancy. A baby is connecting with the Divine and activating the new information it will need to live in the physical world, and a mother is calling upon her empathy, and all the new ways she will need to think, intuit, and behave to be the fiduciary of this new being, and herself. When we see mothers and babies grieve, we don't feel bad or see them as weak, we see the experience as natural and powerful.

However, we still perpetuate a culture where when we see young children (especially boys) and adults cry we judge them. . . and so the attempts at reprogramming begin. It has been because of these multiple attempts to culturally reprogram our bodies and minds to avoid grief, that the real obstacles to wisdom and healing have occurred—and their subtle ripples live on today. Every time we choke back tears, scold ourselves or others for being too emotional, or make efforts to use physical activity to delay the emotional process, we reaffirm to ourselves that we are not worthy of what the Creator is seeking to give us—the new seeds of wisdom for our transformation, and the courage and permission to make whatever changes are necessary for our transition.

I am an Empath (a person who takes on the mental, emotional, or spiritual understanding of another), and as such, I cried every day for the first fifty years of my life. It wasn't a choice; it was just how it was. In my early years, my mother was deeply frustrated with my emotionalism. She would scream and yell at me all the time because I was speaking a language she didn't understand. I think, on subtle levels, she was resentful of my freedom to feel because it had been drummed out of her early on in childhood.

Another thing our culture of stoicism does, is connect high emotion with mental wellness or mental illness. In my story, a grandparent on both sides of my family had mental issues, but the stigma that went along with them in the 1920's–50's was prohibitive of any real assistance or healing. It was no surprise to me that my mother was taught to buck-up or suffer the consequences, as the consequences may have been anything from being isolated in an asylum to receiving a frontal lobotomy. I, however, was never going to be able to achieve buck-up status. It wasn't in my nature, and my spiritual needs forbade it.

The beautiful thing about my relationship to my mother, Audrey, is that we understood each other on profound levels. She trusted me and I didn't judge her. Together, we offered one another what we most needed, but would individually struggle to get for ourselves. Audrey had the emotional integrity of a saint. She may have occasionally suffered through anger, from the peripheral waves of emotion on the surface, but deep down she was still water. I was able to contribute understanding—ever since I came out of the womb, at seven months, I had the spirit of knowing. I think this gave my mother a sense of security that I could always take care of myself if need be.

For every expression of grief I indulged, my inner wisdom was activated. It would awaken in me memories of pure devastation, along with sheer power. The message from Creator was always clear to me: with the gift of your raw power comes ultimate responsibility and consequence. For me, crying was always the stopgap that would drain my rage through tears, forcing my body to relinquish its deepest karmic memories of trauma to receive a life of peace and prosperity.

There are no words that truly convey our cosmic need for and relationship to the process of grief, but with every word in this book I will do my best to explain the power that lies within and is given its first breath in this world through our grief. I will offer the antidote to our cultural resistance of grief and show you many times over how others and myself have used their pain as a direct channel to the Divine and emerged with a clear, concise vision of what was to come next.

Traditionally, there is a neutral demeanor and viewpoint expected of counselors and educators on grief. We are expected to be non-judgmental, and non-religious in our vantages of grief, death, and dying, and to offer a person a listening ear for their pain. Whatever a person walks into a session believing about death, and the afterlife, is not my job to change. I am charged with facilitating each client in their own understanding.

As I said, I am an Empath; thusly, the majority of my viewpoint on grief has been accrued over a lifetime and informed by my experiences. Secondarily, I am a certified grief counselor, which was born out of the recognition that almost all my spiritual counselling clients were grieving in some way, about something. I found, as an Empath, that I attracted clientele to my practice who needed to grieve. If they were uncomfortable or unable to surrender the grief they felt, naturally I would take it on and share in their tears. It is in respect for the many years I have of feeling the grief of others, that I affectionately call myself a professional griever. While I practiced different forms of Christianity in my early childhood and spent a good portion of my adult life studying many world religions, my views are spiritual in nature.

Almost all the information you'll find here is acceptable to the major religions and can be interpreted congruent to religious beliefs. Even my spiritual recollections of my own past lives, and my mediumship work with souls in the spirit world do not require your belief in these things to receive the teachings on grief. Having a different belief than I, will not diminish the understanding nor the explanations of grief you'll find within. However, my vision, education, and voice are needed for every individual to be represented by a viewpoint of grief that aligns with them and their spiritual leanings. In many cultures there exists extreme resistance to life after death, or the sacredness of the grief process, and it is for this reason, and for all people, that I write this book.

We must now be able to parse out an understanding of grief and spiritual transformation that is not lumped in with mental illness. There are many levels and phases of grief that are temporal but not experienced by everyone, therefore not considered normal. We, collectively, must begin to expand our thinking, understanding, and practice of grief in order to meet the mental, emotional, and spiritual challenges of the twenty-first century. There can be no illness, where there is spiritual flow.

The more we allow the transformative process of grief to guide our lives, the more we connect with every level of ourselves and the environment we live in. Imagine if every department of our government communicated or had access to every piece of intelligence garnered by another? Well, it would become obvious which departments work for us, against us, and with us. Grief has the same affect. It divulges to you, which aspects of yourself work for, against or with you. It requires you to change and shows you the best path to stability. It is your inner vision becoming outer sight. Grief is the mercy of the Creator being bestowed upon you in your most receptive moment, and it is your crying-up-to-the-heavens to your one true love. It is the stone and the chisel you will use throughout your life to reveal your greatest work of art—you.

FUN FACT ABOUT GRIEF

When you want to cry, "lean in". Going with the flow of the tears will render your eyes less puffy when you are finished.

Over the years of processing profound emotion, I have used affirmations, herbs and incense burning, candle lighting, holistic natural medicine, and crystals and minerals within weekly rituals to help me work through my grief. The consistent spiritual practice of ritual brought me the understanding and forgiveness that was needed to heal my heart and mind, and offered the space to recover physically from any healing crisis (physical symptoms brought on by extreme emotional changes) through which my body was being prepared for necessary changes the grief revealed.

The practice of any ritual (or religion) helps one to cultivate their own relationship to their deepest self-knowing. There is a need for conscious connection to the Creator and the cultivating of a "desire to know" that supports the emotional process of becoming aware of yourself and your environment. Performing any task with this intent helps us to connect to all who have come before us, seeking enlightenment or change, and inevitably leads us to the path of empowerment and compassion.

It is in this spirit, I offer a ritual at the end of each chapter to deepen your awareness in all the ways you need at this time. You'll find I have made suggestions of flower remedies to use, but you are welcome to substitute other options and brands you may prefer. You are especially encouraged to make these rituals your own as you go along. I have written the rituals to educate and inspire you to innovate and create your own process.

FOREWORD BY NICHOLAS PEARSON

Grief is a strange thing. It is something each of us experiences throughout the ups and downs of life. Culturally, we are predisposed to recognize the big grief-responses that accompany loss, like the death of a loved one or the loss of a career, but there are other kinds of grief. Each has a way of getting inside us and taking root, often without our being fully aware; in today's world, so full of large-scale tragedy, our unconscious sadness builds until it threatens to make inner peace a blurry memory from the far-distant past.

In my own life, I've felt the pangs of intense emotions that come from many sources. Some of those have been white-hot grief that threatened to eat me alive, while others were little things that piled atop one another until they demanded my attention, spilling over to other parts of my psyche. Grief, as it grows within the heart, transforms us from the inside out, whether we are conscious of it or not. Some of my own transformations accompanied this kind of pervasive grieving. The loss of my paternal grandparents—and the accompanying changes in our family dynamic—have changed the way I relate to the world in a fundamental way. Similarly, leaving behind a degree in music also planted a seed of grief, a wild one that pops up in unexpected ways even though it's one of the best and most fulfilling decisions I've ever made in my life. Grief comes from both good and bad, easy and difficult, transitions in our lives.

When Tracee reached out to me about Transformative Grief: An Ancient Ritual of Healing for Modern Times, I couldn't wait to peruse the manuscript. Too many times we think of grief as a mountain that must be climbed or a monster to be vanquished. Tracee, however, introduces grief as an intimate ally and teacher—a spiritual tool that helps us enact deep healing and spiritual growth. She gives us a tour of the potential hidden within and beyond grief, demonstrating the ways it can invite self-reflection and drive inner and outer transformation.

Tracee combines her many gifts to craft a lucid and effective manual for navigating grief of all strains. She discusses the everyday grief that slowly compounds, and she offers us remedies to counteract it. Tracee's words weave a map through the territories of injury and illness, loss, mourning, and death. She shines a much-needed light on the timely topic of transpersonal grief, broaching the subjects of generational grief and cultural trauma to help us all during a period marked by systemic injustice and uncertainty.

From the outside, Transformative Grief: An Ancient Ritual of Healing for Modern Times seems like a valuable addition to any self-help library, but truthfully this book is so much more. It contains secret formulas for transformation coded within simple exercises of meditation, mindfulness, prayer, and self-inventory. Like a medieval alchemist, Tracee reveals the method of transmutation. She shows us how the leaden pain of loss can be transubstantiated into the luminous, golden light of inner peace through the process of grieving consciously. In every chapter you'll find solace in her empathetic, compassionate prose born out of lived experience. Case studies and vignettes from her clients illustrate her theses about the transformational nature of grief, but the real gem—the veritable philosopher's stone—held within these pages consists of the collection of rituals found in each chapter. Tracee offers tangible praxes that draw from a toolbox that feels familiar, comfortable, and magical to me: flower essences, crystals, botanicals, candles, and other simple-but-potent tools. Ritual offers us structure; it marks rites of passage big and small and celebrates the crossing of thresholds between the ordinary and extraordinary. Use these guided rituals to create simple altars or lush tableaus as focal points and sacred spaces where you can ritualize your grieving, your healing, and your transformation.

The world continues to change before our eyes, moving at an unprecedented pace. It's easy to get caught up in the stride as numbness and apathy swell within. Now, more than ever, it's necessary to invoke the blessings of mindfulness, ritual, and self-care so we can grieve intentionally, embracing the transformation that comes when we do, lest we forget to know grief as the ally it can be. My sincerest hope is that Transformative Grief: An Ancient Ritual of Healing for Modern Times will help you experience all your emotions as a radical, alchemical tool to help you change within and without.

Nicholas Pearson, Author of Crystal Basics and Flower Essences from the Witch's Garden

May 2022

GRIEF: THE ETERNAL WELL
UNDERSTANDING THE NATURE OF GRIEF

When I consider grief, I think of music: the melody that gives us context, the treble notes that remind us of possibilities, and the rhythm section that keeps life moving on, endlessly. Grief can be played with all these notes, but the vibration of life that folks avoid the most is the bass line. Those deep, sultry, dark-thumping notes that draw out of us our deepest feelings and desires to be reckoned in the light of day. The way you relate to music will surely give you some insight on how you embrace grief.

Do you avoid it at all costs? Do you overtalk right past your feelings? Do you work endless hours? Do you "keep things light" and focus on the subtle ebbs and flows of the day? All these forms of dodging your grief, until the night arrives, finally bringing you the solace of sleep? You are not alone. Many of us naturally resist grief on the basis of our family dynamic, culture, or mental, emotional, spiritual, or physical condition. We may have been shown or taught that grief makes us weak, ineffective, or selfish. We may believe that our grief is a portal to endless pain that will eventually go away if we wait it out. We may be encouraged not to "get upset" for fear of an escalating physical or emotional condition.

On the other hand, you may be well versed in the emotional highs and lows that grief can take you through. Comfortable with the tears and anxiety you feel as you contemplate life without what you are losing—the anger that overtakes you in brief fits of rage. The adjusting and concessions you negotiate with yourself as you recognize all the life you wanted to have with what you are losing. There are numerous fluctuations within the process of grief, and they will inform your body, heart, and mind in waves of change, at different times.

Take a moment to acknowledge your current understanding and beliefs around grief, and where they may have originated. It is paramount, when making a change, to have a solid comprehension of where you have been and where you are, so that you may receive where you are to go next. **Contemplate your answers to these questions:**

Do I consider grief?

What do I think grief is?

What do I know about grief?

Am I comfortable feeling big emotions?

Have I witnessed other family members grieving?

How did that make me feel?

Did anyone ever talk to me or teach me about grief?

Have I ever grieved a loss?

How do we express grief in my family?

How do we express grief in my culture?

THE PROCESS OF GRIEF

What we believe about grief informs all our systems. At first, our thoughts and beliefs will tell our mind it is out of control; our body: it is sick; our heart: it is crushed, never to be revived. All this because at times, this is how grief feels. The process of grief is essentially a spiritual process of changing from one condition to another, one awareness to another, one set of circumstances to another, or one perspective to another, and there is no absolute timing or order to this transformative process because it exists on multiple levels all the time. Our relationship to loss then becomes our relationship to change—simple or complex.

The Kübler-Ross model[1] postulates that those experiencing grief go through a series of five emotions: denial, anger, bargaining, depression, and acceptance. Over the last several decades, culturally, we have expanded our thinking to recognize that grief isn't only an experience we have when someone dies, but it includes other major losses as well, and that there are not only five phases but seven.

My understanding of grief is that it is far more than five or seven linear phases, but that it moves in an all-encompassing circular motion transmuting and changing our relationships to everything it touches—in a powerful and life-affirming way. My idea of **Transformative Grief** aims to expand the understanding of grief to embrace that we grieve for every change we experience (good or bad), and that this grief exists for all of us, on some level all the time—because we are always making some transition—large or small. All this, despite our relationship to death.

---

1 (Kübler-Ross 1970)

Integrating an understanding of the spiritual process of change allows for a deeper relationship with ourselves and our emotions, beliefs, and patterns that informs how we create space for the release of whatever energy is no longer needed, and how we open to receive the energy that is most valuable at the time. Because we are continually going through some change in one dimension or another—physically, emotionally, mentally, or spiritually—it becomes clear that grief is the way we transform and integrate who we are on every level of our being. It is a natural part of our growth and development.

The anatomy of change

My anatomy of change has less to do with loss but more to do with our awareness of a transition and our relationship to that change, at any given time. There is a rhythm to our awareness of this process that is recognizable by the following dynamic phases.

"The Anatomy of Change: The Seven Elements of Spiritual Process"

[An excerpt from my book **Heal Your Soul History: Activate the True Power of Your Shadow**][2]

Like everything, the dynamic of change is multi-dimensional, and the more deeply we understand the specific steps involved in what it means to transition from one position to another in every way we experience the world, the more confidence we have in engaging fully in those changes. In the seven elements of spiritual process outlined here, there are seven markers of awareness that you will traverse in any transition. Like grief this process is circular not linear as it is always in constant motion, some elements overlapping as we process the modifications, we are constantly making to ourselves and our ways and means. Note if you recognize any of them from your experience.

Ignorance *is the phase of spiritual process where we start to become aware of the impending change in our lives, seeing it happening to others around us or noticing it in our thoughts, feelings, and environment. However, we don't feel it applies to us, so we ignore it. Pay attention to your thoughts and what you notice: thinking that it doesn't apply to you is a signal that you should pay more attention. Ignorance is different from denial: in denial there is no conscious acceptance of what is happening, whereas in ignorance you have awareness of the dynamic but don't apply it to yourself.*

---

2   (Dunblazier, Heal Your Soul History: Activate the True Power of Your Shadow, 2017)

Resistance *is the phase of spiritual process where now the evidence of the change is connecting to our conscious mind through extreme negativity or avoidance. Resistance is often signified by phrases or thoughts like, "I'd never do that" or "That person is so (fill in the blank)." Whatever you are recognizing through a negative perspective or your judgement of others indicates the change that is beginning in your life.*

Conflict/Struggle *is the phase of spiritual process where we start to engage the possibility of the change, and in preparation we will begin to adopt new philosophies that will support the change. We then begin to release old belief systems, people, circumstances, or things that do not support the transition.*

Surrender *is the phase of spiritual process that witnesses a release of the old pattern, person, place, or thing, and experiences a discomfort or lack of understanding of what will be taking its place.*

Choice *is the phase of spiritual process when a decision is made, or action taken that makes a significant, irrevocable transformation. Although any decision made can be changed, you can never un-know what you have learned from the process.*

Humor *is the phase of spiritual process that helps us detach from the old ways and open to a new experience, feeling, or idea. Objectivity through jokes and humor allow us to explore thoughts and feelings about our circumstances without fear. This phase can also bring sensation and perspective that is so foreign to the self they border on the absurd—a feeling that is beyond the expected and sometimes indescribable. At times, a sense of levity we receive in place of the burden that was once there. Humor is the bridge that guides us into a more liberated viewpoint and way of life.*

Completion *is the phase of spiritual process where the new ideas integrate and manifest in the physical realm. They can manifest as wisdom and understanding, emotional breakthrough, a change in philosophy or beliefs, or receiving something in the real world. Completion is the time when all questions have been answered and one can truly move on to the next phase. Completion can take years depending on what is being processed, it means we have moved through the dynamic on all levels. Keep in mind, it is our multidimensional nature to be able to process many things at the same time.*

THE PURPOSE OF GRIEF

The purpose of grief is to deepen your relationship to yourself and broaden your awareness of the world you live in. Grieving changes your perspective of all things, but especially yourself. Once you begin to grieve away the layers of illusion and confusion inherent in loss, a biochemical cascade of hormones is released by the heart and other glands that create a sense of clarity, peace, and well-being.

When you grieve—whether you laugh, scream, or cry—do it loudly with purpose. Crying for ten minutes or more actually changes the brain. It erases neurons (old memories or beliefs) and creates space for new ideas to be populated by your neural circuitry, ultimately sending new emotional signals and responses to everything you do and changing your brains chemistry.

Over my fifty years of grieving daily (as an Empath), many of those years, my constant running thought was *When will this end?* It was tiring and at times difficult to recover from. The blown-up, puffy eyes and exhaustion became a feat to overcome. Sometimes, I didn't recognize myself in the mirror. However, a pattern began to emerge. Once the weariness lifted, a clarity and joy took over. I was no longer easily triggered from the loss, or the dynamic in my life it represented. I had a fresh perspective, objectivity, and many "ah-ha" moments. I even found it easier to get to the humor in any situation.

It is easy to overlook grief as a nuisance and misunderstand the deep transformative power it has, but grief will scrub the mind, body, and spirit of outdated information and emotion. It paves the way for your next level of truth and understanding, all the while creating a new foundation of wisdom from which to live. Some losses we will endure for a lifetime, but through grief, most will be transformed into something completely different and more useful, over time.

My longest and best friend, Nanci, was also my neighbor. We grew up together from my first year of life. Every member of her family was brilliant, which also rendered them somewhat uncommon in the neighborhood. While both our families did what they could to remain as conventional looking as possible, I always felt at home with Nanci and her family.

I can't say exactly at what point I knew there was something "different," because my family was always labeled "eccentric," having lots of characteristics that at times I felt were undesirable, and definitely uncommon. I was the fourth child, unplanned, and followed years behind my three siblings. They were often assigned secondary supervision, after Mom, so Dad was a hands off disengaged father.

He was extremely intelligent, worked in the science and technology industry for the government on complex projects, and spent most of his time engaged in his reading, work, model building, and other introverted activities, including photography. He stayed occupied in the "den," which was lined with books, model airplanes, and other collections, along with a wall covered in his degrees and awards. It is here where I would spend my time with him, one on one, having deep conversations. It was during these moments I would notice the small differences about him.

Early in childhood, things I would observe struck me in a way I couldn't communicate, like the fact his nails were beautifully round, smooth, and clean compared to my brother's, or even mine. As time went on, and I got older, I'd note that it looked like his legs were shaved, but didn't want to look too closely. I didn't always know how to register that kind of stuff. Were those women's pajama pants and a woman's robe he was wearing?

I'm not exactly sure when or how I was told about the cross-dressing. I just know it was the word used to describe the odd behavior I would ask my mother about. (It was the 1970s.) I could talk with her about anything. I'm sure I didn't feel safe asking my siblings. I can't say if it was because I felt they wouldn't be honest with me, and I couldn't trust them? In general, I didn't. I am certain at the time, I knew they did not approve of any of it, so my siblings did not feel like a safe source of information.

Mom would explain that he liked to "experiment" and "experience" what it was like to adopt feminine aspects of appearance. Sometimes, he might try makeup, or jewelry, or clothing, or hair, etc., and that this was known as "cross-dressing," because it was "crossing lines" of expected behavior of dressing. She also explained that he never really had a mother, because she died when he was only three years old of breast cancer. And that due to her illness, she never really held him as a child, so this was a way he tried to connect to the lost mother he never had.

By the time I was twelve, my siblings had all left for college. A "library" had been added onto the back of the house, an expansive room to replace the outgrown den with glass doors to better shut out the rest of the house. During this time, my father began to feel freer walking around and through our home adorned with more aspects of his cross-dressing. For example, he might be wearing ladies' "short" shorts, with the shaved legs and polished toes. He would wear women's loafers or sandals, and women's polyester pants instead of men's, more consistently introducing new things into his ritual.

—Nanci M.

Children are deeply perceptive and highly intuitive; they pick up on the subtle vibrations of information but struggle to make sense of its meaning and communicate their feelings about it. How does a child make sense of the rift between the development of their siblings and their own; a mother's deep compassion for her husband; a society's rejection and judgment of a new understanding of gender; and their own confusion about needing to compete with their father's feminine expression?

It was just after Christmas, and my dad had once again avoided attending a 30-day mandatory alcohol rehabilitation program required to keep his job. My siblings were temporarily home for the holidays, and Dad was in his classic worst form of dysfunctional, ugly, drunk. My older siblings pressured Mom to confront him about it, and we all sat down in the family library to do just that.

During the heated discussion, he decided to look straight at me, the youngest person, and I assume the safest person in the room at that time, and shouted, "And, you know I'm a transvestite too!" Which, no, I didn't understand it at all. Because, at that age, I didn't know that word. It was scary, and I didn't understand all that rage coming at me. I thought it was something new to deal with; he was drunk, and everyone was very upset. It took awhile to reconcile that pronouncement with my understanding of his "cross-dressing." Oh . . . then I got it.

In high school, I became particularly resentful of my father's cross-dressing behavior as I was struggling to find my own identity. I didn't have a sense of my own style or a strong peer group and didn't speak about my father to anyone. I'd come home to bags of Newport News, Sears, and other mail order catalog delivery bags and shoe boxes arriving for dad, in his name, on the porch after school, and drag them in the house. It seemed to just increase in volume particularly one spring. It never seemed to occur to my parents that I needed clothes too.

One day, I was struggling to put together an outfit. As I ran out of clothes to toss around my room, I decided to march down the hall, and explore his closet. "That will teach him to, maybe, think of me next time he's shopping. Especially when he sees me wearing his clothes," I thought. So, I found a big pink sweater. Perfect. I belted it, with some leggings. And knew it was going to make a statement. Next thing I knew, I overheard him bragging about it to my mother! "I noticed Nanci really liked my pink sweater, and it looked so good on her." Ugh. I was furious. And I let him know how I felt.

Looking back, by my high school graduation, I had my own eccentricities. I wore heavy makeup, big hair, and loud clothes. I was a big fan of heavy-metal music and dressed accordingly. My standard go-to outfit became rock T-shirts, studded wristbands, and a leather jacket. Perhaps I was just trying to be louder than my dad, so no one would notice him . . .
—Nanci M.

Nanci's father named his alter (feminine self) Janet, and after the "big reveal" when Nanci was twelve, her relationship with her father changed dramatically. They would pass in the hall in silence, and as he began to focus more on himself as Janet, she never knew who would be home when she got there. Although her father did stop drinking for a while, the world outside still had no idea about Janet.

Nanci couldn't have friends over, nor could they just drop by for fear that Janet would be home in a dress and heels. I remember being about ten years old and hanging with Nanci and her dad in the library. I subliminally took note of his smooth shaved legs and the white terry cloth short shorts he was wearing. But most memorably, I was sitting on the floor near the chair he was in, and as he crossed his leg over the other, he slid his hip down toward the end of the chair, exposing his flank, like a very confident woman would do when she wanted to be noticed.

Other than that, I hadn't been witness to Janet, and it wasn't until our late twenties when Nanci and I first spoke about her father and Janet. Hearing it said out loud settled something for me; it was like a piece of the puzzle was put in its place. Nanci, however, spent a lifetime managing her feelings and grieving the father she didn't have, and accepting the one she did.

All the while, Nanci was trying to find ways to handle a society that did not yet have an open-hearted place for her father and Janet. Over the course of decades, she would revisit her childhood to grieve and reinterpret her relationship to multiple dynamics as they would rise up into her conscious view, elements such as dignity, gender bias, shame, competition, other people's opinions, rejection, judgment, self-importance, confidence, sexuality, sexual orientation, and communication, to name a few.

Life was unpredictable. That was what was so hard. Who knew, like with the alcoholic, who'd be behind the door when I arrived home? I never felt comfortable making plans or having anyone over. I still carry that feeling today about my home. "Text me when you're on your way." "When do you think you might be in the neighborhood?"

So crazy. I know it is from the sense of "What if something wild is going on at that moment and I can't explain?" The nagging feeling I grew up with. I was ashamed as a teen, and angry at what I felt was his selfishness and greed. This really was my position until I finally got out on my own and was able to understand things from an adult perspective and have some control over my environment. My anger gave way to compassion for a man living long before his time.

—Nanci M.

THE VALUE OF GRIEF

Grief changes the way everything in your microcosm is organized—from every cell in your body, to each emotion that arises in response to your environment, to every element of all that surrounds you. There is nothing that remains the same after grief has paid a visit. I like to think of each crying session as summoning the light of the Universe to rearrange all that I have and to dispel the illusions that no longer serve me—marshaling the perfect building blocks of my purpose, only to place them effortlessly in my view.

Another profound value of grief is the way it teaches us compassion through how we hear, understand, and speak our language. Certain words have meanings that deepen over time as our grief-stricken lens of victimization changes to one of transformation and triumph. When our postgrief lens is bathed in a new light of empowered hope, how we hear the voices in our heads and how we hear the words that others speak over us change. They begin to nourish and rebuild our spirits.

Allow me to give you a little primer in understanding the defining language of grief, and how these words can reflect growth over time and expand their meaning:

Apathy comes at the beginning, in the middle, and at the end of grief. In the beginning, as a form of obfuscation of reality to slow down the process of emotion. In the middle, as a way of reassessing the values and beliefs (in the face of loss) that you once held dear. And, at the end, as a form of rest and repose at the completion of a grief cycle— before you begin the mourning process.

Depression is a process that requires you to pay attention to yourself. **Despair** creates a deepening in understanding of your true needs.

Devastation burns away the illusions you have about what you need, who you are, and the truth of your circumstances.

Groundlessness is the feeling, during grief, that so much has disintegrated that it feels difficult to be focused or tethered in your current reality. It is, in and of itself, the very beginning of feeling liberated—a respite from control and an encouragement to go with the flow.

Humiliation is your mind's unconscious way of getting you to recognize your truest heartfelt feelings/needs and the ways in which you may have disregarded them at an earlier time. Your red face is a red flag.

Humility is your first experience of choosing peace in the face of unfulfilled expectations that often cause conflict.

Overwhelmingness in the instance of grief is when your heart is flooded with so much feeling that your brain is unable to decipher its meanings.

Sadness protects the things that are the dearest to you.
Sorrow allows for a deeper experience of self-reflection. The opportunity to become aware of what is missing or what is needed for the heart to be at peace.

At our lowest point in grief, when we have scraped and scratched, dove, and dug all the way down into the depths of our darkest places inside, we gain new sight; like cats, we become able to see and navigate our truth in the dimmest of light. It is in those times that our vision breaks the barriers of every layer of energy. We can see, hear, and feel the vibrations of other dimensions. We become clairvoyant, clairsentient, and clairaudient. We receive the hard-won wisdom we are entitled to.

In the emotional haze of grief, it is common to see loved ones who have died, experience music in a new way, dream or receive past-life visions, and transcend our mundane relationship to the world through an openness to the angels and other spiritual beings. We also begin to recognize the value of all life and connect in ways we may not have before. The voices of the animals and trees become apparent in this new vision.

GRIEF VERSUS MOURNING

Although there is an entire chapter devoted to the process of mourning, I see fit to include a bit about it here, to make clear the difference between grieving and mourning. The act of mourning is the process you must go through to make all the mental and physical adjustments that any loss requires. We must transition our thinking, reactions, and behaviors to reflect the way our life is today.

I love to cook, something I enjoyed doing with my mother starting early in life, and I took over the responsibility after my father died, when Mom lost her interest in family meals. We had a sit-down family dinner every night when Dad was alive—it usually included an appetizer, one or two choices of vegetables, and a meat or main course with something sweet at the end—every evening at 5:30 sharp, with everyone present. When he died, it stopped.

By that time my elder siblings were old enough to be out of the house with their friends and able to provide their own meals. I was left in the house with Mom, who now had a full schedule and wasn't interested in cooking when she got home. I would do my best to keep the tradition going, but often she just wanted a bowl of cereal or a salad for her meal, and that was it. My mother's way of mourning the loss of my father was letting go of or rearranging all the things she did out of obligation to her marriage to him, and cooking was one of those things.

I mourned this loss by struggling to take over the cooking duties and doing my best to encourage meals together, at least between her and me, which didn't always happen. Mostly it didn't. All my life I have made a connection among family, food, and togetherness—along with the sense of belonging that comes with all of them. I have sought to create togetherness by cooking for whichever friends or neighbors are present at the time. I also spent a decade in the food industry as another way of making up for the loss of family togetherness, all ways of mourning the cohesive family relationships I was missing.

Recently (in the last few years) a new layer of grief revealed itself as I had begun a new ritual at the onset of the pandemic, of gathering my friends and neighbors together for a family dinner every Thursday night. It was a safe way to commune with my "pod," as they came to be known in the era of COVID-19. These dinners were potluck, and everyone would contribute something, but I found myself contributing more, most of the time—at least that is the way it felt. Finally, getting frustrated with always being the one to plan and execute these dinners, I decided to stop being the planner. And as I suspected, they stopped.

It wasn't until the writing of this portion of the book that I recognized the power and meaning this ritual had for me, and because I had given it such an important job (satisfying the family dynamic I so desired), it always fell short, and

I was left bereft and frustrated again. Little did I realize that every family dinner I made efforts to plan and provide for was reinvigorating the grief I felt all those years ago, a feeling of abandonment and compounding the lack of belonging. Now that I have uncovered, recognized, and grieved this very important part of my history, I can claim forgiveness, leave behind the old pattern, and find and forge the familial relationships that match my values and meet my needs, accepting all my relations as they are.

WHAT IT MEANS TO GRIEVE AND HOW TO DO IT

There is no right way to grieve—we hear this said all the time. But what exactly does that mean? Grief is a deep and abiding heart opening—based on an individual's comfort level with being open, combined with the circumstances and conditions happening at the time—and they will respond in a multitude of ways. Some people collapse in emotion, others buck up in shock, and still others may respond in maniacal laughter.

However, it is the majority that will feel nothing at all—until they feel it is safe to do so (this is the dynamic that causes what we call posttraumatic stress disorder, or PTSD). Our body and mind's ability to store emotion until we are relaxed and in a place to allow the grief to be expressed. There is no appropriate or inappropriate response; there is only the response you have in the moment.

Like a lotus, our hearts open one petal at a time. We will oscillate to different vibrations of grief as our heart understands the current truths and begins to grieve its way into the transition at hand; the change from one state of consciousness to another. Grief is the path through which your body says goodbye to your spiritual, mental, emotional, and physical pain.

THE THREE CIRCLES OF GRIEF

In the dynamic of grief, there are three realms. Energetically speaking, we can say three different dimensions of grief. The first circle of grief is the process of transitioning through the actual trauma or event. The second circle of grief is processing the consequences of choices made from the lens of grief, and from having experienced the trauma (to be more specific: the consequences of those beliefs, ideas, and choices and their remedies). The final circle of grief contains the echoes of grief that remain in your energy, habits, and expectations, based on the beliefs, ideas, and choices that were made from the original trauma. The circular motion of grief and the multiple levels of energy on which it exists allow for the refining of our character, the understanding of ourselves, and the comprehension of the world we live in.

Circle One: The traumatic event. When we experience any unexpected event, it can be traumatizing—anything from a physical, mental, or emotional assault to an unexpected occurrence that leaves a person feeling surprised or powerless. Grief allows you to become aware of the more subtle energetic patterns that reveal the causes and effects to which we are connected, and sets up the opportunity to become empowered in accepting, grieving, and then resolving our concerns the trauma has revealed or created.

Circle Two: The beliefs, ideas, and choices illumined or manifested because of the trauma. The second circle of grief is the process of becoming aware of how the traumatic event has changed our experience of life—whether it be through new habits or beliefs invoked to protect us on some level, or specific decisions made because of our life experience. Often, these constructs are built out of a reaction to the shock, sadness, or fear a trauma can promote. It is common to take the habits these reactions have cultivated and adopt them as our belief system and perspective about life. Doing this has consequences.

Circle Three: The consequences of thoughts, beliefs, and actions derived from trauma and their remedies. The third circle of grief comes when we have so fully processed the grief of the trauma we experienced that we become aware of the habits or beliefs that were generated because of it—the echoes of grief that remain in our energy, habits, and expectations, based on the thoughts, beliefs, and actions taken on the basis of the original event. This awareness becomes apparent years after the original event, unless and until the person does specifically focused work on understanding, overcoming, and processing the original event so thoroughly that one does not transfer their feelings from the trauma onto other facets of life.

This rarely happens. More often than not, it isn't until some time later that we begin to be aware that the relationships we've chosen and decisions we've made have been based on theories or beliefs about ourselves, others, and life that no longer feel true. When this realization occurs, it begins the third circle of grief, which ushers in new and productive inspirations that will move us forward into the future and create a new and more peaceful present. This grief occurs as tears of truth and relief or simply an "a-ha" moment.

Some years back I had a client, Sarah, who wanted to stop smoking. She'd been a daily smoker for twenty years and had struggled with quitting the last five. At this point, she'd tried everything: therapy, nicotine patches, behavior modification, and hypnotherapy—nothing worked.

At the time, I had a sweet little office in West Hollywood, on the second floor of a popular bistro. She had made an appointment the day before, and when she walked into my office, with the aroma of fresh-brewed coffee wafting up in the air and the bright-yellow and green couches, the environment seemed to disarm her frustration and anxiety. This was her first session, so I introduced myself and we shook hands. Immediately, she exclaimed, "I need to stop smoking and I've tried everything."

"Okay," I responded. "Let's go back to the beginning. Why don't you kick off your shoes, take a seat, and make yourself comfortable. Now, close your eyes and go back to the day and time you had your first cigarette."

Her eyes welled up with tears.

Her memory led her, quickly, back to a time in her late teens. She was hanging out with a new boy she liked, and somehow ended up in a back alley made of cobblestone, surrounded by many dingy red-bricked buildings from another century. The smells of urine-soaked corners seemed to flood back, and she flinched. The boy had raped her. In shock, and unable to feel grief in those next moments after the assault, she ran to safety, joining friends at a café. This was the first time she picked up a cigarette. Her smoking escalated over the years, to a two-pack-a-day habit.

I directed her to visualize going back in time to thirty minutes before the rape—she described how happy and excited she'd felt as she began to walk with this boy, how thrilled she was at his interest in her. So much so that she didn't notice he was walking her away from the crowds.

She began to cry.

Giving her a few moments to sit in the realization that she'd had some inkling of dread in those moments but completely dismissed them, I waited.

Finally, I asked her to visualize what she would do differently. Right now, if she could go back into those moments preceding the assault, what would she do today?

"Now," I said, "I want you to visualize it. Take yourself back in time and space to that exact moment and tell me what you are doing."

She saw herself walking away from him, staying with her friends, and responding to his urging to follow him, with a polite "No thank you." Again, she burst into tears. It was the first time she'd felt something new, other than shame, guilt, anger, or rage. The energy from this man she'd carried with her all these years seemed to float back to him through time and space. She had taken her power back and freed her spirit from the obligation to remain in pain. For the first time she could envision forgiveness for him and for herself.

After she left the office that day, she never smoked another cigarette. She checked in with me about six months later to let me know she wasn't smoking, that she'd not had another craving. Also, she'd quit her job and was going to school. For the first time, she was free to do what she wanted, unencumbered from the fear and anxiety that had always been present in every aspect of her life.

I know this outcome seems a bit miraculous, but in truth it was the result of many years of work and levels of grieving—never allowing the heart's complete surrender to the sorrow for what had been lost. Without this surrender, the psyche is unwilling to receive the depth of pain we feel, and we manifest habits that keep us from this deep flood of emotion (the smoking was her habit of choice). These rituals have their own set of consequences and only prolong the inevitable, a deep expression of the sorrow we feel.

In this case, the three circles of grief are

First circle (trauma): the rape

Second circle (manifestations based on the lens of the trauma): the smoking

Third circle (consequences and remedies for those manifestations): ill health caused from the smoking, the perpetual feeling of fear, and the lack of self-trust or ability to do anything that felt like a risk

Each one of those layers of grief had to be resolved on every level they existed—spiritually, mentally, emotionally, and physically.

Sarah, at the onset of her grief, struggled with admitting what happened to her; she felt shame, rage, and guilt about the assault. It took time and work to stop blaming herself for what happened, and to accept that the rape was not her fault. Then she needed to process the immense rage she carried toward her rapist. During this period, the smoking was one of the coping strategies she used to quell the constant anxiety and big emotions that were just under the surface.

What came next were all the ways Sarah kept herself safe in relationships, such as isolating herself, distrusting everyone, not communicating her true feelings, or—quite the opposite—transferring her frustration onto others and sabotaging many opportunities for intimacy and friendship. For much of the process, Sarah was unaware of the impact of her behavior. It was through her traditional therapy that she was able to better understand why she did these things and began to open to the necessary change her responses to her life desperately needed.

The point at which she became conscious of every new layer of her process was just following an intense emotional release that cleared the way for new understanding. The final layer to be transformed—the energetic/spiritual memory of the event—was realized when she addressed her smoking habit.

Sarah's willingness to shift the self-inflicted pattern that was in place because of the original trauma was an unconscious message to her: she was ready to find forgiveness for all involved and finally move forward in her life. She was ready to abandon functioning from a victimized point of view. Once the crutch of smoking had been removed, she was free to learn new ways of being in the world.

The circles of grief become the glue that connects every layer of our being to all the dimensions in our lives. It is neither positive nor negative, but a transformative shift into an awareness of our inner and outer worlds. As our culture gains a new lens on grieving, our world will find innovative ways of resolving some of our deepest sorrows and the current impediments to forging a future that serves everyone.

The exercise below is an opportunity to take an inventory of your current emotional intelligence and relationship to grief. Answer the questions and then set them aside for an hour. Go back and reread and contemplate your answers. Are they what you expected? Why or why not? Are they unexpected? Why or why not? Did you notice any specific pattern of emotion? If so, what?

How do you acknowledge personal signs of grief in your life?

Find out by answering these questions:

What do you do when you feel sad?

What do you do when you feel angry?

How do you respond to your needs not being met?

How do you respond to feeling disappointment?

When something happens you are not expecting, what do you do?

Forms of grief—How often do you experience these?

H = hourly, D = daily, W = weekly, M = monthly, N = never

1. Crying

2. Depression

3. Irritability

4. Frustration

5. Anger

6. Apathy

7. Sadness

8. Manic or uncomfortable laughter

DOES GRIEF MAKE YOU WEAK?

Grief does not make you weak; it makes you receptive, flexible, malleable, and open—all elements of spiritual and emotional integrity. Receptivity in this case refers to receiving the new thoughts, ideas, and wisdom that come from letting go of anything that no longer serves you. Grief is the mechanism though which we will cull our current paradigm and transform (with our crying sessions) anything we believe or feel no longer holds true or is simply outdated.

Is crying the only form of grief, you ask? I do not believe so, although crying is inevitable at some point since there must eventually be change on a biochemical level, if we are to be fully liberated from what ails us. Often, tears are evidence of the higher vibrational energy of healing that moves through us during grief. This level of grieving is the process we go through to recognize the reality of what is happening, not only based on how we remember or experience it.

It has been proven that our minds have selective memory when in trauma, but as we move on the path of change, we begin to feel safe and relaxed, which promotes honest memories. Our spirit has a blueprint of everything that has ever happened to us at any time. It is the accumulation of these layered memories that generate beliefs and philosophies about us, others, and life.

The power of this layered blueprint cannot be underestimated. It is the aspect of the human consciousness that we call the shadow—the hidden story that empowers everything we do. The dark side of our consciousness isn't bad or evil; it is powerful and seeks to promote our survival, which is why it is formidable and can be easily misunderstood.

It is our personal mystery: the concealed and sometimes disguised soul information comprising tools, spiritual imprints (soul memories that we are born with), and emotions. These elements become the building blocks or destructive forces we need to refine who we are, our character, and all we will become in the present incarnation.

COMPLICATED GRIEF: WHAT IS IT?

Grief can become complicated by loss that is exacerbated by unresolved personal or professional relationships, unresolved addiction, untruthful beliefs about circumstances and conditions, and multiple losses happening concurrently. This kind of grief can cause deep experiences of self-pity and victimization, leaving a person to feel helpless to help themselves.

Of course, there are varying levels of complicated grief, but no matter; one must be prepared to process each loss on its own merits. One at a time, until all matters have been worked through completely.

Grief can also be complicated when it is related to addiction, homicide, suicide, or unexpected misfortune. Any loss a person experiences connected to a socially controversial event or dynamic can make it more difficult to speak of freely and garner support from one's social systems. I would love to say that most people are compassionate, loving, and supportive about things they do not understand, but they are not. Many folks are locked into judgment about their own self-loathing and can oftentimes be incredibly cruel to those experiencing levels of grief they don't understand regarding circumstances they cannot imagine.

A friend of mine, Sharon, one day after her mother died, was laid off from her job of twenty-five years. Even though there was a paid severance and a need for time off, the complicated grief arose out of the loss of "two families." The profound shift in the emotional dynamic of the *DNA family*, and a total loss of the emotional support system of the *work family*. Both losses created a direct change in her daily schedule, and a definitive change in her daily emotional-support system. The physical, biological, emotional, and mental changes that grief generates can render a condition of anything from extreme emotional grief to denial of any emotional feeling at all, even delusional beliefs about the circumstances.

Other than the rings we saw earlier in the process of grief, there are different, though tangential, circles of complicated grief as well. These circles are additional layers of information and stimulus that intensify the repercussions to a person's bereavement. They will amplify elements such as clarity, actions, environment, current relationships, and how all these will impact and magnify the feelings of grief.

The first circle of complicated grief is the presence of multiple losses one person experiences simultaneously, and is the most potent on its own.

The second circle of complicated grief is the amplification of grief one creates by the choices they make while suffering or because of the lens through which they view life while grieving. The clarity of reason and vision can easily be manipulated during times of extremely overwhelmed emotions. Our brains do not function under duress in the same way they do when relaxed, and this can cause people to naturally transfer their grief onto situations, people, events, and conversations that personify their pain.

I call this "delusional vision," and it is common to some degree in complicated grief. During these times a person's beliefs can become convoluted. A person makes assumptions when there is a gap in their memory or information; their emotions will fill it to what allows the intensity of their feelings to make sense. These assumptions lead them to say things or take actions that further create chaos.

We see a lot of this dynamic in our current political climate. When fear is used as a motivator in the outside world, a person experiencing multiple traumas in their personal life, such as job or money deficiencies, food scarcity, health issues or scares, relationship confusion, or experiencing emotional highs and lows, can easily be manipulated by the outside stimulus to which they are exposed. Especially when this outer stimulus allows a place for them to expend their energy, attention, or grief, despite its truthfulness. For example: the invoking of an insurrection at the US Capitol on the basis of a belief that the election for the newly elected president was fraudulent.

The third circle of complicated grief is the reaction that one must contend with from their environment, friends, family, or onlookers about or because of their grief—or the reactions by others to the losses themselves.

As you can see, complicated grief is a layered topic for which there will be more information in coming pages. For now, it is important to take a few minutes to contemplate the possible layers of grief that may be a part of your or a loved one's process.

Questions to ask yourself to understand your grief

What is the loss you are processing?

Who else is involved in this loss?

What is your relationship to them?

What, if any, secondary losses, changes, or crises are you experiencing?

What is the emotional loss?

What is the reality being uncovered through your grief?

What, if any, are the physical world repercussions?

How many losses have you endured in the last twelve months?

What needs do you have that are not being adequately met?

Does your family or community feel comfortable with emotional expression?

Are you comfortable with emotional expression, big or small?

What access do you have to support your mental health?

GRIEF TRIGGERS AND DELUSIONAL THINKING

Sharon's grief was amplified—five years after being laid off from her job of twenty-five years and losing her mother, she was diagnosed with uterine cancer on the anniversary of her mother's death. All of life happens in a series of cycles—the patterns that energetically guide each of us on our path of self-awareness—the anniversaries, seasons, and times of day of loss that mark our path of grief, leading us to find forgiveness of the loss at hand.

These patterns of grief can follow us through days, months, and years, even moving with our soul into future incarnations until they have been processed, and any remnant of them and the consequences of their presence have been resolved. The "consequences of their presence" is any exhibited behavior or choice made while looking through the lens of loss.

For example, it is not uncommon to do things we normally wouldn't if not for our loss or grief. For instance, friendships being tested or broken (while one party is grieving), dating people outside our value system (while in grief), and, finally, quitting a job, changing jobs, or moving our residence. All these big decisions, often inspired by a need to escape deep feeling, would be best reserved for another time.

The release that comes with grief often promotes a feeling of unrealistic freedom and new awareness that may not be rooted in truth. Often, it is shrouded in a new feeling of confidence and courage that may not be fully grounded in the person's personality and set of values, so making far-reaching choices such as moving, purchasing large-ticket items, or breaking up relationships is not recommended for at least six months to a year after an impactful loss. Unless, of course, the change was being planned long before the movement-inspiring loss, and the freedom that ensues is just what is required for the move forward.

Sharon's attitudes toward politics and humanity became tainted as her grief wore on in a holding pattern. Her anxiety and depression amplified, and she began feeling more and more isolated until it all came to a head when the pandemic hit and she was forced to work from home. The further isolation from the joyful realities of the world and her investment of time in only a few sources of information exacerbated her distrust of people and magnified her depression.

So much so that it made finding help for her condition impossible, in her mind. She sought therapy but turned away multiple options after meeting only once with each. She was in a hole and kept digging. Eventually, Sharon's patterns will lead her to an inner or outer event that will activate her innate wisdom and lead her to the information she needs to grieve and begin a new forward movement.

GRIEF ANNIVERSARIES

Anytime we experience a loss, our spirit records everything about the moment. It remembers what day and time it was, what season it was, the weather on that day, exactly what we were feeling or wearing, where we were, or what others were doing around the time of the loss. Our cognizant minds, however, may not remember anything for a period of time, and for some, not at all. Depending on the loss, some people disassociate from the conscious recognition altogether—but make no mistake about it, the explicit details of the event are seared into our spirit, waiting for their time of recognition.

A good friend of mine, who's been sober for twenty-five years, remembers the events that led to his rock bottom. Every year, as the snow begins to fall, an enormous sense of fear and depression comes over him. So much so that he must remind himself he is safe and grateful to have such a good life.

You see, all those years ago, Joseph was making his way home from somewhere, high and hung over—feeling awful for the previous night's events that loomed in his consciousness, but from which he could not recall any direct memory. Only the feelings of guilt and shame that arose every time he'd go on a bender. The snowstorm was intense on this particular morning as he walked on a deserted gray and dismal street, freezing and feeling ill.

For months he'd been wanting to outrun his cycle of addiction, but to no avail. The parties and the fun were immediately followed by the sickness and deep depression from which he suffered. He was so weary and ready for change. Something about the series of those last few days brought him to his lowest point, and he finally asked for help.

Now, twenty-five years later, when a snowstorm triggers feelings of fear and depression, he remembers what it felt like to feel out of control—not to be able to remember what happened the night before. To this day, he pays special attention to himself on those days and reflects on how far he's come in his life, relationships, and, most of all, his personal growth. Doing so reinforces a new pattern that over time will become the new way of being and feeling. He acknowledges his sacred relationship to himself and takes stock of what he may want to change or appreciate in his life. Every year, like clockwork, when the snow begins to fall.

These anniversaries of transition are the building blocks of our process of change. We hold on to them so that we do not forget the events of the past and our dedication to never again re-creating the pain, suffering, and chaos of our ignorance and folly. Or, merely to remember those people, places, and times through which we experienced great joy. These grief anniversaries are important parts of our mourning, and the structure on which we will build a new life.

HOLIDAYS AND GRIEF

Another potent time for grievers is holidays and birthdays. There is so much expectation of celebration, joy, and revelry that often falls short even when you are not grieving. Those days can become your nemesis. And when you have no family or support system readily available to you, for those who are suffering these special days can be brutal. Now, if you've encountered a loss on one of these days and it becomes a grief anniversary, the reemerging of your pain or depression may be compounded. It is difficult to be around folks in a festive mood when you are struggling to stay balanced.

Conflicts at family gatherings or encountering people in various states of inebriation are an additional dysfunction often found at holiday reunions. So, what are you to do about your grief in these situations? Well, you have a few options: first and foremost, it's important to take care of yourself. The first decision you need to tackle is whether to make an appearance. You have to determine if isolating yourself and not going will be worse than the strife you might encounter when you are there.

The Cathedral of St. John the Divine

The first Christmas after my father died was devastating to me. From the age of twelve on, the holidays became a struggle. Finally, after moving to NYC at eighteen, I was able to begin the process of changing my habits and traditions around the holidays, in hopes that I could find solace in some new ones.

My first Thanksgiving (Day of Mourning) in the city I spent at the Cathedral of St. John the Divine. I'd been living in New York for only a few months and had made friends at the church (at one time they housed a 2,000 lb. quartz crystal that easily brought me a respite from my grief, just sitting in its presence). The church had quickly become my favorite place to go when I was struggling with my deep emotions.

On that day, of course, I cried while slipping on my ankle-length, forest-green, velvet 1920s frock with a matching feathered hat. I arrived a little worse for wear, but it was nice to be around a happy family of my choosing. At least eighteen of us gathered around an enormous dining table in the rectory with the most beautiful mahogany woodwork.

The rectory had been completed in 1862, and I could feel every bit of its history in my bones. That Thanksgiving I also received the privilege of a tour of the inner sanctum of the sanctuary. There was a "catwalk" about 25 ft. up, all around the main sanctuary of the largest Gothic cathedral in the United States. It led to a little private room that held some Gothic heirlooms. I was flooded with a sense of reassurance in the space, and I will never forget it. There was nothing better to pull me out of my depressive feelings than a great spiritual mystery to be discovered. The rectory was magnetically haunted from times past.

The most important thing you can do for yourself when preparing to manage your grief with an audience is to take time to contemplate what you need and what you don't need. Write it down. Write a letter to yourself and define the experience you would like to have, in the most detail possible. Include how you need to feel and what sort of responses you'd like to see from the people you expect to be there. Give yourself permission to take a few hours off from your grief, to enjoy the festivities. You are not dishonoring those you've lost by feeling joyful.

Once you've written your letter, carry it with you to your gathering. Additionally, here are a few things to try to help you get through your holidays.

Find an ally: Make sure there is one person who can be supportive to you at your gathering, and let them know how you're feeling. If you don't have one related to you, invite a guest.

Tell people: Don't be ashamed to, unassumingly, let people know that holidays are difficult for you.

Set boundaries: Don't be afraid to set boundaries with people who may like to joke and have some fun at your expense. Gently and firmly tell them to stop, and then walk away from the moment to give them the opportunity to react and adjust outside your presence.

Go early and leave early: I always enjoy the cooking process and the early setup. I find there are fewer opportunities to get into uncomfortable or triggering situations when I am task oriented.

Go for dessert: Arrive late and limit how long you stay. This will give you a limited time with which to share a few good moments and be on your way.

If you cry: Don't worry if you get emotional around others; allow your feelings without having to become the center of attention. Most people can tolerate witnessing emotion when you don't require or expect anything of them to help you through it. And that is exactly how you want it to be. If your anger is triggered, let yourself move to another space so that you may feel it in a managed way—you always have more self-control then you think. You do not have to stuff it down. Your emotions are yours alone, and you can let them shed as you go along.

If you have been harmed: I see this so often when a person has physically, mentally, or emotionally been harmed by someone in the family whom they are expected to see at the holidays. It is your choice alone to determine what is best for you and your mental health. Forgive people for not being able to support you the way you need, or to acknowledge your pain, or even to recognize the events in question, and do what is best for you. Be honest and tell the truth to whoever wants to know it. If you'd like, make efforts to organize a smaller separate gathering with the people you would most like to spend your time with.

Do something creative: Anything. Try something new and let go of the result. Bake a fallen cake. Burn some cookies. Go to an establishment you've never been to and meet one new person. Google some funny videos. Learn something new. Collect some sticks or leaves from outside and make something, using only what you have in the house. The process of doing one thing outside your normal pattern can miraculously change your entire outlook. It doesn't mean you won't feel your losses, but it will change the way and the intensity that you do.

Run energy: Running energy is a form of visual prayer. Take a moment away from others and visualize a beautiful, warm, golden-white light, like a ray of sun beaming down into the top of your head. See it working its way down through your entire body, through your feet, and then visualize a crystalline core of the earth to which it connects. You can do this throughout your gathering, in the car before and after the event, or if you are alone (it reminds you that you are never really alone, and that you always have spiritual support and love).

Most of all, the spirit of the holidays is not only to spread joy but to cultivate forgiveness and compassion, and that is truer for no one more than those who are grieving. Let patience be your ally. Give yourself permission to turn away from your rage or anger, your sorrow or confusion—just for a few hours. Let a little bit of light and peace into your day and breathe deeply, allowing some of your hard-won wisdom to take root. It is these subtle moments you put your focus on that will be the building blocks of the new traditions you will create for many holidays to come.

THE VALUE OF RITUAL AND ALTAR BUILDING

While grief, in and of itself, is a ritual in cleansing and illumination, as a professional griever I have always enjoyed the power of creating and performing rituals to aid in the conscious marking of my mental, emotional, spiritual, or physical transition. Lighting candles, burning herbs, and constructing altars have been ways for me to connect with the ancients and begin to unravel the process and purpose of my grief, to call on a higher understanding and wisdom, and to gain clarity and peace. Ancient spiritualists used ritual as a form of commitment building, a sort of contract with themselves to show their dedication in having what they are asking for or to gain insight into the transition at hand.

It is the action of collecting the items to be used in the ritual, along with the time and energy it takes to perform it and the reflection it requires, that cultivates a sense of commitment toward the desired results. It also invokes a connection to our direct environment and the universe around us that helps us become more aware on every level. Most importantly, rituals will unify us with our own unconscious information, allowing the elements that are causing strife to become front and center. Once the information becomes evident, we can reevaluate and make new decisions to resolve the issue or imbalance.

A Ritual for Illumination/Cleansing

Affirmation: I am safe to know the truth, I walk toward it with an open heart.

What you'll need for your ritual:
one white jar candle
one fire source (a lighter or match)
a white cloth to place on the sacred altar area
one Lemurian quartz crystal
one medium-sized metal pot to burn herbs (and charcoal if needed)

paper and pen

one glass of water

Herbs you'll need:

Juniper (leaf): This herb helps release old patterns and energies, uplifts the energy of the space (including mental space), and promotes an environment where one can feel safe and reflect in a clarifying manner.

Palo santo: Is a wood high in resin and, when burned, clears a space of any negative energy. It also prepares the way for new innovative ideas and experiences.

Cedar: Cedar helps ground and soothe one's emotions after an expression of grief. It too has clarifying properties to one's emotions and mentality.

The following are additional options for your ritual (flower essences or oils). You may use any brand you prefer and can often find them at a health food store.

Flower Essences

Agrimony Flower Essence: To help one face uncomfortable situations, challenges, and difficulties in life. For those who are in shock or don't want to face grief or any "uncomfortable" emotions.

White Chestnut Flower Essence: Helps one stop negative, repetitive, worrying thoughts that prevent one from having a peaceful mind. Helps nullify the "what if" thoughts one may have while going through grief.

Directions for using the Bach Flower Essences: You may add four drops into a cup of water and sip during the ritual to help ground your energy field and calm the mind and emotions. Or add the drops into a bottle of water and spritz over the altar to set the intention of your affirmation. You may also add four drops into a cleansing bath prior to the ritual.

Begin your ritual by cleaning and clearing a small area in any room you prefer. Collect all the items for your altar and place them in the cleared space. Light the palo santo stick and spread the smoke over the altar space and over your head. (It's always good to be conscientious about others in the home and their olfactory sensitivities. You can always burn your herbs outside or with opened windows.)

Now, sit with your paper and pen (no computers or phones here) and write what you are feeling about your current situation, and what you would like to be rid of on any level. Don't censor yourself. No one else needs to read your writing. Give yourself permission to be raw and truthful, using whatever language you'd like. There are no rules or shame for either.

Once your writing is complete, fold your paper two times and write the affirmation on it. Now, place it in the burning pot. Add a piece of palo santo, some juniper, and some cedar flakes and light all four corners of the paper (this may smoke quite a bit, so you will want to take your burning pot outside).

Once your affirmation and notes are burned, light your candle and let it burn to the socket all at once, or continue with the writing every day until the candle is done. Performing this ritual may inspire a grief response, which is completely appropriate. Allow yourself to feel anything that comes up, and if you are too emotional to capture your feelings on paper, that is okay. The understanding you seek will come in many ways over time. Give yourself permission to go with the flow.

LOSS: LIFE'S MOST EXTRAORDINARY ILLUSION

In life, things aren't always as they seem to be. They depend on our vantage point and lens to become manifest in our view of existence. Often this viewpoint can become a collective one with family and friends or even a community, regardless of the facts. This is what we call an illusion—a deceptive appearance or impression of something like a false idea or belief—our perception of reality distorting the truth just enough for us to, through the lens of grief, begin chipping away at the information that guides our perspective.

While we are grieving, every unresolved illusion we carry can pop up for reexamination and release, a powerful and potent rehashing of our view of the past on any level—energetic, emotional, mental, or spiritual. Grief requires that we, intermittently, go through our feelings and belief systems to see if they still resonate with who we are, the choices we are currently making, and who we have become. If they no longer match the person we have grown to be, we grieve them away and begin to build on the new beliefs that allow us to move forward.

Illusions are a two-way street. They can lead us forward in a positive way or thrust us down a path of bondage, one illegitimate thought at a time—but even our journey into what we fear the most becomes our access to the greater Truth we spiritually seek. Where we put our focus and attention is what picks up traction and momentum until it sows the seeds and reaps the harvest of our beliefs.

Think of illusion as a set of Legos—different colors, sizes, and shapes to make anything your big heart desires. You use trial and error to sort out what fits, feels, and looks the best for your final masterpiece. You start with the blueprint that comes in the box (your soul). Through the creative process to which every aspect of yourself has access, you try on different ways of being and thinking until you land on one that, at first, suits your needs of the moment and then ultimately draws to you the ones that suit the needs of all you hold dear.

Illusion is our ally; a tool to be used to envision what we want and the many paths to achieve it or receive it. The higher we set the standard of how we achieve something, the narrower and more focused our options become. For example, let's say you wanted a promotion at work, and the raise that comes with it. You have many ways to formulate in your mind how you see it happening.

You can ruminate on how you probably won't get the promotion, how much you need the money, and how you struggle with the job you have now—zeroing in on your feelings of imbalance and being victimized by life. You can center your attention on how to sabotage your competition, stepping on whomever you need to because you deserve the job. Or you can pivot your viewpoint to the result, which is for each of your coworkers, as well as yourself, to get the position that brings them the most fulfillment, the salary they want, and the time and environment that supports them.

When you call on the "most for the most," you enlist the highest and best for everyone and leave spirit the job of putting it in place for you. You might find that you end up at another company that offers more money, more authority, a beautiful environment, and a committed support system.

The standard you set at the beginning determines where you put your energy, and the possibilities you can witness before you. Wherever you begin, grief will help change your attitudes and beliefs about what you can have and the ease with which it arrives on your doorstep. None of this is to imply that there isn't work involved, but the confluence of your magical thinking and your grounded awareness leaves you with a vantage point where anything is possible, and the Universe is conspiring to bring it to you.

THE POWER OF DELUSIONAL THINKING

When someone is grieving or sick, especially from a long-term illness (theirs or a loved one's), or an unexpected accident or event takes place, the shock to their system is palpable. It can draw up unprocessed or unresolved loss from the past and skew or blur the facts of the present. They or their family can easily be traumatized over again, by continual misunderstandings that come from misguided perceptions, feelings, or facts.

This is an experience that often occurs with patients of dementia, those in the final stages of cancer, or loved ones who have been through multiple traumas, to name a few. But no matter what side of the tragedy you are on, the perpetual flow of emotion can leave you in a state of resistance, denial, or frustration that can make you vulnerable to misremembering events not as they were, but how you felt about them.

When the body or brain is taxed to the max, all it wants to do is generate the flow of its emotional lowest common denominator (grief) so that it may release the pressure and start the cascade of chemicals that create positive feeling, relief, or resolution. The truth of the facts or beliefs that trigger the movement of grief is irrelevant.

WHAT DO ILLUSIONS AND DELUSIONS LOOK LIKE ON THE VARIED ENERGY LEVELS?

Spiritually speaking, illusions and delusions are a part of the human creative process; illusions are possibilities that may not fully exist or don't fully exist in one's presence, yet. Someone who is intuitive might feel the presence of a clothing design, picture it in their mind (having never seen it before), and then view it in a magazine the next day. The illusion is the burgeoning thought or idea, and the delusion is the thought or idea connected with our feelings about it.

Take this creative dynamic and apply it to one's personal or collective safety. Anytime we are accessing intuitive information from what is happening in our environment, we automatically connect to our fight-or-flight sense that activates hypervigilant perception. If we are afraid of being victimized, have been victimized, or carry any form of social bias, these thoughts and ideas come up in our energy body to be reviewed by our rational mind.

Our physical body also has an energy body, commonly referred to as the aura. Each layer of the aura governs the different aspects of the physical body, the self, and the personality. It is in the energy body that our main energy centers or chakras help us process information from our inner and outer world.

It is through these centers that we process information through the illusions we glean or delusions we feel. They come in many forms, and grief may trigger any of them. When one is in grief, the emotion is triggered to be released. It is useful to recognize these perceptions as they are occurring. Following are the types of illusions one may encounter, where they are centered in the body, and how they might affect us.

Etheric body: Your body double. It is the layer of energy immediately outside your physical body. This is the layer of energy to which delusions belong (it also holds the energy patterns of your physical habits). Mostly, our delusions come up on this level as a safety measure when we are in fear of or have been victimized in any way before. Our mind can conjure the illusion of that possibility to keep us safe. For example: in a crowd of people, when we are feeling boxed in, our energy body alerts us to pay attention to our physique and surroundings.

If we have been psychologically or emotionally abused, we can feel the telepathic intrusion of someone else's thoughts (usually as they pertain to us) at times with physical sensations, and we can use this intrusion as a way of conjuring up the very thought form that will cause a grief response in us. Delusional thinking helps us play out the possibilities of our fears, generally in a safe space. If we weren't actually safe, we would have a genuine physical fight-or-flight response and either freeze or move into action. You can use this densely creative energy to visualize what you need to feel safe, and the alarm system it provides to move you into a state of awareness that shows you the path to safety.

Mental body: Delusions supported by the mental body are either negative belief about us or the world, or ideas of grandeur and miracles. Take, for instance, paranoia: It is not to say that if a person is paranoid that someone is not after them. Paranoia points out you are solidly on the path to find out the truth about what is happening. Paranoia is a heightened state of awareness that cultivates trust. It must be integrated with the perception of the heart to receive the truth.

Visions of grandeur and miracles are often put in the unattainable category, because when we begin, we cannot envision ourselves having what the miracle represents. The time and space in between where we are and the place we intend feels incomprehensible to navigate for us or those around us. Thus, we quit before it is achieved.

Emotional body: Our emotional body supports delusional thinking to help personify our pain and grief. While we are processing our suffering from loss, it is easy to formulate thoughts, feelings, or beliefs about those around us to help us define the dynamic we are grieving.

A client of mine, Jarmon, was working in an organization. He was taking the place of an executive, Bob, who had suffered many losses, including multiple family members in the span of two years. As the transition began to take place, Bob began to resist the process by sending highly critical emails to the board about how things needed to move forward, culminating in several volatile, venomous communications that began to cause disruption and emotional anguish to every director aware of them. When Jarmon had done what he could to set boundaries, in compassionate responses via phone calls and emails, he finally had to stop responding to the flood of emotion coming at him and the others. In the end, when Bob recognized the futility of his behavior, he requested that he not be communicated with again.

As the transition wore on, Bob began to post on social media about how he'd lost his family. How he'd been cast out of the organization and betrayed beyond comprehension—he began deliberately bad-mouthing his successor every oppor-tunity he got to others in the company. My client, Jarmon, was between a rock and a hard place. They were colleagues and not friends, so there was no way to try to vie for Bob's understanding or accountability.

The dynamic Bob was processing through his emotional body was isolation and abandonment. Bob was in such a deep place of victimized pain that the only thing for Jarmon to do was to let things move on as they would, in hopes that as Bob grieved his multiple losses, eventually he would be able to come around to a place of peace with everyone involved.

Bob's feelings of loss were all true; he in fact had lost his work family (much of his own undoing) and his biological family (something he could not control), and therefore he focused his rage and grief on the work family members who were still present, especially his successor, because they were all safe targets. On some level, his spirit knew they would not retaliate. Despite all he'd said and done, they would retain their love and compassion for him.

Sometimes in grief, you cannot stop the moving train; you are only left to get out of its way. However, if this kind of experience is happening with a valued friend or a family member, there is never a time when we are required to tolerate abusive behavior, and you must consider setting boundaries every time a misunderstanding arises. Be clear and honest about navigating the space you need to be able to support your loved one. Ultimately, it is the one who is grieving who is responsible for their own feelings and reactions, and the resolutions to them. Patience is at the heart of this level of expression.

Spiritual body: When we process information in the spiritual dimensions, it can show up as night terrors, dreams during REM sleep, and daydreams or visions. It can also rise up around us in the form of paranormal activity, fluctuations of the electrical systems around us, or connections and communications with other spiritual beings. All these happenings and the synchronicities they inspire are messages to us about our spiritual goals, the state of reality we are engaged in, and what we need to do to resolve it. More poignantly, what we need to grieve to move forward with the new perspective that serves who we are today.

If you are one who has this "spiritual body awareness," you can use it as a powerful source of information and change. For example: waking up in a bad dream or after a night terror, you can imagine (visualize) yourself going back into the dream and changing or resolving what makes you uncomfortable. Remember, you have all the power in the spirit world when you are grounded in your authority in the real world.

THE CONCEPT OF LOSS

Loss is an illusion that stimulates our creative ability to begin to integrate who we are. It is the mechanism through which we witness or are mirrored by aspects to our personality, character, or soul information that we can choose to utilize or release—this is the process of integration. Loss is the event, and grief is the act of fusing or disintegrating these elements to create space for what is to come.

Loss does not exist; it is only a marker of transition to something ultimately better. I know those of you who are experiencing a catastrophic change right now are thinking, "Tracee, you can f@#% right off with that noise." Sitting in the face of loss, we cannot see the future. Our eyes are filled with the blinding light of devastation ripping through our hearts and our lives. I am not saying that the pain that loss leaves in its wake is not real. It is profoundly real—as is the change it inspires in us, for us, and by us.

When we experience loss, it reveals the varying levels on which we deepen our awareness of ourselves, our environment, and others. Grief is the mechanism we use to scrape away each layer of our ignorance, until there is only the Truth. Loss then is our path to being who we are. It is our road to self-awareness and radical acceptance of everything exactly the way it is.

In my younger years as an Empath, I was deeply affected by those in my midst—their behaviors, feelings, beliefs, and ideals could, over a period of time, gnaw away at my sense of self. It placed me in a state of confusion, but it allowed me to learn about the feelings that were mine and about those feelings of others whom I had temporarily owned. It was either that, or I was being thrown into a cycle of struggling with self-doubt that led to a deeper level of self-questioning and awareness, eventually revealing to me who I was and how I was different from those I was surrounded by.

I came to understand that physically losing my father and emotionally losing my mother at the tender age of eleven was probably one of the most auspicious things that could have happened. I understand now that while my parents were as progressive as they could have been (being born into the energy, beliefs, and ideals generated from the Great Depression), they both, in their own ways, suffered deeply from the collective experience of lack, racism, and misogyny, and the dismissal of the value of emotion that was perpetuated up until the sixties and seventies and exists to this day.

I was born psychic, empathic, and multispirited—deeply rooted in the spiritual dimensions of awareness that were perceived as mental illness to many in my parents' generation. Both of my ancestral family lineages had members who suffered deeply from mental maladies and a heightened spiritual awareness that was considered to be illness. If I had grown up with deep emotional ties to either of my parents, I would not have been free to be myself and to embrace the many spirits that clung to me for life in the physical world, and who were my greatest teachers.

As it turned out, I received the indomitable strength of my mother and my father's legacy of humor and compassion, all in ways I could sustain without promoting inner conflict. I was left to the peacefulness of my inner silence and convictions, with no one to counter them for many years. This allowed me to establish the self-trust and confidence I would need for the journey of grief that lay ahead for me. The illusion was that I needed my parents for more than what I had with them. Once I recognized that, I could embrace what I gained from my limited experiences with them and find peace and gratitude in my new spiritual relationship to who they truly were and the energetic legacy they left with me.

LOSS IS AN ILLUSION

To consider that loss is an illusion will be for some an uphill battle. But the idea here is not only to recognize, while amid loss and grief, what is now missing but to create an honest dialogue with yourself about the purpose of the loss on deeper levels and the natural gain that comes with it. When we are not looking through the lens of our pain, lack, or self-pity (all valuable dynamics that we will explore later), the gain becomes more visible. I'd like to contribute an exercise here for you to further contemplate the illusions you carry regarding your own losses.

Choose a loss that you have experienced. You are welcome to choose one that currently brings deep sorrow and grief, or you can choose one you feel more balanced in at the moment. Sit with a paper and pen or computer and answer these questions from an intuitive stream of consciousness. Take four deep breaths to relax, clear your mind, and focus on the subject of each question. Take a moment to contemplate them and write whatever comes to mind. Do not censor yourself in any way. You are welcome to read through your answers once they are written, but save the document to read four days later and see how you experience the information at that time.

What is the loss you experienced?

How long ago?

What circle of grief are you experiencing regarding the loss?

Are you in connection with others that have experienced the same kind of loss?

Name all the secondary losses you experienced because of this one loss (e.g., money, dignity, friends, habits).

What did you gain despite the loss?

Theorize or imagine how this loss could be valuable to you.

Did you experience heavy emotional grief from this loss?

If so, does it feel complete?

What are some of the changes that you've made since the loss?

What focus, energy, or habit have you used to replace the loss?

What is a new truth that came to light after the loss?

Receiving is more difficult than letting go

I was working with a client, Serena, when she exclaimed, "Tonight, I spoke with my husband and shared about my debilitating anxiety, and his response was to suggest having a drink!"

She was so frustrated at always having her feelings marginalized and diminished by his inability to just listen. At least that's how it felt to her.

And then it smacked her in the face: despite her husband's inability to empathize and connect in times of stress (a longtime relationship issue), she realized that he says, "I love you" in many ways other than with words all the time. She realized that she'd been afraid to receive his love because it had historically been laced with his fears and anxieties too—some of which she felt were a lot to handle. This subtle acceptance of the truth allowed her to reveal a deeper truth about her relationship to love.

"I realized that saying, 'I love you' and feeling the full weight of my gratitude for how much I am loved by everyone has meant for me that 'the end is near.'"

She felt that truly experiencing love meant that she would die. She went on to explain:

"Somewhere along the line, I began to believe that expressing deep gratitude, love, and appreciation is something from the movies, my culture, literature, or something we do when people are about to die or are dying. This is the only time."

It occurred to her that this philosophy had fundamentally shaped her behavior and been a filter through which she saw life.

"I would allow myself to experience deep affinity and care from others only when I felt I was ready to die or had died. Of course, it was not true; I was still breathing. However, because I didn't want to die or was not ready to die, it had not been safe to receive or even see the love I had in my life."

Though counterintuitive, it is easier to remain in the energy of loss than to open yourself up to the change that is necessary to receive something you want. Often, we can misidentify the resistance to change we feel as a failure in accomplishing our goals or not receiving what we expect or need. How we perceive our lives and loved ones during a crisis can be varying at best. Thoroughly investigating our illusions around loss can lead to revelatory wisdoms regarding our lives.

Illusions and awareness

The various states of our personal awareness contribute to the multitude of illusory information we carry or receive. It's like when our brain recognizes something that it is familiar with and begins to see it everywhere. In fact, our spiritual and emotional perception has a tendency to see things as we have previously experienced, instead of receiving them as they are and allowing our brain to break its neurological pattern by having a new experience.

The heart in our body and our spiritual heart (the heart chakra, the energy center in the middle of the chest) are the places where we allow new energy in so that we can receive a new experience or witness a new event and the emotions that may go with it, such as fear, joy, surprise, excitement, or awe. When we can create a connection between the heart's openness and the brain's trusty patterns, we call it heart/brain resonance. The phenomenon of this connection allows us to see with new or at least accurate perception.

The purpose of pain

To truly have lost someone or something, we must recognize the loss through our experience of pain. Like the old adage "If a tree falls in the forest, and if we don't hear it, has it really fallen?," pain is the archeologist of the spirit. It continues to dig until it reveals the Truth in between the multiple levels of suffering. Pain exists in layers of vibration. Vibrations that propel the movement of emotion that we call grief. It is an essential building block to the process of human awareness and connection.

Pain is a teacher of epic proportions. She shows us the places within ourselves that need to be brought into balance, where we may need more information or to be honest with ourselves. She can reveal the lies others tell us, or themselves. Essentially, pain creates a road map of physical sensations, habits, emotions, mental patterns, and spiritual imprints that get our attention on any one of these levels of energy, so that we may work to bring peace, grace, or mercy to each one to resolve the pain.

Spiritual pain: Our spiritual pain refers to the karmic imprints we incarnate into this life with—they are the vibrational patterns that reveal themselves through our inclinations, attractions, likes, and dislikes. When these imprints cause us pain, it is because we have carried with us hurt from our past that has not yet been resolved. It is common to recognize such imprints through dreams, psychic awareness, synchronicities, and irrational emotional responses to circumstances where these responses do not match the conditions at hand.

Mental pain: Many people experience mental pain as a confusing cacophony of running thoughts. The pain that is experienced arises out of fear, disempowering beliefs, and the possibility of a loss of control—an inability to control the mind. Mental pain is often not based in fact or truth, but what a person believes has or will happen, and their reaction to it.

Emotional pain: Emotional pain is processed through our heart, lungs, gut, and genitals—this is where the energy stays in the body if it is not processed through experiences such as tears, laughter, deep breathing, or rage. Feeling your strong emotion is necessary for a healthy body, even your rage and anguish. Your goal is to allow the flow of the emotions through your body by not stopping them, not transferring them to others, and not allowing them to propel you into making choices that cause further conflict. Being able to process your strong emotions in a safe, isolated environment is the best option to ensure your success, until you understand more of how emotion works and what patterns, events, and feelings your emotions represent.

Psychic pain: Psychic pain refers to all the energy from others around you and in your environment. Being able to connect to this pain is also called your transpersonal awareness. For example, when there is a major traumatic event such as 9/11 or the COVID-19 pandemic—where multiple people are experiencing enormous pain in our midst, our empathy will open us to receiving and processing that pain when those who are experiencing the trauma personally are unable to do so. This kind of energetic transferring of grief can happen with family and friends, with communities, and even globally. To whatever degree of empathy one can feel, on the basis of their own personal pain, they attract and process this psychic pain.

Physical pain: Physical pain is, of course, the pain we experience in our bodies. However, the pain in our body, whether it has occurred because of some sort of malady or a mishap, is surely connected to all the other forms of pain we have discussed here. The physical body is the final stop on the journey of our pain's message to us. It travels through the many different vibrations of our awareness, seeking our attention to its message. Each level of pain can tell a different part of the same story, in hopes that each vibration can be processed in a way that allows peace to replace it, finally stopping at the physical body to help you with your revelation. You might think that you have pain because of an accident or disease, but it is the other way around. Your accident or disease is evidence of your deeper desire to understand the message your pain seeks to impart.

There is no better time to be born than when we are on the brink of losing everything.

—Simone Biles

The importance of catastrophe

There are many types of loss, or should I say "relationships," to one's illusion of loss. How one perceives the losses they experience, inevitably, has more value than the loss or event itself. Two people experiencing the same event will relate to it differently. Each of us has our own unique way of seeing the events in our lives, often predicated on previous conditions and spiritual imprints.

A spiritual imprint is a soul memory that we are born with—you may relate to them as past lives or simply the inclinations and compulsions you begin with, but no matter how you see them, they are the premising lens through which you view life, as well as the foundation of your grief. If you carry many spiritual traumas, it is possible the bedrock of your point of view will be one of feeling victimized by life. A feeling that everything that happens in life is happening to you and not for you. Every loss occurring on top of this premise only amplifies a feeling of disempowerment.

Each recurring loss can propel you deeper and deeper into the abyss of intense emotions such as self-pity, humiliation, devastation, powerlessness, and apathy. When this happens, every individual will respond from their spiritual imprints, the way they have been nurtured in life and from their experiences, to address these all-encompassing feelings. Some people will be overtaken by anything from depression to mania-related behaviors, or to emotional denial and a breakdown of their physical health. These conditions create the type of dense energy that is not easily moved.

Enter catastrophe. A catastrophe is an earth-shattering event with so much emotional kinetic energy it can move a mountain. These huge events in our lives serve as opportunities to master who we are, by requiring us to engage with ourselves and others as never before. The way we handle a catastrophe can remove our long-held ancestral filters that preordain how we see or respond to what is happening for us, offering us the opportunity to choose what we do next. This will shift how we filter out the energy that is not ours to carry.

In the wake of the COVID-19 pandemic, people got smashed with a crash course in death and loss, and most of all, their illusion of life was shattered. People lost jobs, a daily way of life, each other, access to healthcare for other ailments, and a general sense of safety. This catastrophe put us all in a position to reevaluate our relationships to everything. Some naturally plummeted into anxiety and depression, while others thrived in the isolating climate.

Amy Cunningham, owner of Fitting Tribute Funerals in Brooklyn, was front and center in New York City for the onslaught of the pandemic. She, like many frontline workers, was deeply challenged by her extreme work experiences like never before. Her preparedness and ability to take care of herself and her family while taking care of so many others was powerful.

It's been hard, working nonstop day in and day out, with late nights on the phone. I gained weight, lost sleep, started grinding my teeth, felt plagued by small errors, and awakened out of dreams influenced by my work. I've found meditating to be important; exercise is a must (something I let go), and a low-drama outside life is almost essential, but so hard for many to secure. It would be extremely tough to do this work with a troubled marriage/relationship, or young children. I know people manage it, but I'm not sure I could. I'd go crazy.

I am proud of the way I've managed, but I've paid a toll. In the early months of the pandemic, NYC mental health counselors and therapists banded together and offered sessions for free to frontline workers. I took a wonderful woman up on that offer and eventually started to pay her for ongoing conversation and support. Though I was not among those who went into the refrigerated trucks and trailers to collect and transfer the bodies of deceased people, I was working nonstop and managing many more cases than usual. In other words, I wasn't in quite as much physical risk as many other directors, but I was in steady contact with people grieving intensely and looking for ways to say goodbye.

There were times when I'd get slightly frustrated, because while I am not conventionally observant or religious, I do sense an energetic connection to the souls of the dead. Family members would say, "I didn't get to say goodbye." And I'd think, "Well . . . try to say goodbye. It's not too late. Sit in a chair, tune in to them, and say goodbye." I feel like the dead are always right there for us. We don't have to beg them to be there or show up. They are also so forgiving.

With that mindset, I felt in vague communion with the deceased people I was helping to find a new home. Burial services—where we could gather around an open grave in masks, all safely socially distanced—worked best. Cremations were delayed, and that was bothersome. I helped set up a new kind of safe, outdoor cremation gathering with the casket prior to cremation and got some press for the work I was doing. I felt the love and admiration extended toward me by others. All my training, all my awareness, all my tools for staying sane were of great use to me. Everything in my life led me to that moment. My feet felt planted in a firm place.

—Amy Cunningham
Owner, Fitting Tribute Funerals

Enduring a catastrophe in your life awakens you to what you value, the habits you have in place that serve you and those that do not. It clarifies things in a powerful and essential way. It draws the line of choices and empowerment so that it is easy to see and follow. Grief is the glue that connects each movement inspired by calamity. You can be affected by anything, but you make the choice to resolve it, and when you do, the Universe shows you how. Honesty and the truth then become the inevitable end result of the connection major events require in our lives.

RELATIONSHIPS TO LOSS

Each of us will have multiple relationships to the losses we experience. They will vary in intensity and can be passive; happening in our thoughts, or aggressive; being expressed in our feelings, habits, and behaviors. Some of these relationships include displacement, delusional thinking, overcompensation, busy work, over-eating, supplanting grief with other behaviors, magical thinking, miracle cures, bargaining with prayer and religious beliefs—to name a few.

We may traverse through a few or many of the relationships on this list, and each of them will bring their own revelations and preparations for our forward movement through the loss at hand. Although many of these compensating behaviors may have been considered a part of the "denial" phase of grief at one time, the truth is that each one of these relationships cultivates a new skill set that becomes a part of the new pattern being formed without the presence of what has been lost. These skills become a part of our new relational awareness of ourselves and others.

Displacement: This refers to the nonnegotiable movements that some losses require. Stricken by many of the earth changes we are seeing regularly—the loss of multiple family members that renders a child in foster care, the loss of a home and other belongings, or the loss of an entire community—sometimes people have no control over the events that affect them, only their responses to them. All these calamities require relocation due to an unknown or incomprehensible condition that will need all the focus available. For a while, grieving the unknown becomes the grief ritual.

Delusional thinking: Delusion is emotional visualization that often is inspired by fear and the "what ifs" in life. It is a vibration of creativity that allows a person to walk through what they fear will happen, often as an unconscious tactic to avoid the worst options. One so fully visualizes their fear, they are able to "prepare for the worst" in their minds. Once this is done, they can begin to contemplate something better occurring.

Overcompensation: This is a form of transferring one's grief onto other activities, either to avoid the deeper feelings or to trigger a sense of empowerment in some other way. Risk takers will "throw caution to the wind" more readily and do things that stimulate a feeling of awe, such as skydiving, zip lining, running a marathon, or car racing, as examples. Others will compensate for their grief by cooking for everyone, reading every book they can find, volunteering their time to charity, or cleaning the house relentlessly, as examples.

Busy work: This is an opportunity to avoid feeling the loss of communicating or connecting with others who are doing so. Busy work keeps the mind trained on a mindless activity, since often during grief the cognitive awareness fluctuates on the basis of the intensity of emotionalism.

Addictive or obsessive-compulsive behaviors: Overeating, drinking, drugging, sexing, or fasting all are behaviors that stimulate the brain and the body to overwhelm the feelings of grief with pleasurable endorphins. A modicum of this behavior is expected in waves for just about everyone who is grieving; however, it is important to be conscientious of not letting any of these behaviors become dangerous.

Magical thinking: This is a form of positive creative visualization. The only thing that keeps a person from getting to their goal is to quit. However, since this concerns what we may consider a miraculous outcome, sometimes there isn't enough time to get from where we are to the intended outcome. Or, the message of the magical thinking is a metaphor, offering light on other levels. Magical thinking often comes up in situations where there is a deeper truth that is being avoided. Ultimately, on a subliminal level this truth is the person in question's goal. Magical realms and magical thinking will be looked at on all the levels of perception in further chapters.

Miracle cures: When someone is grieving a dreary diagnosis, one of the ways the spirit seeks to move one from depression, gloom, and death to an outlook of brightness, joy, and life is to offer a positive ritual or task. Whether or not the "miracle cure" is real is not the purpose. In any dynamic of healing or integration, we must overcome our fear of death and recognize the intrinsic power of being human, despite our condition. This is a task-oriented way of achieving that viewpoint.

Bargaining with prayer and religious beliefs: Everyone incarnates with soul patterns that destine them to certain activities or behaviors that they must either overcome and change or submit to and strengthen. These patterns do not fate one to certain events and outcomes, but they reveal a path to the learning and transformation that is intended by the soul. Our spiritual practices and our relationship to the Creator are how we participate in this dynamic.

If we dismiss or avoid a relationship to our higher selves or the Divine in times of crisis, that relationship can turn to bargaining to begin to understand the higher realms and to receive more of what is needed. If one has cultivated a relationship to the Divine, it is the way they will access the truth of what is to come for them in any situation and to transmute their fear and worry into usable energy for their grief and struggle.

THE ANATOMY OF LOSS

Each loss we experience has a specific pattern that allows us to transition on every level of our awareness, I call it the *Anatomy of Loss*. In each aspect of the transition from releasing to receiving, we will gain new insights about ourselves through our intuition, thoughts, and feelings. The depth or intensity of any of them is based on not only the loss at hand, but our previous experiences, current belief systems, current support, and current state or condition.

Life is not so simple as to give us one loss at a time, allowing us to process it fully into an easy transition. No, we are constantly experiencing everything from little changes to major upheavals all the time, simultaneously—all with their own transitional process. A development in which grief is a part of the proceeding. That lends us to embracing the messy, multifaceted experience of going through many of the following phases, simultaneously. However, recognizing any one of them will give us a deeper sense of understanding and compassion for ourselves and others by releasing us from the judgment and shame that often appear with grief and loss. Here are the phases of the *Anatomy of Loss*:

The resistance to change: When we make changes, they are never truly spontaneous. Inherent in transition are the various alarms that go off in our awareness at specific points in the metamorphosis. When these triggers sound in the subconscious mind, they appear as variations of resistance expressed through negative words and understanding, such as focusing on what you don't like, don't want, or can't have. The stronger the resistance, the closer the opportunities for change are in proximity to you.

The intuition of letting go: Always, in the process of transitioning from one thing to another, are the intuitive messages alerting us to the change at hand. They can arrive as subtle thoughts about the change to come, images of that change, dreams about the change (literally or metaphorically), or witnessing those changes in others or our environment. Learning to pay attention to these subtle energetic synchronicities is key to understanding the need for the changes in your forward movement. Our spiritual messaging can be negative or positive, depending on how open we are to letting go of one dynamic, person, place, or thing to create space for another.

The physical release: Another phase in the anatomy of loss is when we remove objects, people, or places from our lives, and a void is created that draws in new and, often, higher or lower vibrational replacements, on the basis of how we are feeling, thinking, and acting in our lives. Clearing away things that no longer have use to us is only a portion of the process. We must also release the beliefs and ideals that attracted those things in the first place.

The transformative grief: The very nature of grief is cleansing, clearing, and transformative. It can be as lovely as a bubble bath and as scouring as the aftermath of a hurricane. In the dynamic of loss, grief is the element that creates space or renews the inner environment to receive new beliefs, ideals, thoughts, and emotions. Before grief, there is the rage of resistance or the anxiety of trepidation to that grief. During grief, there is the experience of ecstatic devastation and an opening to the limitless realms of opportunity. Finally, after grief, comes the release of endorphins and chemicals in the body that allow us to experience peace, calm, and vision (the ability to see new possibilities and innovations that bring us into a state of grace).

The radical acceptance: The state of radical acceptance is to honor everything exactly as it is in the moment: good, bad, or indifferent. This adherence to reality can come before or after the grieving process or be the very thing that promotes the transformative grief to pour out. When we embrace things as they are, not as we would like them to be, we become empowered from a grounded emotional perspective to make changes to anything in ourselves or our life that no longer serves us.

The beginning of a new path: When we make movements away from what no longer resonates with us—as we stay in motion—before we know it, we are fully on a new trajectory of life. This doesn't mean that everything or everyone is new, but that we are renewed, present, and available to respond with a fresh viewpoint, inspired emotions, and new spiritual patterns to promote and provoke a new lifestyle that more fully meets our needs.

A Ritual for Solace

Affirmation: I accept that life is happening for me on all levels; the Universe provides every need. I am safe to release my worry and feel my emotions in the safe harbor of a loving world.

What you'll need for your ritual:

one blue jar candle

one fire source (a lighter or match)

a multicolored cloth of your choice to place on the sacred altar area

one statuary item or one item that represents safety and protection for you. If you cannot think of an item that feels appropriate, the ancients used the herb star anise for its protective energies. Place four stars on your altar, one in each corner.

one piece of smoky quartz

mason jar

paper and pen

dried tobacco for offering

one medium-sized metal pot to burn herbs (charcoal if needed)

Herbs you'll need:

Lavender: This herb helps calm the nervous system and cushions the shock of loss. Lavender is a "first aid" plant that helps heal, support, and stabilize the body, mind, and spirit.

Sweetgrass: This wonderful-smelling grass helps prepare the space and body for releasing and opening for peace. The sweet scent helps calm the nervous system.

Juniper (leaf): This tree leaf helps release old patterns and energies, uplifts the energy of the space (including mental space), and promotes a place where one can feel safe and reflect in a mindful manner.

Optional:

Flower essences

Rescue Remedy Flower Essence: This remedy helps support the physical, emotional, mental, and ethereal body during challenging times such as shock, trauma, loss, and accidents.

Directions for using the Bach Flower Essences: You may add four drops into a cup of water and sip during the ritual to help ground your energy field and calm the mind and emotions. Or add the drops into a bottle of water and spritz over the altar to set the intention of your affirmation. You may also add four drops into a cleansing bath prior to the ritual.

Oils for Solace:

Lavender essential oil: This oil helps calm the nervous system and cushions the shock of loss. Lavender is a "first aid" plant that helps heal, support, and stabilize the body, mind, and spirit.

Rose Geranium essential oil: This oil helps ground and heal the heart and physical body from loss and promotes a safe place within one's sacred space and heart. Promotes self-care and self-love.

Directions for using essential oil: You may dab one drop of oil on pulse points (make sure to do a small patch test for sensitivity). Or add three drops into a cleansing bath before the burning ritual. You may also inhale from the bottle as you go through the ritual.

Begin your ritual by cleaning and clearing a small area in the main living space. Collect all the items for your altar and place them in the cleared space. Place the herbs in the mason jar and hold the jar in hand while repeating the affirmation (you may also say prayers of your choice for healing). Exhale your breath onto the herbs to release the energies of the affirmation.

Now, sit with your paper and pen (no computers or phones here) and write what you most need right now. Is it emotional, mental, spiritual, or physical? Once you've written it out completely, go back and rewrite what you need in ten words or fewer. This is an exercise in precision and directness.

Write your statement on a separate piece of paper, fold into halves twice, and place in the mason jar with the herbs. Light your candle and let it burn to the socket, or a few hours a day until it is complete. You can take a few moments every day to sit with your altar and reflect on how you feel and if there are any changes in your thoughts, emotions, or behaviors. Once the altar is complete, offer your tobacco to your outside garden and burn the herbs and paper in your burning pot, outside.

Performing this ritual may inspire a grief response, which is completely appropriate. Allow yourself to feel anything that comes up, and if you are too emotional to capture your feelings on paper, that is okay. The understanding you seek will come in many ways over time. Give yourself permission to go with the flow.

EVERYDAY GRIEF
THE ULTIMATE TEST OF STRENGTH

Each day, without fail, the sun rises again in the east and welcomes in another day—regardless of what we are going through or how we feel. Daily we experience many continual trivial and valuable transitions, and while these changes throughout our week all garner emotions—as a culture, we have been incentivized to ignore the relentless emotional messages. This societal conditioning, whether to be polite, to remain calm, or simply not to feel too much for fear of judgment or reprisal, puts us in a position to be unaware of the burden that is storing up just waiting for the right situation to release its weight.

How many times have you yelled at the automated customer service at the end of the line, "Representative!!" Or hurried off the phone in frustration when you couldn't get your issue resolved. A small occurrence in the scheme of things, but powerful nonetheless, and depending on our biorhythms or condition, it just may be the event that pushes you over the emotional edge. At any given time, our central nervous system can be overloaded, which leads to unexpected emotional responses and ill health.

As we grow and develop as humans, it deserves reminding here that the human brain is not fully developed in impulse control until we are at least in our twenties.[1] That means we struggle with processing the information we need to make solid decisions that are in our best interests. Learning to grieve regularly and giving ourselves permission to express our more subtle emotions as they arise is the way we access the insights we need for our growth. And if we are resistant to that process, it results in reactive behavior and hastily made choices in response to stimuli.

---

1   (Psychology Today, n.d.)

STRUGGLING WITH EVERYDAY GRIEF

No matter the reason, stuffing down these temporary expressions of emotion causes an enormous stress on the physical body, and these repressed utterances only build up in the emotional body to be experienced at another time, when an overload or deeper trauma requires an emotional release.

Everyday occurrences that cause us to store emotion can include events such as missing the bus, not getting the reservation or appointment we need, being promoted (or demoted), breaking a sentimental item, receiving bad news, or facing a world filled with racial injustice or gender and sexual bias, to name a few. Or, worst of all, you wake up in the morning and the coffee pot doesn't work and all hell breaks loose. Most often it is these small, seemingly benign events that build up day after day until they break though the dam holding back the flood of emotion.

Our everyday grief does not always culminate as deep emotion. We can struggle with little to no sleep and bad dreams, a perpetual negative attitude or fearful running thoughts, and low energy and depression. If we are not accustomed to expressing emotion, it is sometimes satisfying to make efforts to verbally chop up all that emotion under the surface by incessantly talking about our problems, in hopes that eventually we'll feel better.

Awareness is key here, learning to be mindful of the subtle feelings that rise up as the events of your day unfold, or that you notice yourself deliberately ignoring as you go along. The practice of mindfulness invites a new energy flow to move through and show you where and when to allow your everyday grief to be expressed. Creating a mindfulness regimen will help you cultivate awareness of the impact these simple daily events have and their value, as you experience and process the perceived loss.

Mindfulness practice

The practice of mindfulness is the process of becoming aware of all your thoughts and feelings. Mindfulness is a form of active meditation that you can do while multitasking: walking, housework, or any other solitary activity. To begin, you merely take a few breaths and tune into the thoughts that arise as you work. Then you pay close attention to the feelings those thoughts inspire, and instead of forcing yourself to ignore them, change them, or criticize them—you feel them. You allow the emotion to rise and fall without judgment or reaction. You simply acknowledge their presence, witness their value, and experience them at whatever intensity they arrive.

In mindfulness, it is natural to have peaceful emotional expressions. When there is no mindfulness, there is usually shame, frustration, misunderstanding, and no patience or compassion. Sometimes we feel guilt or fear that the painful release will take "forever." We work up so much anxiety about our grief or angry emotions that by the time we feel them, they are complicated by multiple events and many dismissals of their original presence. This leaves us in a position to have no clarity on what we are feeling and why. When this unexpected emotional response occurs, often the release is triggered by someone or something, possibly having nothing to do with the actual trauma being processed. It is easy for the bereft to transfer their grief onto an unrelated person or situation as a way of releasing their emotion.

Cultivating a mindfulness practice helps us become clear on what we think and feel, to be accountable to the truth of it, and to process it solely so that we may become present to our relationship with our self and others.

An exercise to understand the process of mindfulness

Go outside for a five-minute walk, up and down the street or to the end of your block and back. From the moment you step outside, speak out loud, everything you see. Just one single word after another, doing this for the entire time you are out of the house (tree, house, sidewalk, etc.), escalating in detail as you go. Once you are back in the house, make note of how your brain feels, how your throat feels, how your eyes feel, and how your heart feels. Are there any subtle changes? Do you feel invigorated or tired?

In every waking moment there are thoughts going through our heads. We are so used to this influx of information and stimulus that we lose our awareness of it and its impact on our energy levels, attitudes, and emotions. By speaking out loud everything you see, you understand the kind of pressure we put ourselves through in our thought patterns, silently, all the time, except possibly when we are sleeping, and even then we are processing other information. When we lack awareness in this process, we do not allow for a complete flow of energy, and there is no release—only thoughts on a loop in our heads.

OVERCOMING FEELING VICTIMIZED BY LOSS

When you experience many small or large losses in succession, they build until you experience a forceful rush of grief. Often this experience is accompanied by feelings of perceived victimization: the events in your life are happening to you—bad things are coming at you and someone else is to blame. Overcoming these feelings of victimization, layered with the emotions of betrayal, resentment, bitterness, mistrust, or guilt, can feel like a high mountain to climb. But in truth, we must look only to ourselves and our feelings or habits of empowerment that preceded the grief response.

If we have always felt dismissed or disempowered in our lives, those feelings will only be amplified and become the mind's priority for expression up until the extreme breakdown of grief. Why is this happening to me? When will it all end? What did I do to deserve this? Bringing the mind into the process of grief only elongates the time it takes for us to allow the expression of our feelings. This is the time to make an important decision and tell yourself:

I alone am accountable for my life and how I experience it. I can change myself in any way I want, to find peace.

On the other hand, if you've always felt empowered in your life, able to be accountable for yourself and the events in play, the temporary bout of self-pity may be an internal alarm system letting you know that you must now pull back your sphere of influence with others and learn to set and hold boundaries, since you are not getting your needs met. The scales of give and take within your relationships have become unbalanced, and you must now shift your focus to taking care of yourself until those imbalances resolve. In this case you must make the important decision to tell yourself:

I am safe to focus on myself, and those who will remain in my life are meant for me.

In the early days of becoming cognizant of my deep empathy and the ways I took on the energy of others, feeling victimized was powerful medicine. At first, it really does feel like things are happening to you. It taught me much about boundaries and how to be accountable for all the emotions I processed, mine or those of others. At that time, I struggled to be in crowds of people. I found myself running errands between five and six in the morning, just to avoid them.

The illusion of need

In life, we are conditioned to understand our needs through a lens of what is available to us, what the environment or culture around us may dictate, or what our biological leanings indicate at different ages. Ultimately, the value of the "feeling" of need is a mechanism we're born with, intended to keep us alive and in a body. This unconscious survivalist inclination is not accurate to most of the physical, mental, emotional, or spiritual needs we experience, yet it is often the place from which we respond to our world to get our needs met. We interact with our relationships, the attention we get, the jobs we do, or the objects we have as if we cannot live without them. This viewpoint creates the buildup of fear around everything in our lives and its inevitable, impending loss.

Much of what we have and experience in life we can do without, but rather than looking at life through a lens of abundance, we pay attention to the fear of not having enough—the innate fight-or-flight directive that underlies all we do (unless we have consciously shifted our focus). This natural adherence to "staying alive" rather than living fully begins to color our emotional and intellectual viewpoint on all aspects of ourselves, others, and our world. It is what generates our illusion of need.

The truth is, while we process our fear of death, the experience of grief becomes the path from one state or condition to another, and the many levels of perspective from which we view the journey. Grief transports us gently and fluidly when we accept our sorrowful emotions, or violently with resistance when we do not. Our destination is to the release of one dynamic or memory, and the introduction of another person, place, or thing that better suits our needs. It is our spiritual, mental, and emotional faculties that facilitate this transition, piece by piece over time. We express these transitions on the different levels, through how we comprehend and manage our needs. Our needs fluctuate as our conditions change.

Getting through life with difficult people

Our most impactful teachers in life are our relationships to others. They require us to take constant inventory of who we are by reflecting to us glimpses of ourselves, and that awareness comes through us in our everyday grief. This inner conflict informs how we will relate to others in all situations, especially difficult ones. The most important thing about working or dealing with difficult people is not to take them personally. First, let's define "difficult." Things become demanding in the face of conflict and struggle. A person in strife is also a person in trauma. My tagline: *Drama Equals Trauma*. Remember that and don't react.

People experiencing trauma are usually not at their best; they're hurting, confused, overwhelmed, and sometimes angry. They don't often, in those moments, have self-awareness or care about their impact, or how they are perceived. Your best strategy with a person in this condition is not to match their intensity. Here are four steps to turn down the temperature of your dealings with a person in conflict.

Take deep, slow breaths. The amount of energetic influence we have on others, either singularly or in groups, is powerful if we accept it. When we shift our demeanor and slow our breath rate, those whom we are speaking with will naturally do the same.

Speak in a lower-volumed tone. When people are upset, they automatically speak in a higher pitch and volume than when relaxed. When you shift your tone and volume, those with whom you are speaking will have to work harder to generate the energy needed to sustain their timbre, and people in crisis are already weary and don't necessarily want to sustain their big emotions; they simply want to be heard.

Do not take what others say or do personally. (Even when they make it personal.) When someone is in trauma and experiencing a grief reaction, it's easy for them to misread intentions and target others with their strong emotions. This is the time to use all the compassion you can muster not to take their words or actions personally, and to stay calm and remain in the situation to listen. If this isn't possible, take the opportunity to let your cohort know that you're happy to speak with them later when they feel calm. It is important not to condone abusive behavior from anyone, no matter their circumstance. Setting composed, firm boundaries energetically helps your counterpart manage their strong emotions better.

Listen to them. People struggling with losses, large or small, want and need to be heard. Often, they are making efforts to express beliefs or feelings that will reflect to them the deeper understandings of their circumstances. They are not necessarily seeking *your* understanding and acceptance; they are seeking their own.

We all have bad days or unfortunate times in life. When we can have compassion and empathy for what another is going through, it teaches us to love ourselves more deeply and to cultivate patience for ourselves and others. The peace that comes from taking the position of empathy for another is for our benefit; it allows us to remain relaxed, intuitive, present, powerful, and healthy—in the moment and over time.

How do I get through life when it centers on loss?

Having a life that centers on constant transition (whether it be a temporal circumstance, a life pattern, or a choice via a job, etc.) and reckoning with loss daily isn't easy for any of us. However, some folks can see in the dark more easily than others. Chances are, if you're reading this, you're one of those. To be of service in this way is not only commendable, but an honored position. It takes great strength and courage to live this life.

When you are under consistent pressure or duress, your self-awareness is invaluable to you; learning meditative practices such as mindfulness or learning to be conscientious of your "self-talk" is paramount to your wellness. To practice self-kindness or give yourself space from others will help sort the many stressors of the day. It may also serve you well to gain a responsible sounding board such as a therapist, counselor, or mature trusted friend to listen to your feelings and experiences; it is a powerful way to cultivate your self-awareness. And, finally, journaling daily or weekly by writing down all your experiences will give you the opportunities you need to process any daily grief that comes up.

I was speaking with Dr. Shapir Rosenberg, a palliative-care physician, and I asked him, "How much training was offered or required through your education or by the licensing authority in managing your empathy and emotions for your patients?" His response stunned me. "None," he replied.

Even with the current cultural awakenings to emotional intelligence, there are still not many opportunities in medicine to discover the spiritual and emotional bond between a caregiver and their fiduciary. Even so, inspired professionals on the front lines of death and dying are paving new paths to understanding and teaching the compassion it takes to work with those in crisis. I asked Dr. Rosenberg how he manages his emotions and the grief of his patients:

I dive right in there with them. They are in a very delicate and profound time in their lives, and the emotions they feel are sacred. I really value that and want to share it with them.

—Dr. Shapir Rosenberg

Jobs that require daily grieving

All the folks working in service industries must have a special outlook on grief, and in many jobs they are trained to set their feelings aside, or it is encouraged in an unspoken way. Emotions are like water; they will collect and build until they break down the wall that holds them. Any high-stress job being of service to people is going to be wrought with frustrations, miscommunications, and power struggles. Here is a short but incomplete list of jobs that necessitate daily grieving:

Police, firefighters, and first responders

Coroner

Funeral directors

Retail workers and Service providers

Medical professionals

Military

Law enforcement and adjacent service providers

Caregivers

Teachers

Artists

Of course, there are beautiful miraculous moments in a life of service as well, but those tearful moments are not wrought with judgment. However, bring on a sad or angry situation, and "Crying makes you weak."

Understandably, no one wants to have a full breakdown midshift, so it's valuable to have a plan in place at work, and a strategy out of work to acknowledge and embrace all your feelings. Crying and screaming are outlets to depressurize the physical and emotional body; learning to manage or master them is essential. Grief breaks the cycle of rage, so it is common, especially for those who have higher levels of testosterone, to stay in the condition of anger if they have resistance to the more fluid emotions.

Empathy is our ability to connect to one another via our energy channels (chakras). Here is some vital information to simplify the understanding of the energy centers that connect to each layer of the aura and to which aspects of another's perspective they will connect us.

First and Second Energy Center: If we connect on first- or second-chakra levels (they govern limitations, everyday needs, emotions, sexuality, and survival), we will experience deep emotional empathy, sexual attraction, pain, or power struggles with others.

Third Energy Center: If we connect on third-chakra levels (this governs how we present ourselves in the world), we can empathize with another's strategy in life, such as beliefs, ideas, and habits, or we can judge those things in them.

Fourth Energy Center: If we connect on a heart chakra level, we empathize through compassion, love, or romance.

Fifth Energy Center: When we connect on a fifth-chakra level, it governs our throat and the ways we communicate. We will naturally connect and be able to listen and understand one another.

Sixth Energy Center: When we empathize from the sixth chakra, we share similar vision or can psychically "see" another's circumstances, often without emotion.

Seventh Energy Center: When we connect from our crown chakra, there tends to be a sense of mutual respect, common perspective, or similar life path or goals, such as being of service.

In addition to release, crying and empathy are also ways that we commune with the higher spiritual realms. It can be used as a form of prayer and to access guidance and wisdom. When we connect with higher vibrations of Truth, it opens our heart and releases tears, so that is what I call them—tears of truth. Most people will experience them during happy or shocking events such as weddings, or when a much-loved surprise caller makes an appearance, or we can experience them during meditation or other activities of reflection, even watching a video or listening to music.

The goal of experiencing deeper feelings is to become receptive to a higher perspective and insight, so working through your concept of vulnerability is important here. Many people equate feeling vulnerable to being unsafe or out of control, but in fact, when you are in an emotionally vulnerable receptive state, you are the strongest, most clear, and most prepared you will ever be. It is in this space that we have access to all the information and wisdom we need about our current circumstances. It is an extreme level of focus that is trained on visualizing the best possible outcome. All we must do is ask ourselves for the highest solution, and spirit can show us our current options within the space. This is our ingress to the true magic of the Universe.

During the pandemic, I had gone to pick up a few groceries and was standing in the checkout line. I noticed that Ray, the young man at the register, had let his mask fall under his nose. I immediately felt incensed. And then I laughed to myself. "Don't be one of 'those' people," I thought. So then I looked again at Ray. I could see he was visibly exhausted and possibly at the end of his shift, and it was busy. As I approached my turn to place my groceries on the conveyor belt, I called on the compassion I needed in the moment.

"Oh my goodness, Ray," I said. "I can't imagine having to wear that mask for so many hours in a row."

Ray brightened up a bit, affixed his mask above his nose, and said, "Yeah, it's rough."

"Well, thank you for your service, Ray. I hope your shift ends soon." His eyes smiled and he asked if I needed bags.

If you work in any of the fields we've mentioned, it is imperative to create a plan for high-stress reactions while working and a strategy outside work to process through all your emotions in a deliberate way, not leaving any option for buildup. And if you are one of the people receiving service, remember the power you have in being a part of the solution.

SELF-CARE AND EMOTIONAL-PROCESSING OPTIONS

The need for self-care cannot be underestimated. Considering ourselves in little ways, from the foods we eat to choosing compassion over judgment toward ourselves and others, is paramount to our overall wellness. In times of loss, we may not always have access to nourishing foods or bright and shiny feelings, but we always have access to gratitude. The one emotion that keeps things fluid and moving forward.

Not the "Thank you so much for this cluster #@$% happening in my life; I am learning so much" way, but the "Thank you, me, for not giving up" kind of way. Gratitude is a leveling emotion that promotes openness and courage. It is your willingness to remain open and fluid no matter the circumstances that allows for your access to the energy and information that will get you through it. Below are some other elements of self-care to consider:

Surrender

The most important skill set you can have is *surrender*. Yes, learning to surrender is a skill set. In this context, surrendering has many other facets than just letting go. It is the act of allowing yourself to release and receive. To free yourself of one belief, idea, or emotion is to create space for the new one. Getting to know your triggers (staunch beliefs, ideals, and judgments) and learning to manage them is a form of surrendering to what is.

Treat Yourself

Treat yourself to something that is good for your body, soothing to your emotions, or inspiring to your soul that does not include fatty, sugary foods; alcohol; or drugs. You can use any one of those things in moderation, but you must have a relationship to your body, mind, and spirit in a holistic way and have go-to habits in place that serve your highest self.

Get a Sounding Board

Working with a counselor (religious or secular), a friend or coworker, or a support group is paramount to your ability to be objective. To see your feelings from another's perspective or hearing yourself speak out loud allows you to become witness to yourself and your feelings. It creates the space to gain new perspective.

Alone Time

Being alone is a powerful time to become mindful of your thoughts and feelings, not those of others. Even taking this time to get extra rest is important for your emotional and mental health. If you work a high-stress job, you should be sleeping for an entire day at least every two weeks. Not only for physical rest, but for the rejuvenation your brain and heart need to decompress. Sleeping for an entire day does not mean you are depressed or that there is something wrong.

Meditation

Learning the art of emptying your mind is an important skill set; spending from five minutes to an hour in meditation will help you be able to take authority over your mind and emotions on command, which is powerful medicine when you are subject to confronting people on the job daily, with whom you do not share the same values, beliefs, religious views, or politics. You must be able to empty yourself of judgments on the spot, if necessary.

Music Time

Music activates the right side of the brain, the "intuitive" side. It helps you access higher thinking and wisdom and can get you in touch with your grief and offer gentle release. Mix it up a bit by choosing something different from what you are used to.

Singing

To sing, no matter your skill level, is a powerful way to honor your presence in the world. It also connects you with your voice and sets you up to easily place necessary boundaries in all situations.

Creative Time or Journaling

We all are creative beings (even when you don't think so). Creativity is the way we access subliminal information from our outside world and higher selves. So, spending time crafting or writing is a mindful task that connects you with your deeper possibilities.

Physical Activity in Nature

Hug a tree. Take a hike. The natural world and all the plants and animals in it are our kindred spirits and there to support and inspire us on all levels. Getting a dose of that at least three times a week, even for five minutes at a stretch, is valuable.

Sexuality

Sex is a powerful healer, and when practiced with love, value, and consideration, it can work miracles. Especially masturbation. Using your sexuality to become present in the moment or to visualize and connect to your most loving self is grounding and healing. The caveat here is to be careful not to engage in frivolous relationships that can bring more chaos and emotional trauma to your life. Sex for the sake of release, or demanding sex from a spouse or a partner, will bring additional burden to your circumstances, whether or not you are aware of it.

For those who work in environments where there is daily change, the grief work is continual. These positions in life are to be of service, whether because of circumstance or choice. These medical professionals, teachers, government employees, retail workers, artists, military, firefighters, and police all sacrifice an aspect of themselves to serve the rest of us—that characteristic is "ignorance." The ability to ignore (deliberately or unconsciously) themselves, others, their environment, or the truth. The people who do this work are faced with the ongoing requirement of self-reflection, intentional or not.

I am not saying that people in these jobs aren't sometimes unknowing or have bias one way or another, I am saying that they are mirrored by their peers on a moment-to-moment basis and have who they are, challenged on every level, until they are forced to cultivate self-awareness. It is the layered deconstruction of the self that grief supports. Our illusions of who we are, what we believe, how we feel, the power we have, and what we want are in constant transition. This is why self-care is necessary.

FACING EVERYDAY GRIEF

Grief gets a bad rap. It's not nearly as scary or uncomfortable when you embrace its rhythms for subtle frustrations and minor occurrences. Using it as a stopgap to release small increases in pressure prepares you for the mind-blowing, heart-wrenching overwhelmingness of trauma and big loss. In fact, everyday grief is your connection to inspiration, innovation, and magic throughout the day. It can allow you access to what's needed for any reconciliation, or the vision to make unique choices and achieve spectacular results in any situation. With grief comes understanding, clarity, and creativity as well as new hope for a fresh outlook and experience.

Grief creates awareness and empathy

The more we grieve, the more aware we become of ourselves, others, and our environment. Only when we begin to understand our environment as it is, not as we wish it to be, can we truly know ourselves. It is in times of great crisis that we are illuminated to the systems in which we engage to run our world. Those systems were created by people in fear and lack, but not without courage.

When we create our vision of the world, it is natural to begin in a state of fear, which allows for a hypervigilance and awareness of our environment as we see it through the lens of our beliefs. Lack is also a part of this equation, because when one is embarking on a new endeavor, no matter how prepared you desire to be, there will always be elements unknown to you.

I watched a movie called *Skinwalker*. A portion of the story was about a native medicine woman who'd died, and what befalls a couple of grave robbers when they steal her personal effects from her grave. She was buried with her sacred medicine bag and other revered items, when along come two fur trappers who steal the medicine bag to sell it. Not understanding this tribe's culture and beliefs, or the spiritual power of this woman's medicine, the man who stole the bag first watched his friend die from a snakebite, and then soon after died a horrible death himself.

In truth, the story was about ignorance, lack of awareness, and respect. The guy who stole the items lacked awareness, and his friend ignored what he knew would befall his partner, showing his ignorance. The moral of this story is to respect yourself and others or you'll die. Of course, my rendition is simplified, but the final understanding here, and the place when grief makes a visit, is eventually in the afterlife. You don't want to wait that long to get the whole picture, do you? You can't know something before you have the space to receive the truth about it, and that space is created by the multiple elements of grieving and mourning.

Being of service

Grief is a layered process. We shed one mental or emotional skin at a time until the heart surrenders to the full meaning of the loss or transition in question, and a good way to accomplish this is by helping others. We need times of respite between grief experiences to connect to the larger world in which we live. To be of service can become a bridge from which to view our own personal past, and a link to witness our present as it is, or a portal to the future we would like to create. To spend time with people in new surroundings with access to the world from their vantage point can be a fulfilling vacation away from yourself and your own life.

The seven traits needed to be of service

1. Fearlessness: To be fearless does not mean to be unafraid; it means we embrace the unknown and walk through the fear. To bring light and understanding into any place, whether one is familiar with that place or not.

2. Can-do attitude: This is the belief that no matter what, you will prevail, coupled with the understanding that your thoughts, feelings, and actions, when in alignment, bring success.

3. Joy: Joy is an integral part of faith. The ability to embrace your power despite not knowing what is to come. It is a choice on subliminal levels, to be the best you can, and to see the highest possible outcome no matter the circumstance.

4. Surrender: Surrender is the act of receiving. Most of us, whether we'd like to admit it or not, must relinquish our need to control everything—even at times ourselves. Notice the connection here between being of service and self-care.

5. Receptivity: To receive is to allow yourself to take in new energy, ideas, opportunities, or physical-world prosperity.

6. Vision: The ability to imagine a world better than the one in which you live.

7. Acceptance: The ability to accept things as they are. We will always see things first through our own personal bias or beliefs. It is the way our psyche and spirit attempt to protect us from the illusion of harm. Once we accept our own vision, the Universe can show us the truth of what we have before us and its value.

HOW TO OVERCOME USING ESTABLISHED BEHAVIORS TO RESIST GRIEF

It is a natural response to stop water from leaking from a pipe or a broken glass. Because of this, we easily relate the same way to grief as leaking emotion, and the autopilot reaction to stop it. In many cultures, we are conditioned to see our need for expressing big emotions as weakness or folly—that somehow the more refined you are, the less you should feel. Instead, we indulge in repetitive, addictive behavior that may distract us from our pain but only creates more in the process. Here are some simple ideas to consider when you are tempted to do any of the following, instead of allowing yourself to feel.

Overeating: Before you dig in the fridge or the cabinet for a snack, consult your body. Ask it what it needs. Ask yourself why you're eating. Take stock of what triggered the desire to eat. (What happened in the five minutes before you got hungry?) Once you've listened to each of these answers, the likelihood you'll need food is minimal.

Sexual outlets: When we grieve, we are highly sexualized. Our sexuality and feelings are centered in the genitals and governed by the second chakra (the emotional energy center of the body). It's easy to fall into new attractions with people or want to express our deeper emotions within a sexual relationship, which in and of itself is great. But it can severely complicate our feelings and relationships, compounding our anxiety. Where it becomes a deterrent is when you mistake your deep feelings for love or attachment to another. This can be a problem for our single grievers.

Entering a new sexual relationship while grieving opens one to taking on the additional emotional and spiritual energy of one's partner. It can misguide communication and further complicate feelings. However, having a consistent, loving, and compassionate sexual partner during grief can be comforting and helpful—if the partners are honest and open and negotiate the relationship equitably.

To determine if engaging in a sexual relationship is right for you during grief, it's important to ask yourself what you need and why you need it. If you're dating, it's important to require yourself and your partner to discuss expectations about the relationship and sex, outside a sexual situation. It is way too easy to go with the sexual attraction and end up with misunderstandings and disappointment.

Substance abuse: Drinking too much and taking unnecessary drugs while grieving only complicate or prolong the emotional shedding process. No matter the substance, the intention behind it is to slow down the emotional experiences of grief and inhibit the awareness that comes with it. This form of denial can have long-term consequences. Remember that to an addict, all drugs are necessary. Take the opportunity before you use a substance to take deep, long breaths and ask yourself what feelings you are looking to overcome.

Allow the specific thought or feeling to rise and fall without reacting to its presence. If a flood of emotion comes, let it move through you, peacefully, while focusing on your breath and heartbeat. Close your eyes if that helps you to hear your heartbeat and feel your breath pattern.

Controlling behavior: It is common for people under extreme duress to make efforts to control others and their environment, instead of making efforts to manage themselves in a way that serves everyone. The idea of control offers a false sense of security and is an unconscious way of feeling safe. Some use controlling behaviors such as intimidation, picking fights, restrictions, anger, or righteous speech to try to preserve elements of the life they feel was present before the loss. Doing this only prolongs the inevitable grief and sabotages relationships along the way.

The madness in the design? People with controlling behaviors often do not recognize their tendency to control. The goal is to take time for self-reflection and to cultivate self-awareness. When we are grieving, it's easy to feel "out of control." Take this sentiment as a message: your deepest desire is to manage your emotions in a way that helps you feel safe and comfortable. It is not a message to control others and their words or actions.

Overtalking: For those who feel unable to allow big emotions, a common way to release that emotional energy is to overtalk in various ways, such as speaking incessantly, leaving no room for discussion with others, speaking with a rapid speech pattern, or repeating the same story, understanding, or belief. Usually, this relentless speech will verbally express emotions but will avoid feeling them at all costs.

In general, if you'll give yourself increments of five to ten minutes, two to five times a day, to take four deep breaths and relax, you will be free to feel and reflect on any emotion that arises at the time. Allowing emotion to flow through in this focused way will create a sense of order in an experience that can feel very chaotic.

A RITUAL FOR COURAGE

Affirmation: I am stronger than I know. I am free to feel without judgment and receive courage, integrity, and wisdom from a loving Universe that is always here to support me.

What you'll need for your ritual:

one orange jar candle

one fire source (a lighter or match)

a tribal-designed 8.5 × 11 in. paper or cloth (any size) of your choice to place on the sacred altar area. (Tribal designs are often based on or echo sacred geometry or elements of the natural world, connecting us to the earth and the cosmos.)

one photo of a person, place, or thing that depicts or represents courage and protection to you a piece of citrine

mason jar

paper and pen

dried corn for offering

one medium-sized metal pot to burn herbs (charcoal if needed)

Herbs you'll need:

Eucalyptus: This herb opens the lungs and helps release grief, sadness, and disappointments that might be stuck in the mind, body, or spirit. Another way to use eucalyptus is to hang a branch in the shower, since the steam will help release the essential oils in the leaves for a fragrant and very purifying shower.

Pine: Stems from this tree open the lungs and help calm the nervous system and mind. It readies one's physical and etheric body for healing grief, to lessen guilt, and to cultivate courage to walk forward. Extremely purifying as well.

Oak: Oak is a tree for strength, courage, resilience, and restoration after the challenges of grief. It helps one to feel strong as one is going through difficult times.

Optional:

Flower essences:

Mimulus Flower Essence: This essence is supportive and gives courage for those who face challenges and fears, and offers the feeling that they can overcome difficulties.

Aspen Flower Essence: This essence is supportive and gives courage to face the unknown of nebulous worries and fears.

Directions for Bach Flower Essence: You may add four drops into a cup of water and sip during the ritual to help ground your energy field and calm the mind and emotions. Or add the drops into a bottle of water and spritz over the altar to set the intention of your affirmation. You may also add four drops into a cleansing bath prior to the ritual.

Begin your ritual by cleaning and clearing an area of your home where you feel safe. Collect all the items for your altar and put them in the cleared space. Place the herbs in the mason jar and hold it in hand while repeating the affirmation (you may also say prayers of your choice for healing). Exhale your breath onto the herbs to release the energies of the affirmation.

Now, sit with paper and pen (no computers or phones here) in front of your altar and contemplate the object of your photo. As you meditate with the photo, ask yourself what about it invokes comfort and safety. Then ask yourself what you need in your life to feel this every day. Write it down. Once you've written down everything that comes to mind, fold the paper into halves twice and place it in the mason jar with the herbs. Light your candle and let it burn to the socket, or for a few hours a day until it is complete.

Take a few moments each day to sit with your altar and reflect on how you feel and on any changes in your thoughts, emotions, or behaviors. Once the altar is complete, offer your dried corn to your garden and burn the herbs and paper in your burning pot, outside.

Performing this ritual may inspire a grief response, which is completely appropriate. Allow yourself to feel anything that comes up, and if you are too emotional to capture your feelings on paper, that is okay. The understanding you seek will come in many ways over time. Give yourself permission to go with the flow.

MOURNING: THE ENDLESS TRANSITION

I looked up the definition of mourning on the internet, to get a general understanding of the information that is immediately accessible to folks, and no wonder people are confused about the process of mourning. I found several sources for a definition, and they were essentially the same: "the action of being sorrowful" and "the outward expression of lamentation like wearing black clothes, etc." I was surprised, to say the least. The only context in which I found a definition for mourning was death.

Fortunately, mourning is a much more profound and complex experience beyond wearing your new black outfit. That's not to say there isn't great purpose in such rituals, but mourning is about what happens when you're not wearing that black suit. We naturally associate mourning with dying, although we mourn in some way for every perceived loss we experience.

When something or someone is removed from our life, beyond experiencing the many layers of grief we will need to make tactical adjustments on mental, emotional, spiritual, and physical levels. It is the process of relearning your life without what was lost. The transition of relating to your life and to what is now missing—and the void in its place.

To mourn your loss speaks to the physical-world transition of any detail that must change now because of the loss. Mourning is the time and space given to grieve. Grief is the change agent that shifts our attachment and changes our understanding of the new mental, emotional, and spiritual relationship we will have with what we have lost. They are lumped together because one does not happen without the other.

PUTTING THE PIECES BACK TOGETHER

Mourning can take weeks, months, or years, depending on the length of time we may have spent with what was lost and the depth of the adjustment needed. It's important to be patient with yourself and others during this very important journey, since it often reveals information to people about themselves, their loved ones, and the situation at hand that may have not been previously known. It is the possibility of these many layers of perspective that deserves our attention and respect.

Look to your physical world

The first act of mourning is to address the elements of life that are critical and time sensitive. It's not uncommon, when we've been grieving, to neglect our work, home, family, or friends. So, the first order of business is to look for any tasks, large or small, that have been overlooked. Jobs such as paying bills, cleaning and sanitizing the home and vehicle, banking or filing tax papers with deadlines, or fixing crucial items around the house. While some people are "doers" when they are grieving, many are not. Taking care of your physical world and making sure all your basic needs are met are crucial.

Most importantly, taking care of yourself is key. It's easy in the face of loss to lose interest in self-care or to compensate for or avoid grieving by putting our attention on less healthful habits. At some point, there is a sense of futility that comes with the mourning process where it doesn't feel like anything matters anymore.

All emotions are teachers, not necessarily positive or negative, but valuable to us in their message. For example: to feel futility is an important freedom-building step, but you don't want to get lost in believing it to be true (nothing is ever futile). The first big rush of recognizing our loss from an objective view is riddled with many more subtle (less rational) emotions such as guilt, shame, or confusion. How we can handle these different emotions is to recognize our feelings of apathy that are generated from the futility we have experienced, and to question the validity of the guilt, shame, or confusion. This helps us experience detachment— the "none of this matters anyway" sentiment.

This more detached outlook is often where we will accomplish a majority of our immediate physical-world changes. We have moved from intense grief and sorrow to weariness or anxiety and apathy. This is where we can begin to sort through our other feelings and manage our physical world a little differently. The intensity of this process depends on the value of the loss and the ability to replace it.

When dealing with how we should proceed during periods of mourning and loss, we should also take note of how we learned to mourn our losses early in life. This will be the foundation of our viewpoint as we get older. The degree of honesty we require of ourselves is an important building block. Diane, who had just lost her best friend of thirty-five years, had begun to reminisce.

I met my best friend when she was sixteen and I was nineteen; we were best friends for over thirty-five years. Jennifer was adopted and had a tenuous relationship with her adoptive father; he was ex-military and very strict. I can recall her not being able to leave the house until her room was clean after he would come in with a white glove to test the surfaces for dust. Her adoptive mother, on the other hand, was very nurturing but enabled her by changing report cards or lying to avoid any fallout from Jennifer's father.

—Diane R.

When a child receives such mixed messages and is taught dishonesty as a coping strategy early in life, it sets them up to bypass their grief and mourning process and not to fully resolve their transitions. This emotional disconnection is the pattern that will unconsciously reverberate long into their lives as they develop.

Take inventory

Next, it is important to take inventory of our thoughts and emotions. When we evaluate our lives with some reflection, it often leads to a grief response, so I believe it deserves mentioning again here that when we cry for a length of time, it changes the neural circuitry in our brains. We release thoughts, beliefs, and feelings because, energetically, they are no longer a match for who we are. Although the process may be subliminal and just outside our conscious awareness, the process of mourning is the light of day after a dark night. It begins to show us what we value now or how our thoughts and feelings have changed; not just about the loss we've experienced, but ourselves and the people, places, and things in our lives. The emotional quality of our views shift as well.

Our life experiences and interactions with people always create imprints in our memory. They can also create energy constructs that feel like shards of glass lodged in our bodies and psyches. They are generated from the fearful, angry, violent, devastated, resistant, or bitter emotional exchanges we have with people, or as residue from specific events. When we mourn, we become aware of any of these constructs we carry. It is through our willingness to inventory our lives: all the memories, thoughts, and feelings—the choices they promoted—and the interactions they created with others. This allows us to be objective and make necessary changes.

Here is an example of a construct:

I was running a special support group for teens who had already been subjected to the penal system. We were sitting in a circle, and I was addressing each child in the circle with whatever question they had for me, when I came to a fourteen-year-old young man, named Henry. Immediately, I was struck with an overwhelming feeling of "not being good enough," but I was clear these were not my feelings. It was as if he had a sign on his head that read such. His question for me was "Why does my father hate me?"

I felt the boy's overwhelming confusion, and it became clear to me: his father hated himself, had not experienced any real nurturing, and didn't trust anyone. It was a potent combination of self-loathing and authority, just enough to propel him to continually tell his son he'd never be anything or do anything with his life. "You are worthless" became the construct Henry carried with him. As I spoke about it, the young man began to tear up . . . and then smiled a huge smile in relief. When I asked him what he was feeling, he responded, "I knew it! I did. I always feel so sad for my dad."

I went on: "Sometimes we must remember our parents are people too. They have feelings and insecurities that don't pertain to us, as their children. I know if your father could tell you he loved you, he would. But, most importantly, you don't have to believe him when he says mean things, and you must tell yourself how smart, strong, and brave you are for facing this truth so early in life. Do you know, most people don't acknowledge such powerful information about themselves until they're forty?!" The whole group laughed, and we moved on to the next in the circle.

Another example: Over my first year of driving a vehicle, I crashed my car four separate times. Who knew you shouldn't drive single-handedly while picking up papers that had fallen to the passenger's seat floor? Luckily, neither I nor anyone else was hurt, just mostly unsuspecting parked cars. Soon, I was to move to New York City, where subways and buses were the mode of transport.

I drove one time in NYC; a friend, Jake, loaned me his car to pick up another friend at JFK airport in Brooklyn. Driving in the city is a unique experience. At that time there were no lines on the streets or avenues, no apparent rules to follow, and you naturally fell into the flow of moving at whatever rate of speed others were traveling—a terrifying experience. Somehow, certainly by the Almighty's grace, my friend and I arrived back to Harlem, where I lived, neither of us worse for the wear. But when I exited the vehicle and locked the doors (manually), I began to shake uncontrollably and then burst into a flood of tears—vowing to never drive in the city again.

I had no idea of the posttraumatic stress I carried from my earlier driving experiences, only to have them exacerbated by the intense need for focus, and the constant threat of being hit by other vehicles in this driving event. Those two factors were responsible for the immense adrenalin rush I received immediately after locking the car door, and I was no longer in danger. I didn't drive again for about ten years, and once I relocated to Los Angeles where driving was a must, and because I hadn't fully processed my previous experiences and relationship to driving, it took me almost two years of walking myself through deep anxiety every time I entered the car to drive, and emotional rushes when I exited the vehicle.

Each of us carries experiences, beliefs about ourselves that come from our spiritual imprints (the fears we are born with), or the emotional energy and fearful reactions of others (constructs). These pesky memories take refuge in our beings until we are ready to feel them fully (grief) and receive the complete understanding of why we carry them (mourning).

If we do not fully grieve, we cannot completely mourn our transitions. The presence of these imprints and constructs offers us subliminal guidance as we walk through life, at times keeping us from repeating our mistakes. But eventually, we will need to pursue and process this energy mapping so that we may be free of them altogether and move forward with the wisdom we gained from their existence.

FINDING THE TRUTH

There is no such thing as "overthinking" something. When it appears we are obsessing on a specific element of a situation, it is because there is an underlying truth we are seeking that is present for us to find. We process our transitions in layers of understanding, one piece at a time, until we have adjusted our perspective of what is happening, eventually to find the Truth. We individually begin with our point of view, based on vantage point and bias, which lays the foundation of the path we take to arrive at the universal Truth. The fundamental elements we all share.

When we've experienced a loss, the journey of grief and mourning leads us on a Truth-seeking escapade. As we grieve, our personal awareness and beliefs shift. We begin to see details we may have not noticed before, or we recognize our past viewpoints, because through the grief, they may have changed. Often there are hidden details about people and events that surface after you let them go.

At one time, I had a boyfriend for about a year who was charming, helpful, and so smart. The more deeply I got to know him, the more the details of his life and his family began to get my attention. Both of his parents had died, and one of the first traumas he revealed to me was that at his father's funeral, previously unbeknown to him, he had a brother from another mother. As I got to know him, the story unfolded that his parents were divorced; his mother had left his father because he was seeing another woman.

I remember him saying one night, "No, there wasn't any overlap in their relationship."

He meant that his father wasn't seeing both women at the same time. It struck me as odd because he knew it wasn't true, and clearly did not remember a previous conversation where he'd explained as much—but was so relaxed and firm in stating this alternate fact, almost as if it were for my benefit. This caught my ear . . . was he seeing someone else?

A few months later, while on a weekend getaway, he'd shared with me his father's funeral program; he carried it in his briefcase. I remember getting a psychic flash of information as I held the paper in my hand. His father's spirit was communicating with me. He showed me the relationship he'd had with the woman he never married; he began it before he met my boyfriend's mother and continued all through his relationship with her, finally moving in with this other woman when his wife finally kicked him out. At this point, he'd also had children with both women.

Soon after, I noticed a woman paying a lot of attention to the man I was seeing on his social media pages, and she began to make attempts to communicate with me. When I brought it up, he said she was a "work associate" who was interested in him, but that he didn't share her affection. He said he wasn't seeing anyone else and that he wanted to see only me. However, every time he spoke (what turned out to be lies), I would see the spirit of his father. At dinner one night, a very sexy woman approached our table to say hello to him.

"Oh, I used to work with her."

His father's face, again, popped into my mind. I knew his father was trying to tell me what his son would not. Of course, you know how this story ended, but to give you the overview, he'd been seeing the woman who was contacting me on social media. We found out when she and I had a friendly banter about our "boyfriends" that happened to have the same name; that's when we found he'd been seeing both of us. And that wasn't all; soon it would come out that he was homeless and in deep financial straits and didn't own a car (all conditions he obfuscated with the help of his friends to continue the ruse).

For me, the interesting thing in this story was that at this point in my life, I'd done so much grieving around relationships in general and so much premourning in this one (through my connection to the truth in his spirit and that of his father's) that it took me three days—three days to process that everything this man told me was a lie. The only thing I was certain of was his name. I didn't need to cry; I only needed to sit in silence and receive the spiritual insights that came as I received facts from the other woman in the situation.

She and I spoke a few times and met once. She was determined to keep her relationship with him as it was. I, however, didn't need to see either of them again. The only real betrayal I felt was from his best friend's wife. I always thought she didn't like me, but as all was revealed, I realized she must have thought I knew of his other relationship. It turned out that of all the people I met while I was with him (and there were many), she was the only one I crossed paths with after the relationship ended. I was able to communicate my feeling of betrayal for her not telling me the truth when she so clearly wanted to.

The grieving and mourning process I experienced was extremely short and peaceful because I had remained present as the stories unfolded within the relationship: the subtlety of the interactions with his friends and especially their wives, the relationship I'd cultivated with his dead father, and especially my boyfriend's level of calm. He had certainly done this before; in fact, it was his way. I found my friends and family expressing more hurt and anger than I felt.

Frankly, other than the complete lie, this had been an easy, peaceful, fun, and inspiring relationship to me. However, when I saw it fully in the light of day, there was nothing else to do but to walk away and not look back. There needed to be no crying, rage, bitterness, or frustration. Once the light shone, it was all immediately clear: he was a liar and there was no changing it. There was no room to be friends, because he wasn't capable of honesty. It was all so simple.

Our willingness or resistance to receiving the complete Truth is the basis of our grief. The grief and mourning process helps us whittle away at the facts as they become revealed, showing us the way to releasing our biases, beliefs, and ideals as the Truth emerges. This is why we each grieve in our own way—we all have our individual relationship to the information at hand and must make our unique journey to the Truth on all levels.

MOURNING IN THE FAMILY DYNAMIC

Every family has their group dynamic set up at the onset, on the basis of the relationship of the two who created the family. Their way of communicating and relating will become the dynamic expressed by the children born to this ménage.

On the basis of the roots of expression, intimacy, and location, each family member will find their way in the transitional process. If the family all live together, each one in the household will likely take on an aspect of moving the whole through each emotional, psychological, spiritual, and physical transition.

In my family, we had very few moments of togetherness where we were all present. We shared thirty minutes at dinnertime nightly, from when I was ages one to eleven. After the death of my father, because my siblings and I were just far enough apart in age, they all dispersed into their own lives, and I was left home alone with my mother, who was a champion at hiding her feelings.

This pattern became exacerbated when as adults, my siblings and I lost our mother. We all were taught by example to hide away and feel our feelings or to stuff them down, since they could be only a deterrent to our goals in life. As an Empath, this directive put me in conflict because my feelings were always too deep and intense to hide completely. I too became a champion hider of emotion during the day, while crying myself to sleep every night.

What my siblings and I did have in common, a legacy from my mother, was her sense of style and a desire to always look our best. This is where the tradition of buying "bereavement wear" began. When my father died, much emphasis was put on getting a new dress for the funeral. I still remember the Laura Ashley frock that I loved so much. I remember spending time with my sisters and my mother in pursuit of just the right outfit to wear. We laughed and shopped and had lunch afterward. It was the one common ground we all could share in a time of such devastation: shopping and eating.

But when my mother died, as it turned out, bereavement wear and food were not enough to keep the family connected when almost everything else was pulling us apart. At this point we all were living in separate states, literally and figuratively. But during my mother's life, she had kept us all in communication, and we took yearly treks home to spend time as a family at the holidays. When she died, she took that tradition with her. While each of us still had to feed and dress ourselves, the mourning transition we learned as children was not enough to keep us in close communication and connection with each other.

THE ART OF MOVING FORWARD

The application of our skill in moving forward is what mourning is all about. How do we keep the best parts of ourselves and create a new relationship to the connections, dynamics, and traditions we must leave behind? It will certainly take our personal ingenuity and commitment to ferret out what we can keep and what must go. On the basis of our spiritual or childhood patterns, what we do next is often unconscious when we have learned to bypass our grief and cope by an "any means necessary" strategy. As we learn about Diane and Jennifer's friendship, we see how Jennifer learned early in childhood to lie as a coping strategy to move forward.

Jennifer was a beautiful girl and woman. I have literally seen men almost crash their cars when they would see her walking. Everyone, men and women alike, would stare at her as we walked through a store. I asked her once how she could not see it; she did see, but she had to walk with blinders on, wherever she was, instead of reacting to it.

Jennifer's adoptive mother died when she was twenty-one; at this time, Jennifer was already married and had a three-year-old. Her parents had already divorced, and she was estranged from her father and had no other family but an adopted brother, with whom she was not close. She and I were like sisters, and I felt at times she knew me better than I knew myself. Shortly after her mother was gone, Jennifer and her family moved to Oregon. We remained close and I moved out there for a short time. While living there, Jennifer started up an extramarital affair, and it ended up leading to her divorce.

From my perspective, that was the time when it seemed Jennifer started making bad decisions, and she often ended up down on her luck. There were situations when she needed money or had to scramble to find a place for her and her daughters to live. Being so far away, there was only so much I could do, but I always worried and would never feel settled until she was.

In 2016, her daughters (all grown) had been living in California. Jennifer had no one in Oregon, so she moved to California to be with them. Her plans fell apart when she arrived, and she was stranded with no money or place to stay. Then, while driving on a California freeway, her car broke down. She sold it for parts and now had no transportation.

As often happened in our relationship, she reached out to me. I was the fixer. I was the one she leaned on for emotional and financial support. I was the one she relied on to get what she needed. At the time, I was able to pay for a couple of extra nights at her hotel, but told her she needed to get to New Mexico. She could stay with me. In New Mexico, she had friends and job opportunities. Soon after arriving, she began working as a nurse in the county jail.

—Diane R.

In this case, Jennifer was still struggling with her childhood coping mechanisms, which were based on what she witnessed growing up: trying to feel good enough for her father by not directly addressing the relationship pattern with the opposite sex in which she engaged, and turning to the resolutions and nurturing of her enabling female friend as she did with her mother.

When making efforts to start fresh, the only thing that matters is what you do next. You alone have authority over it. Faith plays a big role (our intuitive relationship with what is yet unknown) in this part of the process. Once you set the standard for what you will or won't do, it is that standard that sets up the pace and options available to you. The difficulty here is following your gut to the standard in play or choosing another standard regardless of whether you can see its reality, its possibilities, or the options it will provide by choosing it. Faith is our intuitive way of deciding we need the circumstances that peace, prosperity, and love will provide. The act of trusting it will be more than enough to allow the Universe to create it for us.

HUMAN BEINGS NEED SUFFERING

Agony is the one thing all beings have in common. It is the meeting place of unity, progress, and innovation. When we arrive at suffering's door, it invites us in without question. Sometimes it locks us away inside our own private room to grieve in silence, and sometimes it holds up a mirror so that we may see ourselves in the light of day; either way, the heartbreak we feel eventually gives way to revelations about ourselves and the lives we are living. Human beings need suffering to reveal the hidden power we were born with.

Nothing is softer or more flexible than water, yet nothing can resist it.

—Lao Tzu[1]

Suffering is the path of wisdom

When distress comes along in any situation, it becomes the fork in the road where we are required to choose a path: wisdom or ignorance. We must either embrace grief and allow the watery flow of emotion to chip away at our pain one layer at a time—until the wisdom we seek becomes evident, or we will begin to split our consciousness between what is true and what we are choosing to see in the moment.

1 (Tzu, n.d.)

There is no cause for alarm; we do it all the time. Our culture practically demands it of us. And shall I say here that ignoring the truth only makes it louder and elongates the journey to it; finding it is inevitable. But you need to know about this fork in the road, since you will find it many times over in your life. You will need to assess which direction, no matter how uncomfortable, will serve you the best.

This choice will be informed by the natural flow of energy that moves through our bodies (kundalini, life force energy), through our minds (thoughts and ideas), and through our hearts (emotions). All of these serve as an integrating force to purify the body, calm the mind, and open the heart.

When we shut down any part of this process (which we do by will, naturally), we limit the ways and opportunities we have, to resolve issues. When there is no movement in our body, heart, or mind, we resort to the energy of our lowest common denominator within our environment—the low-hanging fruit, if you will—but to choose the most accessible path often brings more chaos and suffering.

However, those who haven't grieved their spiritual or emotional trauma tend to attract opportunities to do so. It is sometimes called trauma bonding. There are other types of personalities that do not experience empathy or pain, and those people thrive on risk-taking behavior and chaos to feel the excitement of adrenaline. These two types of people tend to find each other in a room.

In the story of Jennifer and her best friend, Diane, we've found that Jennifer has struggled from the childhood emotional trauma of an ultrastrict father and an enabling mother, which left her with the superpower of finding others to resolve her problems and enabling her unfortunate habits. No doubt, there were other spiritual dynamics at play of which we are not aware, but nonetheless, Jennifer always sought to remedy her situations through her attention seeking and relationships. Diane remembers:

Jennifer had been working as a nurse at the local jail and began to tell me stories of how she met an inmate there she really liked. He was getting out of jail; they took him to a facility in a small town to be released. She bought him clothes and shoes and drove to pick him up. He had family in Albuquerque but became a staple in our house. He was a decent guy, and we all liked him. However, as Jennifer tended to do, she sabotaged the relationship by sleeping with his best friend.

After, she began telling me about another inmate that she liked. I should say that Jennifer never really "liked" anyone; it was love from the outset, and it was always the best thing she had experienced, every time. This inmate was telling her that he was a trust fund baby and would talk about all the places he was going to take her and all the things he would buy her. This appealed to her because she found her worth in name-brand items; she always wanted the best things.

She stayed with me for a year and then moved herself into a casita. She was over the moon for this new inmate and would regale me with the stories, but her daughters and I were wary of her relationship with this man. However, if we voiced our opinions to her, about him, she'd become angry or shut down communication all together (this was a pattern).

In our relationship, I found myself walking on eggshells all the time. I didn't want her to abandon our friendship, as she'd done in the past.

One day, she took me ring shopping; the boyfriend told her they were getting married as soon as he got out of prison. Things began to escalate, compounded by her financial struggles. Knowing her situation, this man told her he would have his cousin give her money, but she needed to prove her love to him. I found out later how much she was keeping from me. What was happening now was bigger than anything I could have helped with.

Finally, she quit her job and told me it was because her supervisor discovered her relationship with the inmate from all her calls to the jail.

Soon after, I received a communication from her to say she was taking a position in a California prison. It was going to pay her more than double what she was making, and it was temporary. She planned to come back after she had money saved. It was all very hasty, and something did not sit right with me about it. She continued paying the lease on the casita, but was very quickly gone. Not too long after, I received a call from her property owners—they informed me the FBI had called—they were looking for Jennifer.

—Diane R.   ·

I know when we hear stories of suffering and circumstances we cannot imagine—it's easy to judge. But to walk the path of enlightenment, the individual must have a burden to overcome and release. They must have something heavy from which to become enlightened. Those who suffer to this degree are cultivating the wisdom they will bring into future lifetimes and experience, and they also have the important role of processing the pain of others and teaching through the wisdom the rest of us receive from witnessing their story.

MAKING BIG DECISIONS

When one is mourning from a deep loss, there is often a feeling of freedom that comes in as the grief lifts. You may feel you can do anything, after enduring such a profound time. All those events or experiences that you once said no to—such as purchasing big-ticket items, getting engaged, changing residence, or quitting your job—may come up for review again. There is no reason not to do it, you'll think. I've always wanted to move to (fill in the blank). I'd really like to have a new car or a house in the mountains . . . (you'll think). Remember, now is not the time.

Additionally, participating in risky behavior such as a criminal enterprise or anonymous sex can become a possibility if given the right conditions. And then there is the list of over-doing-it behaviors (e.g., eating, drinking, and drugging). There is never a good time for any of these, but it is fascinating how overcoming a major loss can inspire courage and even fearlessness for things that may have never been an option before. If you'd like to soothe your apathy and newly found courage by becoming a "risk taker," write a book, take up dancing, or paint your walls a bright color.

Fearless apathy

At the end of a major cycle in life such as graduating, setting and enforcing a long-needed boundary, getting a divorce, or overcoming an illness, we go through a period of chronic apathy. Depending on how long the cycle lasted, the period of apathy will vary from weeks to months. It is an opportunity for the heart, mind, body, and spirit to recuperate or adjust to the learnings of the previous cycle. It's like an emotional winter: a time of rejuvenation and reflection. But if you are unaware of the meaning and value of this time, your apathy and lack of emotion can turn into fearlessness and risk-taking behaviors.

Our emotions reveal to us our conscience. They let us know when we are hurting or there is any sort of spiritual shift or intrusion. The conscience is the aspect of ourselves that mentally and emotionally works as an alarm system, to pay attention to the ways in which our choices, words, or behaviors are affecting others or ourselves. Our intuitive standards bring us another level of self-awareness and can help us become clear about our environment as well.

When we are in this period of apathy, unless we are deeply aware of our psychic channels (an unemotional, intuitive channel for receiving information), we may miss important clues to the natural recognition of the impact of our choices and behaviors. Or, when we receive these intuitions, we do not care about them. This is the period when much of our physical-world transition takes place, and it's important to rely on our old values as a marker to the new values that may be emerging as we are making life-changing decisions.

The only time it may work out beautifully to ride this wave of false bravery is when you have been planning a change all along, and the impetus to complete it comes on the tail end of a loss or end of a cycle. Maybe you'd been planning to leave a partner or marry one? Go back to school for a degree or quit a job? Anything you were making efforts to do prior to another major transition can often become easier in the flow of this new sense of liberation in your life. You can feel safe to capitalize on it. The main point here is to make sure you have fully thought out any major changes, choices, or purchases for which you cannot change your mind later—and that you are clear on their impact for all involved.

Finding forgiveness

The most important phase of mourning is forgiveness. In this context, forgiveness is evidenced by the detachment from the loss, all the circumstances around it, and the opening to something new. When we forgive a loss and the conditions surrounding it, it means we forgive ourselves, others, and the Creator for such an experience. We will do a deeper dive on this level of forgiveness in other chapters, but it's important to understand that on a spiritual level, it is a part of our natural mechanism of accountability to take authority over any situation by acknowledging our role and contribution to the process.

When we do this, we recognize the pattern that connected us to the situation to begin with, and we forgive it and all involved so that there is no further mental, emotional, or spiritual connection to the dynamic or event; this is the ultimate act of compassion and self-love. When we fully forgive others and ourselves for our condition, we are freed from further bondage to it.

GRIEF IS THE PORTAL TO MAGICAL DIMENSIONS

The idea of magic is the way we recognize all other dimensions of life force energy, and when conceptualized as interconnected, we have the beginnings of an understanding of the Creator and its creation. When you use your intent, emotion, and actions to activate life force, you manifest those intentions, since all your energy is in alignment with the outcome. This is an example of our creative power.

The connection between creativity and grief

There is a reason we say, "when your creative juices are flowing," because we recognize that creativity is fluid and moves in ebbs and flows, affecting and informing everything around it. Our emotion, specifically grief (the many deep emotions we experience), is an agent of movement and change. It displaces old, outdated energy, ideas, beliefs, and feelings with new, creative inspirations and innovations better suited to our current conditions.

Our grief activates our creativity, which is always online and seeking to expand. When we focus it with intention and action toward an outcome, we align with the magical realms to magnify and attract anything that can fulfill the completion of our project. However, this may not appear as smooth as its fluidity would suggest.

When we have elements of our condition, personality, or life that are opposed to the outcome we seek, they must be reconciled. We must make changes to ourselves and eliminate the people and things in our lifestyle that hinder our progress. The process of finding focus and intent tells us exactly what those things are.

Using imagination and ritual to create a new reality

The main effect you are creating during your mourning process is walking through the options and possibilities of your new reality. We can use creative rituals to help us imagine what our new choices may bring, and their impact on us, our friends, our family, and our environment. We can take the new ideas that come through grief and create a ritual (any of your choosing; altar building is my thing) to connect our subconscious self to the magical realms of creation that support and inform our journey.

Your ritual must have an expressed intent. Write out what you want or need in clear, concise language in as few words as possible. Now, choose a ritual activity to perform, to cultivate your commitment in having what you say you want. This activity can be any of your choosing. One of my favorites is a Colombian ritual of walking with a suitcase around your neighborhood on New Year's Day to manifest more travel in the year to come, or burning a bayberry candle to the socket to have money year-round in your pocket.

Ritual is not superstition; it is an active commitment toward your goal that will reveal any obstacles or resistance you may have to receiving what you want. It also uncovers possible consequences that should be considered before making important choices. Another important factor in creating an effective ritual is that it should be fun and consistent.

The purpose of your ritual is to begin a new habit or spiritual pattern; performing your ritual at the same time every day is helpful to align you with your commitment and with the Universe that supports you. The insights you receive can come in the form of synchronicity, intuition, or dreams. But without fail, the information always arrives. This process will also help you become aware of the subtle vibrations through which your Universe will communicate with you.

A RITUAL FOR REJUVENATION

Affirmation: I am always renewing myself and have the complete support of everything in my world. I am safe to try new things.

What you'll need for your ritual:
  one yellow jar candle
  one fire source (a lighter or match)
  a sparkly cloth (any size) of your choice and color to place on the sacred altar area
  one item that represents joy
  one piece of obsidian and one sunstone
  mason jar
  fresh cooking sage for offering
  one medium-sized metal pot to burn herbs (and charcoal if needed)

Herbs you'll need:
  Mullein: This herb is grounding and supportive and offers strength during mourning. It has a "fatherly" energy to it.
  Yarrow: This herb is rejuvenating and healing, and supportive during a time of transition. It helps protect the mind, body, and spirit so one doesn't feel vulnerable.
  Lemongrass: This refreshing, lemony-scented plant helps rejuvenate the senses and allows a clear mind and calm heart to go through the process of mourning.
  Lemon verbena: This herb helps the mourning process by letting go of blockages or negative patterns that may prevent one from healing.

Optional:

Flower essences:
   Walnut Flower Essence: This essence is good to aid in any transition and helps one close a chapter and embrace a new path and direction in life.
   Directions for using the Bach Flower Essences: You may add four drops into a cup of water and sip during ritual to help ground your energy field and calm the mind and emotions. Or add the drops into a bottle of water and spritz over the altar to set the intention of your affirmation. You may also add four drops into a cleansing bath prior to the ritual.

Begin your ritual by cleaning and clearing an area in the center of your home. Collect all the items for your altar and put them in the cleared space. Place the herbs in the mason jar and hold it in hand while repeating the affirmation (you may also say prayers of your choice for healing). Exhale your breath onto the herbs to release the energies of the affirmation.
   Every morning for seven days, take your special item and move it to another room for the day, and if you run out of rooms, start at the beginning again. In the evening, place your special object back on your altar. Light your candle and let it burn to the socket, or for a few hours a day until it is complete. Once the candle is finished, burn your herbs in the burning pot.
   If you'd like, take a few moments every day to sit with your altar and reflect on the joy in your life; what strengthens it or what diminishes it. Once the altar is complete, you may burn the cooking sage with the other herbs in the pot.
   Performing this ritual may inspire laughter and feelings of embarrassment for what may feel like a ridiculous ritual, and that's okay. Joy can never thrive where judgment lives, so allow yourself to laugh it away or allow yourself to feel anything that comes up. The release and rejuvenation you seek will come in many ways over time. Give yourself permission to go with the flow.

LOSS OF A PARTNER: A PROFOUND TASK

A few years back, Holly, my lifelong friend, reconnected with me. It had been about twenty years since we'd had any real communication, mostly because of her relationship; it was complicated. Little did she know then, when they met, how much the isolation and mental abuse he (now her husband) perpetuated would wreak havoc on her psyche and self-esteem. His abrupt death from liver cancer just before her fiftieth birthday sent a shock wave through her life, and emotions unlike anything she'd seen or experienced before—all with her eleven-year-old daughter in tow.

Relationships are the lifeblood of any story we tell. We mark our weeks, months, and years with them as if they are placeholders for our evolution. We engage in connections to all things—people, places, and objects—to form attachments, and then scrub them away with our grief when we are finished. From an outside vantage point it's all very clear: through our relationships, we explore who we are and witness who we are not—with every bond we forge.

In other words, from an intimate point of view, processing the loss of a relationship from death or disrepair is life changing. We are no longer who we were when the relationship started, and in the weeks and months after the loss, we are forced to reconcile exactly what that means and why.

There is no limited time frame through which our grief pours out. It trickles like a leak, babbles like a brook, or hits like a tsunami whenever it feels like it—until there is no more water to flow. Of course, it seems logical that the time it takes to grieve a relationship is directly proportional to the length of time we carried the connection, but that isn't necessarily the case.

You see, we attract different partners or lovers in our lives to reveal different aspects of our spirit, each association uncovering a bit of our heart and soul at a time. Whittling away at the unneeded parts of our personality to reveal the love we have to offer is but one of the many unspoken obligations of the relationships in which we choose to participate. The excavation of these energy patterns is a lifelong process that will forever be linked with the one who caused or was present for the revelation. And it is this kind of connection we will grieve most.

LIFELONG FRIENDSHIP

When Holly and I met, we were still teenagers making our way alone in the Big Apple. We clung to one another through the many trials the city had to offer, especially through all our relationships of our early twenties; our link was disrupted the day I met the man she would soon marry. There was an instant repulsion between us that I didn't fully understand until about six months after his death, when she found my phone number in an old box and decided to call. It was then I understood that I could have never been present for the continual criticism and psychological abuse that was to unfold in their relationship over the years—being a silent witness was never my strong suit.

From the time Holly met me, I was in a constant state of grief. Although I was fun at parties, before and after the party came the endless shedding of tears and the many tragic adventures that unfurled in my life. Although I always seemed to be protected physically, the emotions I felt were deep and sometimes dangerous. In the first place, I was processing the grief from the early loss of my father, the emotional loss of my mother, and the rape by a trusted friend that had propelled me to New York City.

In the second place were layers of spiritual trauma that were waiting for just the right circumstances to receive their opportunity to release. Grief for me wasn't a singular occurrence; it was a lifestyle. A way of life, in fact, that is hard to watch and even harder to understand, unless you've experienced it yourself. So, while Holly and I aligned on many levels, we each had our specific paths that would not intersect again until we were grown women with two more decades under our belt. It was Holly's profound grief at the loss of her husband that connected us once more.

MANAGING THE VOID

The void created by the loss of a long-term partner is profound. Everywhere you look is where they used to be. There is an enormous empty space in your life, in your heart, in your behavior, in your beliefs, in your thoughts, in your routine; I could go on, but I know you get it. The void left behind by your beloved, even if the partnership was not romantic, leaves you with an enormous amount of space to question everything about your life and yourself. I think it is the one thing in grief that people are the least prepared for: emptiness.

There is a reason many spiritual traditions practice the art of emptiness: learning to override the human need to fill space is complicated and relentless until you take authority over it—over yourself. Mastering your behavior, changing your habits, and taking your power back from the relationship compromises you have made; this is the task at hand.

Every relationship must have compromise to survive, and while a good relationship does not breed contempt for those sacrifices, that is exactly what they are. The contempt may only have begun to arise in the space where your partner used to be. The overwhelming flood of all the choices you have made, out of love or otherwise, begins to resurface—prompting a deeper understanding and wisdom about those compromises.

Grief is the mechanism we use to uproot the results of our choices and to move on from their authority over us. All we must do is step away for some perspective, and the wisdom reveals itself: the answers to all the "whys" that became the building blocks of the life we had that has now come to an end through the loss of our partner. Practice is the way you will manage the void you find after any loss—every day becoming more familiar with the empty space left behind.

TAKING CARE OF THE DAY-TO-DAY

The first and most important chore after the death or loss of a partner is to make sure the day-to-day tasks are being taken care of. The first concerns are the basics: money, food, childcare, pet care, and your job. Are the bills on autopay? Has the paperwork been filled out with any critical deadlines for insurance, social or government programs, or medical bills? When you are a person walking through the grief of a loss, even the essentials can lose their importance. Apathy is one of the most powerful emotions we experience, and can be overwhelming enough to create further discord if your basic needs aren't looked after.

The next priority of our daily existence is embracing and managing our emotions. Sometimes there are secondary losses that come with losing a life partner, such as they weren't honest about their/your current financial reality, they didn't take care of bills, they were not insured or they let the insurance lapse, or they had undisclosed relationships and other secrets in their life that become revealed in their passing. Also, you may lose a group of friends you gained on the basis of your relationship.

If you or someone you love is experiencing this type of emotional or physical betrayal, it's natural to feel shame or humiliation (because you did not know what was happening, or you feel judged by others or yourself). The presence of these two emotions is meant to uncover a person's true needs, not to lower their self-esteem. Whatever your loved one did or did not do is not your fault. Offering yourself or your loved one compassion and nonjudgment is paramount.

Anger

Anger is another valuable emotion during the truth-finding phase of the aftermath of losing a partner. It brings potent focus and hypervigilance to the details of the situation and, if managed, can serve you well. Again, compassion, nonjudgment, and patience for the person experiencing waves of anger can only support the process. We tend to shy away from emotions that make us feel uncomfortable, and to abandon ourselves and others because of the illusion of social protocol. Do not let this be you. After a loss, the truth is necessary; find a way to get comfortable with your discomfort. Let the anger inform your journey of recognition, not control your mind or alienate the people in your life.

The things we feel anger for are the elements of life with the most value to us. Are you angry at the emotional betrayal? If so, your heart needs you to pay attention to how you love yourself and set and reinforce boundaries. Are you angry about financial betrayal? If so, security is your currency. What do you need to do, right now, to rebuild your feelings of security within yourself? Are you angry about the injustice of the events in your life? If so, empowerment and confidence are your currency. How can you begin to respect your needs and release yourself of the opinions of others?

ASK FOR HELP

Our humanity is layered, and we must honor our mental, emotional, spiritual, and physical needs. We are the ones responsible for recognizing and seeing that our needs are met, so asking for help from others is an act of self-care. Making lists or delegating tasks is a way that we can help others support us through the initial shock, and often the long process of mourning the loss of a life partner.

Here are a couple of lists that can be useful for those in your support system:

Physical necessities

Money: Make a list of bank accounts and passwords. Who has power of attorney? Has autopay been set up? Create a calendar of bill-due dates.

Food: Make sure the refrigerator is full, or take care of paperwork that ensures there is enough food. Write down food preferences and food allergies for others to do the shopping.

Shelter: Make sure the mortgage or rent is on autopay. If there will be a gap in the availability of funds, make sure to call all necessary parties and put your needs in a written request.

Child or pet care: It's important to have the names of backup babysitters and dog walkers who can be available on short notice should the need arise, as well as specific food needs and other supplies.

Quality-of-life necessities

Housecleaning: Do yard work; take care of car detailing and maintenance. (A clean, organized environment helps a grieving person manage their emotions and helps with focus.)

Emotional support/journaling: Speaking to someone other than family or friends, in addition to journaling, is helpful to process the loss and gain deeper understanding of the events or the process.

Pet and child companionship: For many adults, having to manage children or pets while in grief is very difficult, so setting up playdates for children and pets can be a way to ease the needs your children or pets may have.

Prepared meals: Meals that can easily be baked or microwaved with no prep time are helpful to encourage proper nutrition throughout the grief and mourning process.

A few names of maintenance people: The stress of small things breaking in the house while one is grieving can set off a firestorm of emotion and sometimes create more chaos.

Consider that taking the initiative for someone who is grieving is a powerful way to show compassion and support for their process. Make sure to ask the person if it's okay for you to take care of some of these household tasks, and if they have any special requests regarding you doing so, such as time, service provider, or special brand requests. Overlooking the inclusion of the person you seek to help can alienate them and increase the powerlessness they already feel. Also, you don't want to leave them with the open-ended *make sure to call if you need something*—since this once again puts the burden on them to take care of things.

REGAINING YOUR IDENTITY

One's personal identity has gone through some transformations in a long-term partnership. No matter how you slice it, having a witness to our lives informs the choices we make, sometimes who and what we are exposed to or like, and sometimes what we can access. After the relationship ends through death, divorce, or separation, a person has a lot of space to reevaluate everything about their lives and themselves.

Filling the space

As talked about before, many questions come flooding in to fill the void of the space left behind by your loved one. Questions such as "Who were you when the relationship began?," "Where did you meet?," or "What did you do for yourself at the time?" Now, you are left alone with the choices you made, and to face the answers to those questions. Depending on the ease of the relationship at the time of the loss, a person may not only be grieving the loss but also reconciling all those personal decisions that being in the relationship required.

I worked with a client, Renny, who had been married since she was twenty years old and now found herself at fifty, finally getting a long-overdue divorce. The man she was releasing herself from was a brilliant eccentric-narcissist who had controlled every element of their lives and her for over thirty years. Because she'd entered the relationship without much life experience and at such a young age, there wasn't much room in this relationship for maturing and developing her personal identity. What she had become was the caretaker to a controlling person who sought to keep her esteem bound to his needs, and little else.

Now, to her, it didn't feel this way every minute of every day. His continual criticisms of her, combined with the temper tantrums he'd throw anytime she expressed any desire she might have had, kept her from emotionally maturing her confidence. Finally, once she'd left the relationship, there was this enormous space open for her needs and wants, and the overwhelming trauma of the fear her world would fall apart if she explored them.

Any relationship we engage in, on a higher level, is intended to help us transform who we are or our condition and help us process any spiritual trauma we may have brought into life. Or, to begin to develop the mental, emotional, spiritual, or physical muscles that may have atrophied because of it. In Renny's case, having grown up with many siblings, she loved to do for others; inadvertently to the detriment of herself. So, thirty years in this relationship left her with a painful inability to set boundaries, and the relational development of a twenty-year-old at fifty.

Our energy bodies

Our energy body (aura) holds every choice we have ever made. All we have ever wanted for ourselves, how we've negotiated our lives thus far, and any regrets we carry. Of course, our spirit holds all the goodness that the relationship fostered as well. While this can be comforting at times, our biggest concern is recognizing the habits we have created on the basis of the needs of another, that are not in our current best interest. Take a few minutes to connect with who you were before the relationship in question began, who you've become within the relationship, and any changes you'd like to make, by answering a few questions:

1. Name three things you really liked but eventually gave up because you were in this relationship.

2. List three things you like about yourself.

3. List three things you do not like about yourself.

4. Would you have had the same career, if not for your partner? (this includes being a domestic engineer)

5. Name three nonnegotiable traits your partner possessed.

After you've answered the questions, take a few minutes to journal about those answers: how you feel about them, do they surprise you, and what you might do differently today. On a deeper level, the partners we choose reveal our inner workings in a powerful way. Do your best to recognize any guilt, shame, humiliation, or disappointment you may feel, but by no means attach yourself to it. Those four transitional emotions are meant to help us see how we need to take better care of our own needs in the future. We are all works in progress, and our significant partnerships offer a blueprint to our becoming.

COMPLICATED GRIEF

As we've spoken of before, complicated grief is the layering of the multiple spiritual, mental, emotional, and physical conflicts that are piled on top of the loss—in this case of a partner—and there can be many. In Renny's story, she was left with the sole care of her children, who often repeated their father's behavior. She needed to square away a new job and place to live that could sustain them. She also had a desperate need for love and affection but struggled with the changes in the dating culture, which were far more relaxed now than when she dated thirty years ago.

Additionally, her lack of confidence in setting and affirming boundaries, along with communicating her feelings—both of which she struggled to do—complicated the initial grief of letting go of the relationship. Add to this the unbearable freedom and space she was now afforded living without the criticism of her husband.

The void that was created from the loss of her life partner became a vacuum for all the deeply seated emotions she had stuffed down from her relationship. Feelings of rage and contempt began to surface, quickly becoming overwhelming. She had not ever experienced such powerful emotion and was at a loss of how to manage it, all the while keeping in stride with her other life obligations.

MANAGING BIG EMOTIONS

One of the most basic elements of our emotional development is learning to manage big, sometimes overwhelming emotions. If you were nurtured in a family or with care givers who felt embarrassed or shied away from showing emotion, you may have struggled or are still in conflict today about giving yourself permission to grieve. Letting yourself scream and cry at the top of your lungs is one of the most empowering expressions of emotion you can have. It is your soul crying out to the cosmos for love, support, and transformation.

It relieves your body, resets your mind, and opens your heart to a new way of being in your skin. To let yourself feel anger is a note from the hidden self of new and valuable information that comes into your awareness as the anger or rage subsides. Often, feeling big waves of resistance is the precursor to the arrival of grief and sorrow. When we pay attention to these emotions and their messages, we begin to experience liberation from them.

A note on anger

Anger and rage are two expressions of force we are not taught to manage well in childhood, often being told it is impolite or offensive. Where or how you were brought up, anger may have been used as a form of threat or intimidation to direct discipline. Traditionally, boys are taught to use athleticism to engage the energy, or it's sometimes dismissed altogether with the "boys will be boys" sentiment. Often, girls are taught to suppress anger completely or are isolated and ignored until they have found a way to calm themselves. Both strategies leave a huge gap in understanding the purpose of anger.

The energy of anger is a master teacher of self-awareness and the presence of grief. When we feel anger, it is an emotional message from our unconscious, getting our attention about what lies beneath the focus of our anger. Other forms of anger are aggravation, frustration, irritation, and avoidance. What makes us mad shows us where we must grieve and find forgiveness.

Below are some ideas to begin that process.

Breath work

Learning to manage a high level of emotion is layered and takes practice, compassion, and patience. The first order of business in managing big emotion is practicing diaphragmatic breathing—taking in deep breaths through the nose (all the way to the gut). The diaphragm is a muscle; when using it as a focus, it allows you to take a lot of air into your lungs and energy into your body. Release that air with a push, blowing it out through an open mouth.

Get the message

Our emotions are the message bringers from our higher self; understanding them and their meaning for you is paramount. There are a couple of things to consider when contemplating this communication. First, where in your body is the emotion centered? Your throat? Heart? Gut? Every emotion we feel is intended to help us bring in information and wisdom about our circumstances. For example, let's take the feeling of humiliation or embarrassment. They reside in the heart and show you where you must begin to take better care of yourself.

In Renny's story, occasionally when one of her children would criticize her in the way her husband had, she would feel immense humiliation and then rage. Feelings she'd always squashed in the relationship with her husband, but now in a situation with a person where there was a different power structure (her child), she began to feel humiliated.

That humiliation offered her the opportunity to recognize all the years she allowed her husband to mistreat her and how she had neglected herself. It gave her the freedom to learn how to do something different. She could now practice setting boundaries by using her emotions as a guide.

When we embrace the power and purpose of our emotions, they become road maps to the messages from the Creator. They show us where we've been and where we must go to wield their force in a supportive way. As we move into the flow of our feelings, consciously, they become familiar friends and tour guides to our needs and desires. They allow us to see our talents and what in us needs work. And they can guide us to the people, places, and things that can best serve us.

Resolving leftover conflicts

When our partner is gone, sometimes the conflicts we had are not. We are then left with the intimidating task of resolving those conflicts by ourselves—finding resolution and forgiveness without an apology. In our culture, apologies are little more than a way to reconnect. They aren't always given with sincere remorse or a guarantee that what the apology represents won't happen again. And if our partner were alive or present to offer one, most likely we'd end up in the same position, only down the road a bit. Alone, we have to learn how to forgive ourselves for the experience we endured. Ultimately, we must find a way to claim forgiveness and peace on our own.

Talking about forgiveness, if bitterness and resentment are the glue that keeps us attached to a dynamic, then forgiveness is the salve that removes the glue. Remorse is not a requirement to achieve forgiveness; understanding how you participated in the dynamic is the only prerequisite. Our willingness to dive deep into what happened and why we valued it is key, and needs only our heart, mind, and emotion to connect.

Your mind needs the facts, your heart needs understanding, and your emotions will be the change agent to access all of it. Take time to sit and write out all the facts about the situations that still evoke anger for you about your partner. Make a list of everything you can remember, allowing your emotions to rise and fall as you write.

This means letting the anger turn to tears, and then deep breaths, all while continuing to write. Neither ignore nor indulge your emotion; just let it move through you at its own pace. If you find there is just too much to get into at a sitting, remember—you are in charge. You can choose the rhythm of your healing and process. Begin with one memory a day and walk through it fully. Here are some questions to get you started:

1. What is the memory?

2. Where were you?

3. Who else was there?

4. Was it day or night?

5. In what season did this occur?

6. What are the emotions you feel about it?

7. Where are they centered in your body?

8. What are they telling you about yourself and your needs?

DISCOVERING YOUR INDEPENDENCE

Independence is something we always have. However, it is common when in a relationship to shift to the viewpoint of our partner, turning our attention away from our own leanings and independence to become unified with them. Sometimes this is a deliberate compromise we make; other times, it happens unconsciously over time. Reawakening to our own true feelings and beliefs is an inevitable part of our mourning process as we let go of the relationship we had with our loved one and reestablish the connection we have with ourselves without them.

Receive the world

Beginning again to receive the world through your own lens can be painful and refreshing at the same time. Your grief will clear a space for you to find safety and companionship in yourself. You will reconnect with and witness your environment in brand-new ways. Once again, the friends and family in your life will change, the same as when you entered the relationship. This can be scary, unnerving, and deeply sorrowful, but rest assured: there is great purpose in every person who moves back in or out of your life.

There is always a larger paradigm at work that energetically guides your divine interests and the soul patterns echoing beyond the life you had with your partner—manifesting what comes next for you. Often, we aren't aware of this vibration because our attention is trained on the feelings of loss as certain people leave our lives; our awareness hasn't fully shifted to what may just be on the periphery. All you need to do is ask your awareness (intuition) to transform the perspective.

Develop your truth

Our truth is based on our viewpoint and perspective, and nothing else. When we invite our intuitional awareness to engage in helping us navigate from one way of life to another, it will naturally expand the understanding of the transition with many more details or creative ideas to inform our choices. This helps us begin to imagine a life beyond the change, and a new sense of freedom and empowerment that will take its place.

Take five minutes every day to envision something new: a dream coming true, a vacation you've always wanted to take, or a new response you'd like to have to a chronic painful experience. Our imagination is the most powerful tool we have, to create the blueprint we want for the journey ahead. No matter how you may think of yourself, we are all creative beings. A little visualization practice will bring you big results in navigating your awareness to any new topic of your choice. Here are some starter visualizations to get warmed up on. Grab a pen and paper for this one. Read the visualization example, close your eyes, and picture it in your mind. Then write every detail that comes to you.

1. Picture a tree in your mind. Now, write down what it looks like (type, height, color, shape, condition, and where it's standing).

2. Visualize winning the lotto! (Where are you? How much do you win? Who's with you? What is the first thing you do after leaving the lotto office?)

3. What is the one thing you want but don't yet have? Visualize having it. Write down every detail: Where are you? Who are you with? What do you have? What does it look like? How does your body feel with it in your hands? Name three emotions you have when your desire is manifested.

4. Think about a conflict you have or had with another person. Now, visualize you and the other person meeting in a room and resolving the conflict (you are safe, at peace, and protected). Write down how you both came to a resolution.

Remember: when you are imagining your way to a new life, you get to choose the circumstances and conditions in which everyone relates or arrives. Only you. What is the highest and best you can imagine for yourself? How would you view life if you were physically safe, emotionally free, mentally present, and spiritually fortified? If that is your starting point, where can you go from there?

When is it safe to let go?

When all the conflict is resolved or we begin to let the good memories fade from the life we shared with our partner, is it okay to let go? The short answer is yes, but often it can feel like a betrayal of what you once shared when you no longer give time or energy to its memory. There is a spiritual reason why most marriage vows end in "Till death do us part." It is because once something is truly dead (no longer functioning with purpose in your life), it doesn't serve you to continue offering your life force to it, in thought or deed.

While we spend our energy on a life or person who is no longer present, we are still living that life. It is important to know that. It can be a valuable choice when there is still much work to do regarding that person. You want to make sure you do not take the struggles, habits, or bad memories into your next phase of living, but most importantly, you must stay connected with consciousness. Do your grief and mourning work deliberately and with presence. Do not give a second of your time to the judgmental opinions of others. Only you know the work to be done and the process you must take to complete it. Time is not a factor; only the work is.

Once you feel fully confident, with no lingering questions about any aspect of the relationship, you are ready to move on, leaving the relationship behind on all levels. This doesn't mean that we don't engage in other relationships during this process or that we will never think of this person again; it is only a spiritual, mental, and emotional marker of our freedom. And while there is fear, shame, or guilt on any level, there cannot be freedom.

Choosing love again

Will I ever love again? This is a question (or choice) people often make too quickly after the loss of a romantic partner. They either don't want to feel the pain they experienced in the previous relationship or because of the loss, or they don't believe they will ever find someone as amazing as their partner to love again. Make no mistake about it; if you want to love, you can—and you will.

While amid the gut-wrenching pain of heartache, it feels impossible to imagine that a time will come that your heart will feel strong and open, ready to give and receive once more. This viewpoint comes from not being complete with the work of grief and mourning.

It bears mentioning again here that grief changes the brain and releases the deep pain and traumatic memories from our neural circuitry. This creates a space for new habits, choices, perspectives, feelings, and beliefs to be imprinted into our daily life. This process takes work. It doesn't just happen with time; the release muscle must be exercised, a little every day, to build up strength and endurance. We make this transformation happen by choosing it. We can ask for help from our Creator, our friends and family, or professionals, but we will always do the work ourselves.

Once the layers of change have been worked through, we are free to love again, fully, and with confidence.

A Ritual for Forgiveness

Affirmation: I forgive myself and all others for my relationship choices. I am safe, whole, and independently powerful.

What you'll need for your ritual:
one purple jar candle

one fire source (a lighter or match)

a paper or cloth with a scenic view of your favorite mountain, ocean, river, tree, or any other natural element, any size of your choice, to place on the sacred altar area

one photo or item that depicts or represents something you might have done if your significant other hadn't come along

one piece of lepidolite

mason jar

paper and pen

fresh or dried lavender for offering

one medium-sized metal pot to burn herbs (charcoal if needed)

Herbs you'll need
Rose: Rose helps one heal the heart after loss and readies oneself for forgiveness; it is a heart opener and healer. It also promotes the movement of the energies within the body. Another way to use rose is using rose water as a spritzer on oneself, in the house, and on the altar. You may also add some to your bathwater for a purifying and healing bath.

Dandelion flower, leaf, or root: A resilient plant full of medicine, dandelions are one of the first plants to appear after winter's snow, foretelling spring. A supportive plant that allows one to stay strong and resilient and helps in releasing the past.

Olive leaf: This leaf helps with peace and forgiveness and allows one to feel nourished and supported during a difficult time. Peace goes hand in hand with forgiveness, and olive leaf helps us with that.

Optional:

Essential oils for solace:
  Frankincense essential oil: Frankincense is a powerful ancient oil that oscillates at a high vibration but is also grounding. It helps support one through loss, clears the mind from feelings of guilt, and helps move one toward the future. You can also use frankincense resins to burn on charcoal throughout ritual.
  Directions for use of essential oils: You may dab one drop of oil on pulse points (make sure to test in a small area for sensitivity). Or add three drops into a cleansing bath before the burning ritual. You can also inhale from the bottle as one goes through the ritual process.

Begin your ritual by cleaning and clearing an area near the front door of your home. Collect all the items for your altar and put them in the cleared space. Place the herbs in the mason jar and hold it in hand while repeating the affirmation (you may also say prayers of your choice for healing). Exhale your breath onto the herbs to release the energies of the affirmation.

Grab a paper and pen, or your computer or phone for this one, and sit in front of your altar and contemplate the object of your photo. As you meditate with the photo or item, ask yourself how you might have wanted your life to be different. First, close your eyes and visualize this happening, then write it down in story form. The characters are you and the people in your life, or you can make up new ones to tell your story.

Once you've written down everything that comes to mind, fold the paper into halves twice and place in the mason jar with the herbs, or save the document on your desktop and print out a copy to place in the jar. Light your candle and let it burn to the socket, or for a few hours a day until it is complete.

Take a few moments every day to sit with your altar and reflect on how you feel. Are there any changes in your thoughts, emotions, or behaviors? Once the altar is complete, offer your lavender to the burning pot with the herbs and paper, and light it up outside.

Performing this ritual may inspire a grief response, which is completely appropriate. Allow yourself to feel anything that comes up, and if you are too emotional to capture your feelings on paper, that is okay. The understanding you seek will come in many ways over time. Give yourself permission to go with the flow.

SIX

LOSS OF A FAMILY MEMBER:
DISCOVERING DEEP EMPATHY

Whom we consider family is as unique a group as constellations in the sky. Our family isn't necessarily bound by blood, but often by the soul patterns that give us a common ground. In this chapter we will focus on grief regarding anyone you consider to be family. When we lose a close loved one in any way and for any reason, it can be earth shattering. Change in these core relationships will often transform our personal view and worldview, and grieving them will be palpable.

On a spiritual level, we choose the family we end up with because we align with one another physically, mentally, emotionally, or spiritually. This connection doesn't necessarily mean we get along with, like, or even agree with these people; it means we are similar and have a trait, belief, or spiritual pattern in common.

Inevitably, our family members are our biggest teachers of the dynamics of living—on the basis of our conditions and circumstances. The family unit reveals to us who we are and what we need. So, when a member of the family is physically removed from our life, everything else changes. This may not change who we are, but it will certainly change how we get there.

EMPATHETIC GRIEF AND THE ROLES WE PLAY

Of course, there are many factors that contribute to how we relate to the loss of a member of our family. For example, our age, living arrangement, current relationship status with the loved one, and proximity to them (physically, mentally, or emotionally), as well as the other relationships the loved one was involved in.

My father died when I was eleven years old and my sisters were fourteen and sixteen. Each of us had a completely different experience because of the developmental level of the specific ages, each of them unique in their experience and perspective of life. A father's relationship to his daughter is the first male/female love experience she will have. If the girls are heterosexual, that is a powerful position to be in, since they will subliminally or consciously model their relationship choices after that central relationship.

I was prepubescent and detached enough from my father; therefore, I didn't feel abandoned or betrayed by his death. I was more deeply affected by the fact my parents hid his condition from us. After my parents told us about his cancer diagnosis, he was gone in a few short months. For me, the most traumatic part of the process was being an Empath and a beacon for receiving the untold facts and emotions of the other members of my family.

Around the age of ten, I had a vision that told me my father would soon die; this was the only time I cried for my loss (although it hadn't yet happened). From that point on, I cried the tears of my mother and sisters, who for many reasons were unable to fully grieve.

The empathy we experience within the family dynamic is unique for everyone. Naturally, each member of a family or personal community plays a role for which they are most suited within the group dynamic. There are roles that exude leadership, empathy, compassion, intelligence, and fortitude. However, each family member will eventually run the scale of these emotions in their own time. This may differ from what they might portray during the process of the loss.

In my family, through the sickness and death of my mother, each of us took on the role for which we were the most comfortable and skilled. My eldest sister was the bookkeeper, my middle sister was the medical advocate, and I was the spiritual connection and advisor. In the last few months of my mother's life, she became very aware of the spiritual dimensions of existence. I would speak to her telepathically every day, and she would tell my sister I had just been to see her, even though my sister knew I wasn't in town. My mother wasn't delirious; she was connected to me and really searching to get a glimpse of what was to come next for her.

HOW TO GIVE SUPPORT TO SOMEONE
WHO IS GRIEVING

The key to giving support to one who is grieving is to give with a glad heart. It serves no one to pretend you want to or know how to support the emotionally despondent if you do not—there is no shame in this. Honesty always works for the long term. If you do not know what to say to someone who has just experienced the death of a loved one, say that to them.

"I'm sorry. I know you are hurting, and I don't know what to say."

This kind of honesty is deeply comforting to someone who feels that nothing you can say will comfort them or take their pain away. When someone is reeling from a fresh loss, their heart and mind are blown wide open, and they are possibly experiencing emotions they have never had to broach in any other situation.

For them, feeling those emotions, let alone managing them, is a feat in and of itself, with no room to help you help them. To know this is the best remedy for walking through the many discomforts that come from witnessing someone else's grief.

I remember a conversation I had the moment I arrived home from my mother's funeral. I was exhausted and raw, with no room for the usual platitudes commonly offered—*I am sorry for your loss, but I am sure she is in a better place*, and *she lived a good life; at least she is no longer in pain*—one of which was given me by a good friend upon my entrance. I was childishly angry at her folly and inability to connect with the deep pain I was feeling, but recognizing she'd not had any real experience with this sort of loss, I said, "I know you're not sure what to say to me, and that's okay. I do not need you to comfort me in that way."

"I'm sorry," she said. "You seem so angry."

"I am deeply angry right now, and it's not about you. But I find your discomfort in dealing with me—irritating. What I would like from you is to feel free to makes jokes. I've always enjoyed your sense of humor, and I could really use some of that right now."

"Oh, the living gift?" (that's what we called her ability to make fun of simple things).

"Yes! The living gift would be perfect."

Once she was clear on how I felt and what I needed, she could support me in a way that came natural to her. And immediately my anger fell away. It had been showing me, in this situation, I couldn't put my needs aside for someone else's discomfort. Now that I communicated it, I no longer required the anger; I realized I must find ways to communicate my needs.

What if you are under enormous stress and do not have the time or energy to support your loved one in their grieving? This is an important question, since many relationships are put to the test during periods of grief. It is common for folks to just drop off all communication with friends or family who are grieving because they are going through something themselves and do not have the wherewithal to witness grief.

Whatever the circumstance may be, if the relationship is important to you, find a way to communicate. Say in the simplest terms possible that you have a situation happening that is keeping you from offering your full support at this time, but you love and care for them. Acknowledge what they are going through, unequivocally.

The death of a family member may very well be the most powerful grief event some will ever experience, and it needs to be acknowledged and respected as such. So, if you're the one in a support position, it's imperative to find a way to communicate your love through honesty. Say what you can and cannot do, but do something.

Find a way to support your loved one in a manner that is natural to you, taking into consideration the circumstances at hand. It's not important to please everyone (some people, while grieving, cannot be pleased), but the relationship will live to see another day at least—and it will be based on a foundation of honesty from which to grow.

EVERYONE GRIEVES DIFFERENTLY

If grief had a marketing slogan, it would be "Grief: Your Own Way!" You hear it said all the time. It may be the one thing everyone knows about grieving. What it means is that there is no "right" way to grieve, and that every individual will, over time, pass through the multiple lenses that inform our relationship to loss. Some people are quickly and deeply emotional, and some stay in a state of shock and show no emotion at all. It can take years for a person to move through all the levels of their loss transition. Make no mistake about it; each person will eventually traverse the multiple dimensions of grief expression.

The reason it can take years? We all have a main lens through which we understand life. This lens may be mental, emotional, spiritual, energetic, or physical, and on the basis of this lens, we will begin the process of our grief. However, ultimately, we will need to process our grief through all five lenses for the process to be complete. Here are the different starting viewpoints explained.

The mental lens: A person who is mentally focused will process their grief through their intellectual understanding of it, and once they feel a shift in their comprehension of the situation or acceptance of it, they often feel the grief is complete.

The spiritual lens: People who view life through their spiritual lens may not be consciously connected through their emotional body. It may appear that they feel "happy" about everything because they are not reactive in their responses. They often bypass their feeling center to recognize the big picture, lesson, or deeper truth about loss and death, and it may take time for them to feel the heartbreaking aspect of the loss.

The emotional lens: Emotional grief is the lens most people think about when considering grief. The crying, heart-wrenching pain, and rage of loss. The emotional lens can also be the subtle and more-gentle emotions of vulnerability and sorrow, or the combination that promotes depression.

The physical lens: Traditionally, we consider grief to be emotional, but if we are unable to release our grief in any effective way, it may become physical grief and present itself as a strong physical imbalance, or malady that pops up over time or seemingly out of nowhere. Often this grief is not recognized as such because we are conditioned to dismiss the power and purpose of grief. Physical grief can present as something simple, such as a twenty-four-hour flu, an accident, a broken bone, or it can be a tumor or other more serious disease, depending on how long the other forms of emotional grief have been avoided. It is often during the recovery process from these experiences that one is able to make amends with themselves and others regarding the loss being grieved.

It is also common to unconsciously choose situations in life to trigger grief that was unable to be processed at the time of the loss. A client of mine had experienced the loss of two family members within six months and was really struggling with her grief. It presented in a deep need to make efforts to control something in her life, so she elected to have a facelift.

Unbeknown to her, going through this surgical experience triggered many of her ungrieved memories of surviving cancer. By choosing the elective surgery, it helped bring to the fore the deeper reverberations she had of feeling a loss of control during her bout with cancer—which she could now confront. There is a sense of empowerment that comes from our choices, even if they result in difficulty.

The energetic lens: The energetic lens refers to our energy body double, the layer of energy that surrounds our physical body. Some people can express rage and grief energetically if they struggle to communicate it in other ways. I've known people who've shorted the electrical system in their home or vehicle on multiple occasions.

Energetic grief also presents in the form of accidentally breaking things, dropping them, or slamming doors and cabinets. If you suffer this form of grief, your best response is to immediately go outside in nature or be near a body of water or large tree. The water or tree will relieve you of your energetic burden or help ground your emotions.

Naturally, we will move through all lenses of grief, whether we are aware or not. Practicing mindfulness helps us pay attention to the subtlety of each lens and find acceptance and forgiveness for those things needed to make change in our lives. When a family member dies or goes away, we must first accept they are gone to reveal the lens through which we viewed our relationship with them and how we were able to value them in our life. Often, it is the ways in which we did or did not honor them that bring us the most grief, since they are mirrors of our own beliefs about our treatment of ourselves.

This ancient Sun symbol used by the indigenous New Mexican tribe, the T'siya, delineated life revolving around the Sun in cycles of four:

The four directions: North, East, South, and West.

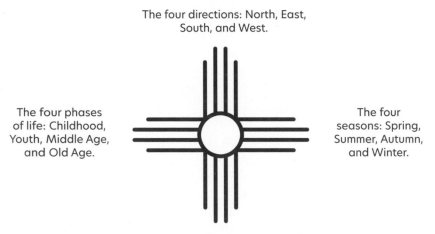

The four phases of life: Childhood, Youth, Middle Age, and Old Age.

The four seasons: Spring, Summer, Autumn, and Winter.

The four parts of the day: Sunrise, Noon, Evening, and Night.

The recognition of these cycles as a template to stay in balance with ourselves, the Earth, and the Creator is the meaning of this diagram.

Take five to fifteen minutes to lie flat on the floor, on your back. Place both hands on either side of your belly button, and like the Zia symbol shows in fig. 1, use your four fingers on each hand to lightly stroke your stomach from the navel outward and then from the navel upward, and from the navel downward. In this activity, like the sun, your navel is the root of your power and the center of your world. Practice this motion as you connect your spirit with that of the Earth.

The Tsi'ya people revered the sun and understood that all life thrived based on the earth's relationship to this fiery planet. The Zia symbol (as it is known today) represents the sun in its center. The four rays moving upward represent the four directions: north, south, east, and west. The four rays moving to the left represent the four phases of life: childhood, youth, middle years, and elder years. The four rays moving to the right represent the four seasons: spring, summer, autumn, and winter. And, finally, the four rays moving downward represent the four parts of the day: sunrise, noon, evening, and night.

This meditation will allow you to get in touch with your body, emotions, mind, and spirit and the planet Earth that sustains you. When you are relaxed and centered, the information or feelings you need most to connect with will reveal themselves to you.

MANAGING A CHANGE IN FAMILY DYNAMICS

Families function as they do because of the combination of personalities that make up the group. When one or more of those personalities is removed, the dynamic changes. This is true of any collective. If the matriarch, patriarch, or leader of the family or community is no longer present, a void is created that other members may not be able to fill. In fact, there is a natural power structure and hierarchy that is formed in groups when the leadership roles are changed; the group may not continue to function for lack of leadership.

The archetypes that function within the group in other subordinate roles, rightly, will change the group dynamic and their specific function but don't necessarily threaten the cohesiveness of the family. Archetypes include the helper, the submissive, the dominant, the intellectual, the caretaker, the business-minded, the philosopher, the communicator, the rebel, or the builder. Each of these roles can be compensated for by combining skill sets of other family members, but not the leader of the pack.

In Chinese astrology, the expression of power in the five natural elements nicely illustrates relationships in a group dynamic (see fig. 2). The balance of the group is based on each member and the element that reveals their nature: fire, wood, water, metal, and earth. Each of these elements strengthens and creates (productive cycle), diminishes and insults (exhaustive cycle), or destroys (destructive cycle) the other elements. As it is in families, each member will support, oppose, or neutralize the personal integrity of the other members. This energetic structure is how and why spiritual families are brought together to keep the whole in balance.

The expression of power in the five natural elements

When there has been a loss in the family, to consider the holistic group dynamic that is generated by the individual relationships can help resolve many of the day-to-day conflicts that easily arise within the collective grief.

In my family, when my father died, we quickly fell apart; within a few years, the cohesive family relationships fell away. Of course, we all stayed in touch, but the emotions that had once held us together became the energy that separated us. We did not grieve as a family, and the few family traditions we had, such as nightly dinner together, ceased to be. Soon it was only my mother and I left in the house, and our birth elements (hers was water; mine is fire) all but ensured our relational fatigue.

I was a deeply emotional child who was in grief often, and with the onset of puberty, my emotions and inability to speak while emotional was the exact situation to bring out in her the worst response for me. She would get angry or ignore me until I settled myself emotionally, which was when I was able to fall asleep.

This led to very little regular communication between us during my high school years and later, when I moved out of the house immediately after graduation and moved across the country.

While I know the lack of communication made both my mother and me sad, we did not blame one another. Ultimately, now, as an adult Empath, I understand the ways in which the lack of communication in my formative years truly served me. The most important relational dynamic we both shared was faith, which ten years later connected us in consistent communication once again. We deeply loved one another, but neither of us had the ability to overcome the weight of the grief my father's death created.

HELPING YOUNG CHILDREN WITH GRIEF

The most important way to help a child grieve is to communicate honestly about the facts of the situation (no matter what they are). Be an example: let them witness your grief—its beginning, middle, and end. Children feel burdened when they are put in a position to take on a parent's grief because the parent is "trying to be strong" and not being honest about their feelings.

I know there are a few different theories out there on how much information a child needs about loss and death, and my philosophy comes from three roots of understanding. 1: I was that grieving child; 2: children know when their parents are lying and often have a deeper understanding about loss and death then they can communicate; 3: the young people of today, no matter their developmental age, need a complete understanding about what has happened, a feeling of safety despite their parents' grief, and a defined path forward.

Children do not need to think that their parent knows everything. They get the same sense of security knowing their parents have expressed their uncertainty of how to grieve, but that they will all move forward together as a family through communication. Young people, spiritually, have soul imprints to help guide them as well. Regardless of their age, they have a powerful role to provide in the family if they are given the space and opportunity to do so.

It is important for you to let your child know what you, as a parent, are going through (not necessarily in full detail, but the overall essence). It's okay to feel fear, and to let your children witness your feelings of fear—but it's imperative to let them know that the presence of fear does not mean they are unsafe.

It means that what you are facing right now is new to you, and your fear produces hypervigilance that keeps you present and aware of the details of your environment, your condition, and any new information you might need. Sometimes, it is those feelings of fear that keep everyone safe. On the other hand, if you are a parent who is experiencing extremely volatile emotions, it is important to get outside help to learn to manage them in a way that does not create further fear or discord for your children.

You might feel that you need to use a more childish language with young children, but I don't recommend it. When you speak about a topic fully, using the language you know to use, the intent of the communication is received completely by the child, and they will have an intuitive understanding of it. They most likely won't be able to repeat it back to you or communicate their comprehension, but the seed they need is planted; there is nothing missing from your communication, which is what makes them feel safe. The way that intuitive people (including children) can recognize an untruth being told is that they naturally compare the energetic signature of what you are saying with the vibration they feel from you or the environment, and if they do not match, they know something is amiss and they will not feel safe.

Making emotions a daily, matter-of-fact conversation with your children helps open a rapport that can be the bridge for communication on particularly bad days. Speaking with your kids about the different lenses through which they will look at grief, and helping them identify which one they are now using, is a great way to help them comprehend that every person will respond differently to grief. It also helps them understand that another's emotions are not about them, and helps cultivate a response of compassion to other family members who are in pain.

PARENTING WHILE IN GRIEF

Parents have a unique conundrum when it comes to grieving: they have the responsibility of keeping the family going in the physical world while doing it. Some parents will feel the pressure to "buck up" and set aside their feelings of anger and sorrow to stay vital and focused at work. Others may buckle under the emotional pressure or find themselves dealing with their feelings in a passive-aggressive way.

If you are the parent who is mourning a loss, or know one, the directive is to ask for help—clearly communicate what you need and how you need it to anyone who can help you. Grief and pride cannot share a bed. As a parent who is grieving, there may be some work in figuring out exactly what you need, so I've prepared a short questionnaire to reveal your priorities.

Physical needs

1. Do I have a bill calendar? (Creating a bill calendar or setting up autopay for all bills is ideal.)

2. Is there a list of medications for all family members, including pets?

3. When are medication refills necessary?

4. Do I have the childcare or pet care I need?

5. What are the standard weekly chores that need to get done?

6. Is there a master copy of all family-member schedules?

7. Is there a list of work numbers and emergency contacts?

8. Are there deadlines or paperwork to be filled out to ensure the family has the financial means to be taken care of for three to six months?

9. Is there a phone list of friends, family, or service providers to help with any of these things?

Emotional needs

1. Setting up a weekly support meeting within or outside the family is helpful.

2. Have I communicated how I feel to everyone, and do I know firsthand how they are feeling?

3. Communicating to your loved ones about how you are grieving is important. On a scale of 1–10, how true are these statements for you? You can also take this as a verbal inventory at a family meeting, so that everyone has an idea of how the others are processing the loss.

a. I am very uncomfortable with my emotions and prefer to feel them when I am by myself.

b. Watching others grieve makes me want to cry, and I don't like that.

c. I am used to crying and don't have a problem allowing the tears to come, whether I'm alone or not.

    d. Currently, I am not feeling anything and am very focused on my work and keeping the household running.

    e. I am feeling very angry about everything.

    f. I don't feel any different but am not sleeping at all at night.

    g. I have a lot of anxiety during my waking hours and wish I could sleep all the time.

    h. I find myself wanting to talk to people often and feel very lonely when I am not interacting with others.

    i. I find myself wanting to escape my life as often as possible.

    j. I am drinking alcohol more frequently.

    k. I am using other substances to distract me from my grief. (If so, what are they?)

    l. My favorite distracting behavior or task is _____.

    m. I would prefer to be by myself all the time.

    n. My life has no meaning.

    o. I think of suicide often.

    p. I want to kill myself and have a plan to do so.

Spiritual needs

1. Are you a member of a church and do you have a support system there? Do they know what's going on in your life?

2. Do you have a system for home meditation or worship? (Creating a system for home meditation and worship that the entire family has access to, such as an indoor or outdoor altar, is ideal.)

3. Do I have an altar honoring the person or pet who has died? (Creating a memorial altar of what or who has been lost offers an opportunity for everyone in the house to connect when they are ready.)

4. Do I have someone to talk to?

Our ability to feel, and the fortitude we have to process grief, is an individual experience. Grief, itself, is filled with many nuances left for interpretation, so how we begin to recognize our feelings is through the practice of allowing them and then labeling the experience. Each person has their own developmental range of emotional intelligence. Taking some time out to inventory your current emotional condition by answering all the questions above gives you an indicator of how you and your family members are doing; it offers an opportunity to self-reflect and self-regulate, or how you can help each member of the family move forward in the grief process.

Remember, emotions are temporal; embracing them and learning to surrender to the grief while managing everything else is the goal. No answers to any of the questions should cause alarm, even the ones about self-harm or substance abuse. If anyone is having thoughts or fantasies about suicide, it is more common than you'd think, and contemplating our mortality is a way we begin to build a sense of spiritual integrity. It is an opportunity to begin an ongoing conversation and to enlist professional help. The benefits of working with a grief professional are the objectivity and nonjudgmental and nonpersonal clarity that come from a caregiver outside the family dynamic.

Create a list of names of people you know who don't shy away from speaking about difficult topics or who aren't judgmental, and who would be able to have conversations with you about what you're going through. Sometimes, it's best while grieving to work with an outer-circle person (a counseling professional, healer, or clergy) so that you or loved ones can be free to communicate how you really feel.

We all have a plethora of feelings and experiences when we grieve, and being a parent it is natural to incur feelings you've not ever felt prior to a big loss. Do not be afraid or feel ashamed of them. Your feelings are your friends and instructors. They will teach you about the deeper levels of yourself and help you begin to expand and grow as a spiritual being. Allowing your children to witness your process, while communicating about it, is positive.

LOSING A FAMILY PET

How you feel about animals and their place in society determines your experience of the loss of a family pet when they die. There is a mass cultural shift taking place, regarding the viewpoint that our pets are our property. Many countries are beginning to acknowledge all animals as sentient beings. It comes as a shock for me that it's taken so long for the collective to recognize all beings as sentient and of value to our ecosystem, or as being intelligent and feeling emotions on every level. But then, I'm the type of person who lets my old cat drink out of my water glass . . .

For most of us, our furry, scaly, or winged friends are our best and most trusted confidants, and their death is crushing. Sometimes we cultivate a deeper emotional intimacy with our pets because of the unconditional love and nonjudgment we receive from them. Certainly, humans have much to learn about life from animals. So, losing a pet in general and within a family dynamic is a powerful experience.

Yvonne's perfect complicated grief

I had met my friend Yvonne (on the trail walking our dogs) just a few days prior to an afternoon when I was compelled to call her; her husband answered—he was in a panic as their dog Marley was taking his last breath. We got off the phone and I began to pray with them for the easy passage of their precious companion. About fifteen minutes later, Yvonne called to say that Marley was gone, and to ask how I knew to call at that time. I told her that I had a feeling to reach out and wasn't surprised that spirit had connected me to them in their time of need.

Yvonne and I became fast friends, bringing much benefit to one another. I had just adopted my first rescue dog, a one-year-old miniature husky, with whom I was struggling to understand her behavior and to communicate effectively. Yvonne is a professional dog walker, and we would walk our dogs together several times a week. She had another dog, Otis, who was well loved by the community in which she lived. He even had his own tagline and poster on the trail. "Otis for POTUS," it read. So when, a few years later, Oti—as he was affectionately called—began to reveal undiagnosed symptoms, Yvonne began to get worried.

You see, she was also in the process of witnessing, unbeknownst to her, the last few months of her mother's life from a distance—it was happening in another country during a pandemic. The stress of these intense situations was pounding away at her emotional integrity day by day. As Otis began to deteriorate, all Yvonne could do was resist her grief. Her heartache would allow nothing else. She took Otis to many doctors and received diagnoses that were mostly in alignment, but none of them mentioned that this could be the end for Otis. Yvonne knows now, deep in her heart, that this process was Oti's final gift of compassion.

Within a month's time, Yvonne's mother had died. She traveled to pay her respects and address her mother's estate and final wishes, and upon returning home from the most sorrowful of goodbyes, Otis's condition began to deteriorate. He needed round-the-clock care, and no one in the house was getting any sleep.

Otis was having seizures, and they were getting more dire as time went on. Yvonne had tried multiple medications, and nothing was working. Her final visit to the emergency room with Otis racked up a sizable bill, but in her mind, Yvonne was still imagining a scenario where Otis would make it out of this horrible dream alive.

Within a few short days, Otis was gone, and Yvonne was devastated. She could barely manage her daily activities. The one thing she adored the most was her car rides with Otis. He loved them so much, and they were in the car together many times throughout the day. Yvonne would look into the rearview mirror, and there would be her happy Otis. It brought her such joy—now the back seat was empty and quiet.

Yvonne could barely stand to get in the car, yet it was a work necessity. One morning it had been a particularly grievous start to the day, and she was on her way to pick up a client when she looked in the rearview mirror and saw Oti's face. She burst into tears and pulled to the side of the road. You see, on that day, she had begged for a sign from Otis. Just one little inkling that he was okay—and there he was. The more she cried, the more deeply she felt his presence and comfort. He was telling her that he was all right, and soon she would be too. He loved and missed her.

For a moment, Yvonne sat in wonderment and confusion. Was it true? Was that really Otis? Next thing she knew, her phone was ringing, and it was me on the other end of the line.

"Oh my God, Tracee, you'll never believe what just happened!?"

"I won't?" And we both laughed . . . because of course I would.

She wanted to know if what she had seen was real, and of course it was. I explained that grief prepares us to become witness to the higher dimensions where the spirits of our loved ones go. It was unique for her to psychically transition that quickly, since most people can take months or years to prepare for a vision or dream of their loved one. Yvonne explained that she'd been crying out for a sign from Otis for several days now, and that she needed to know he was okay, and to connect. She wondered why it happened on that morning and in that way, and I responded:

"Well, your immense grief and desire to communicate created the energetic connection between the two of you, and your grief released you of the picture of how you remembered him and created space for you to see him as his spirit is today."

"But it seemed so real!"

"It is real. It is only our minds that struggle with reality, and for good reason. To be human, it is imperative that we focus on remaining in and taking care of our body—learning to walk between the worlds takes cultivation and skill. Imagine how many people might jump ship if they got to fully experience the freedom of the other dimensions. No one would stay for the glory of the hard times. Otis visited you today, and in the place that was the easiest for you to receive him."

Over the following weeks and months, Yvonne began to adjust to life without Otis as she remembered him. She continued to communicate with his spirit but began to refocus her attention on Oti's sister Angie, and all the other physical living beings in her daily life. But she will always carry with her that moment together on the side of the road and remember just how close he is, anytime she may need him.

COMPLICATED GRIEF

It does bear mentioning here that it is not uncommon to emotionally turn against others during grief, and that includes parents to their children and vice versa. All the feelings of helplessness, aggravation, or rage can come to the surface and be triggered by other emotional family members or members of our community. When this happens, it creates many layers of emotion to be reconciled later, in addition to rebuilding the trust that is lost when someone feels emotionally betrayed.

Yvonne, just days after Otis's death, felt such rage for the emergency room that charged her thousands of dollars in the last two days of his life. It was the one place she could focus her anger for the loss. After some time, she was able to realize that her resistance to losing Otis kept her engaged with the doctors. Did they have some culpability in the situation? Possibly. But how would she have felt if they'd refused her service? Everything looks different in hindsight.

Another powerful, complicated grief scenario that can arise in the family dynamic is when secrets are exposed. There is nothing more painful to family members than being put in a position to hide family truths from their friends or outer-circle family members. Although social mores of the day have expanded significantly, there are still people and cultures who struggle with feelings of shame about sexual identity and orientation, and judgment about drug abuse, criminal behavior, or being a victim of domestic (or any other) violence.

In many cultures, it is standard to keep the knowledge of improprieties or peculiarities of family members within the confines of immediate relations; however, when a major loss or death occurs, sometimes that information becomes public. Families can suffer deeply from the judgment of others when this kind of information is revealed.

FAMILY DIVISION AND THE ESTATE

In addition to secret revelations, money is the other character shaker and integrity breaker within the family. Who gets what and how much can create irreversible divisiveness between siblings and other members of the relative pool. The only real way to avoid this is to make sure every bit of personal property and who it goes to is explicitly detailed in a last will and testament—to let all family members know your wishes before you die. However, this rarely happens (for many reasons to be discussed in chapter 9). So, what can you do to bring down the temperature of this family conflict?

First, do not take what others do personally, and don't expect them to change because the family is in crisis. People don't often behave better when they are grieving. If they were selfish before, now they are selfish and in pain. Take some alone time to decide what you really want and need, and where you are willing to spend resources taking your loved one to court if need be. This may significantly shorten your list of "needs."

I have a client whose blended family of forty-plus years went into a grief crisis when the stepmother died (my client, her two siblings, and her father joined her stepmother and stepsister in a blended family). Even though all community property was legally left to the father (now in his eighties), and the couple had been together and married for more than four decades, the eldest daughter began trying to control how her mother would divvy up the family assets.

In her mother's final days, the daughter became paranoid, bitter, and fearful and generated much conflict with the other siblings by isolating herself. Upon her mother's death, she immediately sued to take control of what had been willed to her stepfather—unceremoniously making any relationship with the other grown siblings, their children, and their grandchildren untenable.

You cannot control what others do and how they feel. All that is left for you is to communicate with compassion, as best you can, and make every effort to ask the uncomfortable questions while everyone is still living. For your final requests, there are suggestions in chapter 9 for building a list to be included in your last will and testament.

BOUNDARIES ARE YOUR FRIEND

Everyone has their own communication style, but learning to set firm boundaries and then enforcing them is key. I used to struggle with this in my teens and twenties. I would feel such emotion all the time that it felt impossible to communicate everything I was feeling—rendering me speechless. I began every statement as a question. If I needed something, instead of asking for it outright I would begin with a series of questions to reveal whether a person was interested or available to give me what I needed. It was a long, tiring way around the truth that mostly left confusion and miscommunication it its wake.

I remember, finally in my thirties, making huge efforts to shift this behavior, but still grappling with it, I had this exchange with an acquaintance I'd met at the gym. I don't quite remember what I was asking for, maybe help with training, but I walked up to him and had already asked three questions that were adjacent to what I really wanted to ask, before he stopped me in my tracks, put his hand up as if to say stop, and said, "What is it you want?"

It really hadn't occurred to me that it was that simple. I could just directly ask for what I wanted and get an answer. I think I confused the idea of being rejected or being told "No" as something personal to me, when truly, just because someone said, "No," it didn't mean I could not have or did not deserve what I was asking for. I felt such relief. From that point forward, I became ultra-aware of my habit of asking leading questions and began instead to ask directly for what I wanted.

The three most effective words and phrases you can know and practice are "*yes*," "*no*," and "*I don't know*." One afternoon I was sitting with a friend, enjoying a cup of coffee, when I asked if she would like a piece of chocolate I'd just pulled from the cupboard?

"You keep it for yourself," she responded.

"I don't want to keep it for myself; I have plenty—take a piece," I said.

"You go ahead and enjoy it," she replied.

The communication went on like this for a few minutes. She was saying no without using the word, and it was confusing me. The emotional subtext that was coming through was that she didn't want to inconvenience or deprive me of my chocolate, so I naturally kept rephrasing my offer to reassure her that was not the case.

Finally I said, "If you don't want any, just say no." And she did, and finally the chocolate conversation was over.

I use this as an incredibly simple example of the multileveled emotional subtext that can be read when one is grieving, and especially within the familial dynamics that arise when there is a long previous relationship to one another within the family. It may seem evident to a person looking through a logical or spiritual lens, but a person looking through an emotional lens feels all the energy in the space, including the subtext of being polite and not wanting to offend. Now amplify this emotional dynamic along with the familiarity of family and the pain of the loss, and it can become a hot mess of miscommunications.

The key to setting solid boundaries is keeping your answers short, concise, and, of course, without subtext. Know what you want definitively or be willing to kick the decision down the road a bit with an "I don't know right now; I will let you know when I do." This kind of succinct communication leaves the ones whom you are communicating with a clear idea of what to do next.

You don't ever need to feel forced into a decision when you are grieving just because others are prepared to render their choices immediately. Allowing yourself to be pushed along by the flow of the needs of others can often cause disturbances or resentments later. If you are not sure what you want, take some time out to journal about the circumstances you are faced with, on the basis of the options in play. Writing down all your feelings will often lead you to the best and most rational decision you can make at the time, and a decision you can live with that considers everyone who will be impacted by it.

HOW WE REMAIN CONNECTED

Even when we are not close with family members in simpler times, coming together during a crisis and finding common ground is a valuable task for everyone, but it takes preparation. It's like getting together at the holidays without all the good food. Many people experience emotional triggers when in the company of their family, and conflicts are bound to arise. Know this in advance and don't expect for everyone to be on their best behavior. When you walk into a situation where you understand the emotional-pain quotient, you are less likely to take their words and actions personally.

Take a few minutes before connecting with your loved ones to make a short list of five things you like about each of them. Doing something as simple as focusing on the positive elements of their personality can create an energy strand or telepathic communication of goodwill between you and them. When people are in pain, they are also possibly fearful, anxious, and hypervigilant for anything they perceive as judgment or disrespect. This on top of preexisting negative emotional patterns can make it impossible to experience easy, compassionate communication without doing the advance work.

Most importantly, know that you are empowered in any family dynamic when you take time out to think things through, understand what you want, and find a way to communicate it deliberately. Show willingness to give compassion, and reserve judgment until you are clear on all communications. Your patience and peacefulness will carry you through the witnessing of the high-octane emotions of others. The personal space you need is created by setting firm boundaries and showing yourself compassion. This in turn creates an energetic aura of peace that draws the best out of others.

A RITUAL FOR WISDOM

Affirmation: I am free to let go of life as it was and embrace the living I have yet to do, becoming present in every moment.

What you'll need for your ritual:
   one yellow or white jar candle
   one fire source (a lighter or match)
   a gold paper or cloth of any size to place on the sacred altar area
   a photo or item of the one you'd like to remember
   a cathedral quartz or smoky quartz crystal
   mason jar
   paper and pen
   dried fava beans
   one medium-sized metal pot to burn herbs (and charcoal if needed)

Herbs you'll need:
Self-heal herb (Prunella vulgaris): One of the most healing plant allies, self-heal herbs help one make the necessary choices and actions to integrate oneself on all levels. The herb promotes healing for all types of loss and clears the way for wisdom and understanding to be revealed about what one must connect with in themselves.

Marjoram: This is the herb with family energies; marjoram may be used for support during loss of close loved ones. Inhale deeply to activate clarity and calmness of mind.

Sage: Sage helps promote wisdom, clarity, cleansing, and stability during turbulent times such as loss. It is most effective during mental, emotional, and spiritual transitions. You may also use as an essential oil.

Optional:

Flower essences:
   Star of Bethlehem Flower Essence: This essence is used for any traumatic shock to the mind, body, and spirit. It allows one to process the blow, so it won't be stuck inside the body. It allows the natural grieving process and helps calm the nervous system.
   Directions for using the Bach Flower Essences: You may add four drops into a cup of water and sip during the ritual to help ground your energy field and calm the mind and emotions. Or add the drops into a bottle of water and spritz over the altar to set the intention of your affirmation. You may also add four drops into a cleansing bath prior to the ritual.

   Begin your ritual by cleaning and clearing an area in your main living space. Collect all the items for your altar and put them in the cleared space. Place the herbs in the mason jar and hold it in hand while repeating the affirmation (you may also say prayers of your choice for healing). Exhale your breath onto the herbs to release the energies of the affirmation.
   Grab your computer or phone to listen to the digital meditation[1], or simply sit in front of your altar and contemplate the object of your photo, while visualizing the golden thread in the meditation that follows.
The golden-thread meditation
   Sit quietly, taking four deep breaths, breathing in through the nose and out through the mouth. Imagine a bright and beautiful golden white light flowing from the Creator down through the top of your head and through your heart, configuring a golden thread. See this thread move through time and space to the one with whom you would like to connect. See the golden thread connect in their heart, and sit for a moment, taking in and savoring the connection. Now say out loud anything that comes to mind. Express any feelings, thoughts, or pain that was left unspoken, or have a simple "catch-up" conversation.
   Feel free to speak how you would like, since your loved one will not be upset, be offended, or retaliate in any way. They love you deeply and long to hear your truth. Allow yourself to receive any responses they have or answers to your questions. Take as long as you like in this state, and when you feel complete with your communication, express your love and visualize

---

[1]Scan the QR code on page 269 or go to https://traceedunblazier.com/product/transformative-grief-an-ancient-ritual-for-healing-in-modern-times/#

the retraction of the golden thread from their heart to yours. Know that you can communicate this way any time you like.

Now, take the mason jar with the herbs and place it on your altar. Light your candle and let it burn to the socket, or for a few hours a day until it is complete.

Take a few moments each day to sit with your altar and reflect on your loved ones. Are there any changes in your thoughts, emotions, or behaviors? Once the altar is complete, offer your fava beans to your garden or dig a small hole in the earth to bury them, and light up the herbs in your burning pot, outside.

Performing this ritual may inspire a grief response, which is completely appropriate. Allow yourself to feel anything that comes up, and if you are too emotional to capture your feelings on paper, that is okay. The understanding you seek will come in many ways over time. Give yourself permission to go with the flow.

LOSS OF A CHILD: THE UNFATHOMABLE VOID

Children are born with a profound and hidden role, an ingrained responsibility in any society: to be the future. We see our offspring as the light, the hope, and the legacy we have worked hard to create or hope our community will become. Indeed, it is a powerful cultural imprint to put on anyone, especially a child. So what happens to these humans, young or old, when they predecease their parents, or the legacy we'd hoped they would conjure for the rest of us goes away? In any community, children are also the metaphorical creations of our work, the practice of our dreams, and the endowment of our vision in the world. There are many ways for parents to lose and grieve a child, and although not everyone will bear a small human, we all create and endure spectacular benefactions along our path, and the grief of losing what is an integral part of ourselves is a powerful, life-changing event. It is in this spirit I write this chapter, and although my focus and languaging is on the dynamic of parents and their children, the information is written for anyone who has experienced a profound loss of their own creation.

When the first child is born into a family, it changes the lives of the parents forever. Not only do their physical routines change, but the parents' entire outlook on all the possibilities of life shift as well, for they are now making plans for a family. The relationship they have created between them changes, and sometimes the fears they may have about the future float up to the surface. The bond with this new, precious being, filled with such light, can bring such terror in the first days.

For a single parent, all these changes can be intensified when there is only one person doing the work that our society tells you should be the work of two. This judgment alone, in addition to any other unmet needs that exist—such as having enough resources, help, or time—must be grieved by the primary caregiver in order to be present for the needs of their child. A special bond can form between a single parent and their only child, a sense that they are in this world to survive all it will bring—together.

For a larger family with multiple children, bringing a new baby into the mix is sure to change the dynamic among family members and siblings. He, she, or they will bring many new and unprecedented surprises, but at least the initial fears about care and rearing have been put at ease; if not in practice, then in perception. For now, their fears have lost importance as the need for sleep takes priority.

All the transformation, on every level, that is brought to bear from the onset of pregnancy is what makes childbirth and childrearing such a profound experience. So, the death of a child is equally life shattering.

TWO KINDS OF LOSSES

The loss of a child, and the circumstances around it, will yet again bring another life-altering viewpoint for the parents and siblings. The loss is profound, and the ones experiencing it will need support to process their grief—to find peace if it is possible to do so. There are two kinds of losses of a child: the loss that is known and expected, such as from an illness, or an unexpected loss, from an accident, homicide, or suicide.

When a child has a life-threatening illness, oftentimes (but not always) the parents can grieve a little at a time. From the first presentation of the symptoms and through the diagnosis, or any possible treatment, there are smaller losses along the way. Parents will grieve not only the possible loss of the child, but feelings of disempowerment, loss of control, inadequacy, or blame; they all come with the territory of a severely sick child.

This also includes depression as an illness. Children who suffer a severe imbalance in their mental health can struggle with daily tasks, education, mood swings, and acutely diminished perspectives they are unable to manage. The parent of a child with depression, or any mental or spiritual illness, will suffer equally in their powerlessness to help.

When a child dies suddenly, the trauma is profound and severe. It may take several weeks or months to work through the shock of the loss, and, depending on the circumstances around it, the parent may be focused on accessing exactly what happened to their child, and possibly seeking justice for their abrupt demise.

If foul play is suspected, the parents are contending with the police, the justice system, or any one of many civil services and media, or possibly none of the above, since our justice system and culture still suffer from deep threads of judgment and racial bias when it comes to doling out resources that are offered in certain cases of kidnapping and homicide.

No matter how a child dies, the future for the loved ones left behind becomes cumbersome and unmanageable under the weight of this loss, especially regarding communication. As with any grief, they will go at their own pace, but often for the immediate family it is hard to discuss the death; every time it is spoken about with someone new, they must relive the news and process the grief and shock of others in addition to their own. No one expects a child to die, and it is always received with a shock and dismay that leaves the family members in a position to relive the news and then process the judgment and confusion in the immediate area.

It's a strange hover between not wanting to be a downer in someone's day and also feeling guilty that if you stay quiet, if you say something like, "I have a younger brother and two older sisters," you are then explaining away a human that has never been forgotten. I am a middle child . . . right smack in the middle of five.

—Boopsie M.

GRIEVING A TERMINAL DIAGNOSIS

There is much to consider when enduring the many grief opportunities of working with children who have received terminal diagnoses. Not only the process of finding acceptance of the diagnosis, but the grief that comes in the days, weeks, months, or years leading up to the death. Living at "death's door" is a profound condition of life. Always thinking about death, experiencing worry and anxiety about it, and the spiritual questions you are left with are but a few of the situations you find yourself in when your child is terminally ill.

It is necessary to give yourself permission to grieve as you go along—the lifestyle changes illness requires, the appointments with doctors, the hospital stays, the medication, the in-home care, and navigating the information and insurance systems all have the potential to be arduous and frustrating. A bit of grief will be required for each. When the authority figures in the child's life communicate about their feelings and show their grief in small expressions as it comes, the child then is free to admit to and experience their own feelings of sadness, anger, frustration, or confusion.

Do not ever worry about being honest with your child or being unable to answer their questions. All they need to know from you is that you are with them on their journey, that you love them despite it, and that you will do your best to help them find any answers or information they may need.

The important thing to do in this experience of grieving is to let your child know you are not mad at them, and that what is happening to them is not their fault. Let them know it's normal to be upset about what is happening, and that it's valuable to let your feelings out in some way as they come up. When you reinforce that the emotions they see you feel are helping you manage your circumstances, and making you a stronger person, it gives them pride to see you figuring it out. This gives them permission to do the same.

I do not have children myself, so I have never been inclined to change my words or speech for a younger person on the basis of their age or development. I have worked with many young people of all ages, and because most of them have come to me to receive help in walking through difficult situations, I find that explaining things to them as simply and directly as the topic allows (even when using language typically outside their development) is the best way to go.

Though a child may not comprehend the words you use, they will receive the meaning on a spiritual level. It also gives them some empowerment within the situation to communicate, ask questions, and ultimately express the very "adult" feelings they may be having. Additionally, it creates a positive foundation for future conveyances and conversations.

What about spirituality?

When children are sick, they often have an intuitive connection to the spiritual purpose of their illness—a sense of a deeper learning to come from the experience. And what if you are a parent or caregiver who does not share these same beliefs? What do you do to help your child with the information that feels right to them, but that they don't quite understand?

Issues of death and dying often parlay into questions about spirituality. And it is not uncommon for the child to have different leanings than their parents or possibly any religious beliefs expressed in the home. It is very important when the child brings up the topic of what happens when you die, or other questions about death, to let them be free to contemplate and speak about it and any understandings or intuitions they may have, without correcting or countering them.

Ask them what they believe happens, and tell them your beliefs, leaving them space to work out any contradictions on their own. Contribute to the conversation what you know to be true, including being honest when you don't have any idea. Somewhere in the spirit of the child is a directive or pattern of information to help them decipher their own relationship to death, dying, and the Divine. Your goal is to help them access it, not override it.

TALKING TO OTHERS ABOUT THE
LOSS OF YOUR CHILD

Interfacing with people after the loss of a child is difficult. After such a profound event, what you value may change, at least for a while. The things that are important to you seem to disappear overnight, and, more importantly, the things your friends and family may value can easily seem trivial under the weight of such a grief-filled burden. From the news of your loss, through the memorial or funeral, you are surrounded by people who see what you are going through, though you may not find yourself speaking about the loss but reminiscing about the person who is no longer with you.

But when that time has passed, and all the people and caring seem to drift back to everyday norms, you are now left alone with your grief. It cannot be said enough that every individual grieves in their own way; some people may remain in shock for months, and others move straight into the deeply emotional responses, but none of that prepares you for running into an old friend at the grocery store and being asked, "How's your family?"

This has been very difficult for me. I really dreaded the once-innocent questions "Do you have children?," "How old are your kids?," or "Where do they live?" After Max's death, the first time someone asked me this, I remember feeling like a deer in headlights. I lied and said we had only one son, Jake. Afterward, I felt so guilty, I swore I would never do that again. I practiced over and over in my head how I wanted to respond: "Yes, we have two sons, Max and Jake. Jake is (age). Max died by suicide in 2015." I can't say I'm completely comfortable answering these questions even now, but it has become easier, and it is important to me to be honest and forthright about Max's death. By doing so, I honor him while helping remove the stigma and shame surrounding depression and suicide.

—Margay E.

Practice compassion

Compassion is the art of taking yourself and others into your consideration. People will show emotion, first how they are comfortable to do so, and second, what feels acceptable in their environment. Practicing compassion is allowing for everyone to feel how and what they do in their own way—not wanting or forcing them to grieve the way you do. It is important to be conscientious of others' grief as well as your own, and to communicate gently and deliberately your needs, or in speaking about the needs of others.

Grief responses in front of others

I've heard from many grieving parents about the guilt they experience from feeling it's easier to pretend like their child is still alive while in social situations. This form of "fight or flight" grief response is normal. When speaking with people you've not kept up with or who may not know your child has died and under what circumstances, it can be an emotional trigger you may not be prepared to handle. While there is no shame in crying in front of others, it is common to go into a state of emotional shock and to say anything to move through to the next moment.

Some people will experience grief as a never-ending rainstorm that blows through unexpectedly and for which there is no preparation. It takes time and practice to acclimate to your new circumstances and the reactions you'll have in a social situation. Listening to the happy stories of friends and family and their children can be unbearable for a while. Remember that you are not responsible for the reactions or discomfort of others in the face of your emotion, and that is okay. You do not need to engage in any conversation that triggers your emotion, and can respond with "I'm not up for that conversation right now" or excuse yourself to another place for a few moments to release the emotion breaking through.

Patience is your friend in grief. If you ever were, you will no longer be able to be everything to everyone; cutting yourself some slack and doing your best to be there for yourself is your primary responsibility. The cabin fever and isolation that grieving can bring may give you the urge to get out and be social, and being out in whatever emotional state you're in is perfect. You will want to be intentional and prepare yourself for the experience. Here are a few things to consider:

1. Long, deep breaths (four seconds in, four seconds out) anytime you feel anxiety or an emotional response coming on can help reroute it to another time.

2. Practice, with a trusted friend, certain conversations or statements that you feel will trigger emotion—saying them over and over will help with your emotional balance while conversing with someone new.

3. Should you cry in public or at a social event, feel free to let others know you're grieving. And know that it is rare in public scenarios for people to acknowledge another's emotional state. Unless you make it obvious to them you want attention, receiving anonymity in the public eye is easy.

4. If you will be drinking or using other substances on a night out, make sure to have a designated driver and let them know you'll be cutting loose.

5. Do not think that an emotional response out in public won't happen to you. Prepare yourself for it.

What about your partner?

Relationships are complicated enough, but under the pressure of the death of a child, no matter their age, the loss can take a toll on the connection between two people. It takes a couple who have cultivated maturity and strong emotional integrity to do what is necessary for one another under the weight of the death of a child—accessing help here is optimal. It is vital to recognize that a third party—whether a grief counselor, therapist, grief support group, or spiritual counselor—will allow both parties to process the grief with others and not each other.

Couples who are processing the same loss will likely do it differently, and it can often be perceived as uncaring, unresponsive, or blame filled. One person wants to move forward, while another is steeped in constant emotion. The pair who shares this challenge will need help, communication, and space to mourn and process the death how they need to in their own time. Consider that this is a lifetime transformation through grief, and there is no rush.

The siblings left behind

Other family members lose their close relationship to the deceased, but also possibly their relationships to parents or other siblings in the way they had existed before. This is a double whammy. They will grieve multiple losses simultaneously and will need to have an open forum in which to communicate about it. Although there may be some resistance from young people to having organized assistance such as therapy or a support group, consider that your children will often get their opinions about help from you. Encouraging support and emphasizing that processing your grief with a third party is strength—not weakness—is a necessity.

Adult siblings, while they may have some experience with other deaths, will also need support in their grieving. It is important for them to be able to communicate their feelings out loud or on paper. Engaging in activities such as movies, television shows, or podcasts that either support or encourage their grief through similar subject matter or triggers is helpful. Ultimately, there will be times when no distractions exist, and they will be left to sit with the pain.

THE IMMEDIATE NEEDS OF THE PARENTS FROM THE DEATH OF A CHILD

When a child dies, depending on the circumstances, the parents may have immediate needs that others can step in to accomplish. Grief can be overwhelming and all-encompassing, and often—in the case of grieving the death of a child—enduring. Here is a list of common tasks for which they might need help.

Daily tasks: Cleaning, cooking, car and home maintenance, bill paying, organization, yard work, shopping

Help with planning the memorial

Managing any financial assets, personal belongings, or housing

Insurance paperwork

Help with grandchildren or pets

Money and resources

Help with any technical support for online presence

Support group or therapy

A place and companionship NOT to speak about the loss

Irreverence and humor are helpful

Memories and experiences of the child from others

WHEN ALL THE SUPPORT IS GONE

In every grief experience there is a rhythm of support from the people around you. Please consider that no matter how close you are, when it comes to the loss of your child, there may be a bestie or two who fall away because your situation makes them uncomfortable, and they don't know what to say or do. When this happens, it can feel like a punch-to-the-gut betrayal of your relationship, but it should not be taken as a personal affront to you. Some people run for the hills in the face of profound emotion or grief, and there is nothing to do but let them go.

Assuredly, others you know and some you don't will fill their space as your grief support team. During this time, it is important for everyone to communicate deliberately. Do not leave your needs or abilities unspoken. When you are the bereaved, one of the most important things to do is to be honest when someone is doing or saying something that is not helpful to you, since their intent is to be of service. As a part of the support team and a person who deeply cares for the bereaved, it is not important that you know what to say or do; just showing up and being present is helpful.

Eventually, however, there will come a day when that support team begins to move back into the normal flow of their life, and you are left with your grief. Some people are planners and will show up in the weeks after the death, to help you with arrangements, and others will avail themselves in the months after the death, but what do you do when there is no longer the help and distraction of friends and family?

I felt relieved and sad at the same time. Relieved because there were times when the calls, texts, emails, and in-person visits were overwhelming, and I wanted only to be alone with my thoughts and memories—to grieve in private. Sad because that was when the loss really began to sink in for me. Without the constant distraction of others, I was forced into a new and different stage of grief. I remember thinking, "Wow, life really does just go on like nothing happened," even though everything felt different to me.

—Margay E.

This period can be difficult in a family dynamic, since the journey of grief is mainly a solitary one. Some family members will be stoic, and others will be puddles of tears all the time. Tensions in the home can be very high in this phase, so here are some ideas to help acclimate to some of the dynamics that are in play.

1. Communication is key. Keep a journal to have an outlet for all your raw feelings. Writing the thoughts you may never speak to another person is cathartic and creates the space for compassionate connection with other people experiencing the death.

2. Have an anger plan. Permission to feel anger in an organized way is a powerful strategy to head off conflict that is inevitable after a child has died. There is no fairness about death—it just is, and your feelings of anger are natural, and for most, a bout of anger will precede the release of their grief. Accepting this and planning for it is necessary.

3. Have a family plan. Have a key word, phrase, or hand gesture you can use that signals to everyone in the room when you are angry about the loss. It's easy when you feel overwhelmed with anger to target other family members with your rage, taking something that they do that is irritating to you, personally, and transferring your real feelings of grief to the situation. If it is more comfortable for you to leave the room to express your anger, using the signal lets everyone know what you are feeling, and that you are okay but need space—when trying to talk through feelings isn't an option.

4. Use the language of death. What this means is to speak bluntly about death and the person who has died. Using euphemisms can often be confusing to children about what being dead means, and can make it difficult for adults to grieve. Many people choose these words and phrases because they don't know what to say, they want to be polite, or they don't want to hurt your feelings by being direct. Death is natural, and final, and will eventually happen to all of us.

Speaking about death directly is the only way to let the bereaved know you see what they are going through. Nothing you can say to a grieving person will hurt them further, but sometimes using words and phrases that make assumptions about where the spirit goes after death, or glosses over the finality of death, can leave a grieving person feeling unseen. When you are grieving a death, where they are doesn't matter, since you are focused on the fact that they are no longer with you.

Use words such as death, died, or deceased instead of euphemisms such as passed away, passed, passed on, resting in peace, eternal rest, asleep, departed, gone, lost, or slipped away. Being deliberate with your language around death and grief helps everyone understand and accept what has happened.

Even when you feel your deceased loved one "is in a better place," "is with the angels," "met their maker," "went to heaven," "is in Abraham's bosom," "traveled beyond the veil," or "is going home." These phrases, meant to promote comfort, often don't and again may leave the one who is grieving feeling unacknowledged for the depth of their pain.

When the bereaved use these phrases, it may be because of their own unfamiliarity and discomfort with death in general, which makes it harder to grieve. However, there is no need to correct them. You can use the direct language yourself to encourage them to feel safe in accepting the death and finding a way to approach their grief.

When you no longer experience comfort from friends and family

In this phase, there will be days where progress is getting out of bed in the morning. Wanting to sleep all day is a natural grief response, and honoring it, if your life allows, can be helpful. Many people see this as an emotional indulgence or depression (and depending on the circumstances, it could be), but what a person who is grieving is trying to do is to connect spiritually—to peace, wisdom, and their loved one.

Prayer is another way to do this, but for those who do not naturally turn to ritual, sleep is what we unconsciously associate with spirituality, dreams, creation, and other relationships to the Divine where we may connect to the one who has died. We go to sleep hoping for some message or insight that will help with our pain.

The solitary journey

Ultimately, your grief transformation is a solitary journey. The people with whom we relate can trigger our grief, but our beliefs, thoughts, process, and deliverance from grief are things we will face in times when we are alone. It can feel isolating, and it is not uncommon for many relationships to break up or take a back seat to grief. When this happens, remember that there is a natural cyclical timing for everything, and what is happening in your life is for your benefit for the time.

Dealing with the guilt

Guilt is a powerful emotion that comes up around death, but especially around the death of a child, or in complicated grief when there are extenuating circumstances around the death that leave unanswered questions or leave the bereaved feeling powerless. The energy of guilt alludes to the idea that one had some power within the circumstances of the death but did nothing.

The spiritual truth is that if something could have been done, it would have been done. So, as the guilt-ridden bereaved, consider that your feelings of guilt are showing you where in your life you must take better care of yourself and possibly make some other form of change to feel empowered in general.

After Max died, I think Stuart and I understood quickly—on a primal level— there could not and would not be any blame for Max's death by suicide, whether on him, me, or Max. It was as if we both instinctively knew we were in for the fight of our lives and would need each other to survive.

—Margay E.

SPIRITUAL CORDS

When a child dies (or any close loved one, for that matter), there is a spiritual cord of energy connecting the two of you. This cord does not always go away in death. It will remain in place while both parties (the living and the soul of the dead) still long for one another. Grief allows for the shedding of emotions and beliefs that obstruct one's view or understanding of the presence of this shared spiritual energy. It is common for people to grieve for a few months (even up to a few years) before they are able to connect to the presence of their loved one.

Even those who do not believe in any form of life after death can have this experience of "feeling" the presence of a loved one, or the paranormal activity of communication with the spirit of the deceased. Your belief system does not dictate what is possible or true; it only guides your awareness of it.

Having this ultrasensitive awareness (even for a time) during the mourning phase of your grief does not mean you are mentally ill or in spiritual danger in any way. It is your person communicating to you from the dimension where they exist, to help you with your grief, and often to communicate the things they were unable to in their body.

HOW TO GO ON LIVING WHEN YOUR CHILD IS NOT

It may feel like an impossible task to go on living when your child is not, but live you must. Your child does not want to be the cause of your downfall, or the reason for an embittered attitude toward life. The purpose of grief is to help you reconnect to the spirit of your child and yourself in a new way, and to address your outer world with more insight and empowerment.

The death of your child is not fair, but it is real, and there are ways other than misery to honor not only the death of a child but the short life they lived. A common phenomenon is deep-seated feelings of guilt for moving on, loving the children who are alive, having more children, or feeling happy. One can grieve and be happy; one does not discount the other.

The issue is a matter of trust. When you are managing any loss, you are working to rebuild the trust you had to yourself, others, and the Creator. You can look to the feelings of guilt and around what topic you may have them, to figure out where you need to build back your trust.

A Ritual for Acceptance

Affirmation: I accept everything as it is in this moment and embrace my divine strength to nurture myself.

What you'll need for your ritual:
  one blue jar candle

  one fire source (a lighter or match)

  a blue-colored paper or cloth of any size to place on the sacred altar area

  a photo of your child

  a piece of pink or gold kunzite

  paper and pen

  five dandelions or dandelion leaves

Herbs you'll need:
  Honeysuckle: This flower helps soothe painful memories of the past and helps the mind, body, and spirit to move forward with acceptance.

  Blue vervain: This herb calls in strength during challenging and painful times and has strong sacred wisdom energy.

  Chamomile: This herb helps soothe hurt and painful feelings within the body and relaxes the nervous system—it puts innocence and trust back into life.

Optional:

Flower essences:
  Sweet chestnut: This helps with extreme mental, emotional, and spiritual pain. It begins to break down the feeling that there is no way out, and allows access to the spiritual wisdom needed to release one from their anguished pain and suffering.

  Directions for using the Bach Flower Essences: You may add four drops into a cup of water and sip during the ritual to help ground your energy field and calm the mind and emotions. Or add in a bottle of water and spritz over the altar to set the intention of your affirmation. You may also add four drops into a cleansing bath prior to the ritual.

Begin your ritual by cleaning and clearing an area in your main living space. Collect all the items for your altar and put them in the cleared space.

Take a ritual bath by running warm water in the bathtub and holding the herbs in your hands while repeating the affirmation (you may also say prayers of your choice for healing). Exhale your breath onto the herbs to release the energies of the affirmation. Now add the herbs to the bathwater (place herbs in a piece of cheesecloth, or cover drain with a cloth when releasing water from the tub).

If you don't have a bathtub: Heat some water on the stove in a large pot and follow the directions for placing the herbs in the bath. Boil the plants for five minutes, let the water cool, and pour the water into a foot tub or other container large enough for both feet. Sit, soaking your feet, for as long as you'd like, and then pour the water down a drain or in a garden.

Journaling

When done with the bath, put the used plants in your garden as an offering. Grab a paper and pen and sit in view of your altar and contemplate your child. Write down these things:

1. Three things you miss about them

2. Three things you don't miss about them

3. One thing you wish you had said to them while they were living

4. One thing you had hoped they could have accomplished in their lives but did not get the chance

5. What was the most powerful thing your child ever said to you?

Be prepared to feel deep emotions as you walk through this ritual, but don't worry if you do not. You may even feel stumped trying to answer the questions, and all of that is okay. Do what you can, and you can repeat another time. If you can get in the flow of writing, feel free to write about any part of your experience and your feelings. You can use it as an opportunity to dialogue with the spirit of the deceased.

Now, take the paper and fold it into quarters and place it under the candle, lighting it and letting it burn to the socket, or for a few hours a day until it is complete.

Take a few moments every day to sit with your altar and reflect on your loved ones. Are there any changes in your thoughts, emotions, or behaviors? Once the altar is complete, give your dandelion offering to your garden or dig a small hole in the earth to bury them.

Performing this ritual may inspire a grief response, which is completely appropriate. Allow yourself to feel anything that comes up, and if you are too emotional to capture your feelings on paper, that is okay. The understanding you seek will come in many ways over time. Give yourself permission to go with the flow.

FACING DEATH: FINDING YOUR TRUE POWER

Looking at death is a sacred privilege: a powerful, enduring, revelatory look at one's life in the face of death. Most people are living to die. Every choice they make is with the underlying knowledge of their impending demise and how to stave it off just a little longer. We may not think of it in those terms, but we are all mindful of our deaths—deliberately or unbeknown to us.

Spiritually speaking, we all have a preordained relationship with death. We have lived and died in other incarnations and carry with us the energetic imprints or memories of our multiple births onto this Earth plane, and transitions from it. Regardless of your religious beliefs, or what you call this phenomenon, we all have a conscious or unconscious knowledge of our soul and spend a lifetime getting to know ourselves and cultivating our spiritual gifts—commonly known as the shadow-self. These patterns propel us into interests, belief systems, ideals, knowledge, and compassion for others that the life we have does not require.

Certain scenarios—such as the love or hate of other cultures and religions, having skills we've had no exposure to, or loving people we've only just met—reveal just a bit of the broad spiritual universe we each contain.

We spend our time promoting or neutralizing every pattern on the basis of what serves us in the present. The trauma of death is to help us focus on the eternity of life. For those of you who may be reading this and feel that when you die you turn into dust and that is it—nothing else comes after—perfect. Whatever you believe in your present moment will be your teacher in what comes after.

DEATH ALWAYS REVEALS ITSELF

My mother, Audrey, was diagnosed with lung cancer in February 2004. Two years previously, I'd received multiple dreams and visions alerting me to her forthcoming demise. There were several precognitive pieces of information leading me to the details of her death, which I took in but kept them secret from myself. One of these was shopping for and finding a Christmas gift for her that year, but when visualizing the sending of it, I said to myself, "Well, you'll just have to take it back anyway; you might as well keep it here." I filed this away into the recesses of my mind immediately.

Another hint of what was to come occurred two years prior to her death, when my mother had come to Los Angeles. Many friends and family had gathered over drinks when she pulled me aside, looked me straight in the eye, and said, "I'm going to need you to take care of me."

"Hahaha." With no context given, I responded jokingly, "Don't you want your favorite daughter to take care of you?" (as we had kidded many times before in reference to the middle child, my older sister).

"No, you will have to take care of me." Her tone shifted to an intensity I rarely saw from her.

"Okay, Mom; no worries. I'll take care of you," I said, a bit befuddled.

It all became clear the day after she'd received her diagnosis, when I arrived at her home in Albuquerque. I had stopped at the health food store on the way from the airport, not fully understanding her diagnosis but feeling positive that good nutrition would be helpful. As we sat in the kitchen chatting, I offered to make her a green-foods shake, and she reluctantly acquiesced; it was an acquired taste for sure. However, after taking one sip of it, she again looked me in the eye; she handed the glass back, saying, "No."

In that moment, I understood. I flashed on the multiple psychic moments of connection I'd had with her over the previous two years, about what I understood now to be her end-of-life process. I was not there to take care of her health; I was there to take care of her death. She had chosen me to be the custodian of her spiritual process.

The one thing we had in common was our faith in each other and an honesty about our own limitations. My mother trusted me completely to get her through the remainder of her days, to walk her through her fear, and to take her through each step of her transition with joy and dignity. In that moment, that's when the real work began, and the true relationship between my mother and me could be realized.

I was filled with a deep sense of gratitude, honor, and sorrow, and—over the coming weeks and months—it would become the abiding peace that carried us through. I began to understand that everything I had learned thus far in my life would all be used at this time: keeping my sense of humor, not taking things personally, not indulging in self-pity but embracing patience, and, most of all, I would have to depend on my physical, emotional, and spiritual stamina. It all seemed to fall into place as I watched my mother gracefully face death head on.

When I speak of death, I will speak simply. Death is defined as the moment in time when a physical body dies, and its spirit moves on to another dimension. Many cultures and religions have their own way of approaching death, but it doesn't change what happens. The physical body dies, and the spiritual body moves on into the ethers or beyond. Before that special moment, there are many ways our consciousness (our mind, our emotions, and our spirit) begins to bring us on a journey between the two worlds. Affectionately, I call it the *Death March*.

In all the deaths I have been privy to, through the experiences of others or that I have myself witnessed in this world and other dimensions, they've all had something in common: people experience a final process of shifting, changing, and reducing ties to this physical world and the folks in it. Simultaneously, they open their mind and heart to the possibilities or realities of the other side. Whether the death is expected (through an illness) or unexpected (via a critical health event, accident, homicide, or suicide), I find that everyone begins to wrap up their lives—sometimes reducing personal effects or completing relationships—all to create space for their spirit to take over when the time of their death arrives.

The death march

In death, there is a process of letting go—mentally, emotionally, spiritually, and physically. It is a time of reconciling one's relationships to all things: going through and giving away personal items and taking a stand on long-held feelings and beliefs—when fear or politeness previously may have been an obstacle. It is a time for the resolution of one's relationships—to themselves first, and to others and the world second. It can be a beautiful time of confidence and self-actualization.

Contemplating your own personal end times is a powerful way to find forgiveness. A reconciliation that may have been shrouded by rage, anger, bitterness, or apathy somehow becomes simple in the perspective of your last moments of life. You let go of the attachment and judgment you once held for yourself and others, and you gain the understanding you need about your circumstances (or you release yourself from the need to know). The process of life is about asking the why of things; death is about releasing yourself from it.

WHAT HAPPENS WHEN WE DIE?

I wanted to include information about the death and dying process in this book about everyday grief because the less we know about the things we fear the most, the more we unconsciously withhold our permission to express emotion and naturally remain in fear, distrust, or agony. Unless you have witnessed the death of a close loved one or had a connection to hospice, it is likely you have not been exposed to what happens to the body and spirit in the process of dying.

As witnesses to losing our loved ones through illness, we will process each phase of their dying through our grief. Grief helps us accept, draw wisdom, and then understand what is happening for our loved one. I find that the more information you have about death before dying occurs, it allows you a deeper level of understanding of this sacred time.

The dying process can be immediate, as in an accident when a person's spirit gets bumped from their body and the body dies. Or it can take days, weeks, months, or years for the body to degenerate and for the spirit to decide to leave. When a person is dying from an illness, the energy begins to reduce in the extremities first: the fingers, hands, arms, toes, feet, and legs. They all go numb because blood flow prioritizes the essential organs to preserve life. When this happens, the person who is experiencing it is not distressed, since they have shifted their consciousness to outside the body.

There are three fundamental pathways to death: cardiac failure, brain death, and respiratory failure. The body cannot sustain life with the nonperformance of any one of these systems. There are two general phases of dying: preactive dying, which is typically seven to fourteen days prior to death, and active dying, which is normally two to three days prior to death. The body changes in specific ways during each of these phases.

Preactive Dying

Weakness and lethargy

Increased sleep

Progressive disorientation

Restlessness

Limited attention span

Decreased interest in food or fluids

Difficulty swallowing

New loss of bladder and bowel control

Increased dependence on caregivers

New bedbound status

Active Dying

Clouding of consciousness and inability to maintain alertness

Decreased responsiveness to external stimuli

Unfocused pupils/gaze and glassy eyes

No interest in food or fluids

Abnormal respiratory pattern

Agonal breathing (shallow gasping breath, once every 15 seconds)

Terminal congestion that causes gurgling; it is not distressing to the person and is normal in the dying process

Hypotension (very low blood pressure; for example, 40 over 20)

A weak and irregular pulse (rapid then slow and vacillating)

Progressive cooling and mottling of the skin (the skin becomes peaked and prune-like)

It is important to remember that this process is very normal and not distressing whatsoever to the dying person. I know firsthand how torturous it can be for a family member to see a loved one in agonal breathing. As a witness, you think you've seen their last breath and then . . . several seconds later comes another. By this point their spirit has left the body, and the body is reducing in energy until there is no more.

Spiritually, in the last few months it is common for the person who is dying to practice leaving their body: to become multidimensional, to have a broader awareness or relive emotional dynamics that have brought strong unreconciled feelings. So, most often, by the time the body's death is complete, a person's consciousness has fully vacated, and they are communing energetically with their loved ones or have moved on.

My mother, Audrey, while dying of lung cancer that had moved to the brain, really enjoyed her multidimensionality. About four months before her death, she'd become deeply aware of my presence when I was with her and when I was at home in Los Angeles. She began to experience me the same way, no matter where I was located.

All throughout the day I would find myself having telepathic conversations with her, sometimes about not much of anything, laughing or joking about something silly. I had told her early on that when she died, we would probably speak more than ever. I'd laugh and say, "I'll talk to you later," while tapping my forehead with two fingers. This was to let her know that I'm always in her head and heart, and that the time and space between us doesn't matter.

The first time I told her this, she thought it was hysterical, and from then on made a point to say it to me often as I left the room, or every time I left to go home to Los Angeles. "I'll talk to you later," while tapping her forehead with two fingers.

During the nine months she was sick, I would travel to Albuquerque to spend two weeks at a time with her, and the other two weeks of the month I was at home working. One day, I had just arrived home in L.A. when my sister had gone to the hospital to see my mother.

Mom: "Tracee will be right back; she just went to lunch."

Sister: "No, Mom; Tracee went home yesterday."

Mom: "No, she didn't. She was just here."

Both things were true. I indeed was sitting on my sofa in Los Angeles, but I was having a conversation with her in my head that was clear as day. I could see my mother, Audrey, in my mind and was imagining our conversation. For Audrey, however, I am sure it was as if I was sitting right by her bed. Once you begin the journey of the awareness of your own consciousness and the power and strength it has, even more so outside the body, everything becomes real. You don't need to reach out and touch it to make sure.

The final four days of her life, Mom lay in her hospital bed in the den of my childhood home. She hadn't moved in that time, but she was still breathing. Her neck and face had begun to don the look of death as her chin swayed upward and to the side. Friends and family were dropping in and out to say their final farewells, and a low-key party was happening just outside on the porch. As the sun began to set on each of those nights, it was difficult to relax. My sister and stepfather took turns remaining vigilant, sleeping in the recliner by her bed. I was posted in the bedroom I'd grown up in, which was now my mother's office.

Each night, usually between 11 p.m. and 3 a.m., Mom would float back to my room in the 1950s-styled blue nighty she was wearing; she would stand in the doorway until I woke up. Some nights she would dance a jig until my eyes were open. The first couple of times, I shot up to my feet and ran to the den, where I found my sister sleeping and my mother still breathing. Audrey was dancing in her newfound freedom. She was excited to share it with me, but it took me a few days to catch on. I knew it wouldn't be long before she left her body for good.

Her final night was a hysterical comedy of errors. It was a Saturday evening—

we all gathered around her on the bed with her barely breathing body. Each of us told her how much we loved her and that it was okay to go. If she was ready to "go to heaven," we were ready. Within moments, my mother began to retch and choke. What did we do? We all flew into an emergency protocol, clearing her airway and adjusting her so that she could breathe more easily. Evidently, we weren't as ready as we'd thought. We all had an uproarious laugh about it, as we sat around waiting for her to die . . . again.

It wasn't until the next day, around 5 p.m., that both my sister and my step-father took shifts, not giving a moment's solitude to Audrey. Finally, my sister rose from the chair she'd been unable to leave for several hours (to grab a snack from the kitchen; she'd not eaten all day), and that became my mother's moment of truth. Again, she began to choke and gasp—and she was out. She was dead but not gone (just out of her body for good), because for months after her death, I would see her in her little blue nighty—sometimes dancing her jig, sometimes ballroom dancing, but always smiling, laughing, and joyful.

Sometimes in death, both things are true: I was her loving, empathic daughter in pain and in grief, struggling to let go of the mother I felt I was just getting to know, and I was the spiritualist-shaman being witness and guide to my soulmate and beloved on her final journey as Audrey. Both roles were profoundly heart wrenching and satisfying at the same time. Sometimes our loved ones experience pain and joy because they are ready to go but grasping at life at the same time. Ultimately, what appears to be conflict and struggle will give way to surrender, wisdom, and peace—whether in this life or the next. Always.

WHEN A DAUGHTER LOSES HER MOTHER

My friend Margay and I have been through a lot of grief together. We met in high school and instantly had a lot in common: we were both the youngest of three siblings, and daughters of single mothers. In our households, all the other siblings had moved away, and we were left alone to find our way through our own sadness—with mothers steeped in grief. You could say we "trauma bonded" and were brought together to take care of ourselves, our mothers, and—from the day we met—each other.

Luckily, we both had an irreverent sense of humor as it regarded our devastating plights. While our mothers both suffered from depression, it took different forms—but their mission of finding a man, they had in common. It's not that they weren't independent women, it's that they were brought up in the 1950s, and having a man to take care of you was what was expected.

That ideology was a teenager's dream—if they were busy dating, they weren't busy paying attention to us—and both Margay and I delighted in it. On nights that Sharon (Margay's mother) wasn't going out, she'd be in the bed watching television, so the price of admission to take her car for the night was to bring her a Blake's Lotta Burger, a Coca Cola, and two packs of Marlboro Lights. One night, Wayne (my mom's beau) suspected we'd be drinking and driving as we were headed to a party, so he offered up his huge truck with a camper shell; we still laugh at the irony today.

Margay's mom, Sharon, was spectacular: she was petite at 5 feet tall, had a huge mane of hair (with which she used an extraordinary amount of hair spray), applied fantastic blue eyeliner to bring out her blue eyes, and had a pair of breast implants gifted from her fifth husband. I only ever saw her in two types of clothing: fancy nightgowns during the day when she was depressed, and scrubs when she was working in a lab. The coolest mom anyone could have, I always appreciated her silent compassion and acknowledgment for my deep empathy. I always felt she saw me. Sharon and I had a lot more in common than I understood at the time.

During her life, she suffered with mental illness and was highly medicated a lot. Wishing for death, for her, was a pastime. It was never fully clear, until Margay told me the story of her final days, the dichotomy between who she created herself to be and who she never got to be . . . and all the love and struggle in between.

Sharon had been in hospice care for quite some time when one of her doctors recognized she wasn't dying but was so medicated that it was killing her. Over the next few months, she was taken off all her medications and had her breast implants removed. Immediately, she began to get better. She went from having a few months to a few more years to live.

Two weeks before she died, Sharon and Margay had gone to her doctor's appointment. She sat on the paper-covered table in a big white tee and baggy jeans with her boyish figure, no fake eyelashes, and a short little buzz cut (all her big hair had been shaved away). She had been returned to the person she always was deep inside—and never more peaceful.

On her last day, Sharon lay in the bed in her final splendor as her daughter rubbed her blue feet. Margay remembers being alarmed at just how blue and cold they were. Her mother hadn't made a sound in hours. "Mom," she said, "are your feet cold?" For one last time, the light came back to Sharon's eyes. "No, hon; they're not cold at all."

WHAT HAPPENS TO THE SOUL IN THE DEATH PROCESS?

The soul can begin its departure days and weeks before death. It varies on the basis of a person's readiness to make the transition into spirit, and its effect on those who surround them. The soul can come and go as it pleases and often does in those last few months, practicing and experiencing what it feels like to be out of a body.

When a person is in their final transition, there is often an ethereal feeling in the room, for they have brought the awareness of a thinned veil between worlds. You may even feel the presence of the loved ones and the angels who have come to receive them. No matter what you believe in life, in death we all have teachers and guides who show up for us in the end of one cycle and to begin the next.

Not every person will have the clarity or awareness of these spirit guides and their communications in a cognizant way, but certainly their presence will be felt. Depending on the state of one's mind and heart at the end, there may need to be some additional spiritual awakening to take place after the body has died, and the person's guides are there to offer that assistance. It is often very difficult for a grieving family member to play that spiritual role for the deceased.

A few years back, an acquaintance of mine had lost her son to an overdose. From that day forward, this young man was in what some of you may call "limbo," basically in the dimension of energy just outside our own physical plane. His death was a surprise to him, and since he was medicated during the transition, he needed help with his spiritual sight and awareness. His soul was being tended to by spirit guides, who were working very hard to get my attention.

Immediately, I was alerted by a friend of the family about what had happened (even though I had no close ties with them), and within days I began to see their son in my dreams. Eventually, he became strong enough in spirit to show up in my waking visions. I would be watching television, and in my periphery I would see him in a room waiting. This, no doubt, was also occurring for others as well (whoever was available to hear), until finally, about four months later, his mother called me, wanting to understand what happened and to communicate with her son.

It was from that point on that mother and son began to speak in a new spiritual language, so that he could better understand what happened to him, and to help his family grieve his abrupt death. Soon after, his mother became an advocate to bring awareness to the danger of drugs, as a way of honoring her son and working through her grief.

THE EMOTIONAL BODY DURING THE DEATH PROCESS

Our emotions are powerful things: they help us communicate new and broad ideas, express traumatic or joyful feelings, and can turn public opinion on a dime. When a person dies, depending on their state of awareness, reconciliation for the life they have lived, and their physical brain health, their emotional-energy body (a layer of the aura or energy system of the body) may need to express certain memories or experiences that have not found peace.

Something as simple as a person entering the room can trigger an outburst that can sometimes feel scary to the observer. A person in the dying process will be aware on vibrational levels, not necessarily conscious ones; they may or may not know what they are doing. For many, sometimes this can be caused by what we call dementia, but not always.

Several years ago, a client I was working with was simultaneously taking care of his dying grandmother, and during the final two weeks of her time on the planet, this grandmother, every night in the wee hours, would become tormented: screaming, crying, and wailing in agony. My client was so disconcerted and devastated to be awakened each night to his grandmother's pain that he brought it to my attention.

It was clear that she was enduring some form of spiritual attack at night, very possibly brought on by the intensity of her surroundings (there were a lot of drugs and drug-induced behavior in the neighborhood). My client and I spent our session praying for his grandmother, and that night she was calm and slept peacefully all the way until morning. Every night until she died, her devoted grandson prayed for her peace until it came for good.

RESPONDING TO A TERMINAL DIAGNOSIS

When someone receives an inevitably fatal diagnosis, it marks the most powerful time in their life. Often, where and when the condition is recognized isn't where the information is relayed to the patient. It is common for a person to begin their journey in the hospital emergency department, for tests to be done, symptoms to be acknowledged, or pain to be managed, and the terminal quality of their condition to be discovered. However, it is standard for the ED staff to make a referral to another doctor who will sustain the new relationship with the patient over the life of their care. This is where the news of the diagnosis will be delivered to the patient.

Often, patients hear things differently from what is being told them. Patients naturally resist the fatal reality of their condition and seek multiple opinions, which is normal and should be received with support and compassion. Another contributing factor to this air of resistance is that some doctors use either euphemisms or technical language the patient doesn't understand. Studies show that patients and family members want to know the truth. Doctors, however, are not immune from their own grief and triggers, and this humanity can sometimes be expressed through their own desire to shield a patient and their family from the deep pain they know this news will cause, by using language that obfuscates the reality of the finality of their diagnosis.

Dr. Shapir Rosenberg, a palliative-care physician, calls it the "collusion of silence" between a doctor and their patient.

They do it so that people don't experience the pain of future loss, but inevitably, to cope and adapt to the reality of their impending death, they will need directness and support for everyone. With care, compassion, and love the caregivers can shepherd the family through the preparation of letting their loved one go.

It is in the physician's purview and, in my opinion, their obligation to speak honestly and support families through their diagnosis and illness, because not doing so inflicts a kind of harm. It robs the family of those precious last few moments they have together. As a palliative doctor, I know the cold statistics of someone like me walking into the room, and its strong suggestion that a person's life is ending. I walk with that awareness through the hospital, and it lends a perspective and urgency that possibly other doctors do not experience. It means that time is of the essence.

—*Dr. Shapir Rosenberg*

Trusting oneself implicitly, on a spiritual level, is what a terminal diagnosis is about for the individual receiving it. Now, you may be expecting me to say something "spiritual" like, "*Everything happens for a reason*," or "*Miracles happen*," right? Don't worry, you won't get such platitudes from me. It's not that I don't believe them to be true for some, but even so, they are not helpful at the onset of an inevitably fatal diagnosis, and their message is not one of the physical world.

To be alive and considering your mortality is a powerful experience. You have to begin not only the process of understanding what is happening in your body, but the slow roll of powerlessness that must be overcome emotionally. Then, there is the matter of the loved ones in your life; you must contend with them and their knowledge, and the attachment they have to the way things are right now.

When my mother received her diagnosis, 1 knew it would ultimately cause her death. I had been receiving dreams, messages, and visions during the previous two years that it was her time to go. I was able to grieve on my own, along the way, so when the diagnosis came, I understood what it meant and its finality. Those few precious moments with my mother were my last. It all settled in for me the day I arrived at her home after she received the news of her condition. She seemed fine; maybe her energy was a little lower than usual, but other than that, she was great. However, I could see something different was happening.

What I remember most about that week was arriving back in Los Angeles and jumping on a call with my dear friend and mentor, Daisy. She was joyful and giggly as usual, which was slightly awkward for me since my heart had just been ripped out of my chest. The second sentence out of her mouth was "When it's time, I'd be happy to help you and your mom through the death process."

I was shocked, since her words felt so cavalier. How could such a spiritual person not see the pain I was in? How could she lack such empathy for me? I felt betrayed and was so angry I got off the phone. We barely spoke again for the duration of my mother's illness.

Later, what I learned in those moments was that people receiving such powerful news need to be able to process it in their own time. I knew that this disease would take Audrey's life, but I too needed a safe place to grieve with a witness, and clearly that would not be Daisy. I still needed time to process my mother's life and was not yet ready to process her death.

The other thing that became clear for me at the time was that when you live life through a spiritual lens, you don't necessarily feel the empathy some people will need from you. Being spiritual is not necessarily a "feeling" or empathetic viewpoint. No, it is usually a much-broader perspective where death is a sacred joyful rite of passage, and grief is not necessarily felt.

When a person receives a fatal diagnosis for themselves or a loved one, it is devastating. Your heart cracks open and pours out all its sorrow onto the ground, and the last thing you need is someone giving you gracious, positive platitudes that don't connect with the real pain, fear, or anger that you feel.

For the person receiving a terminal diagnosis:

1. Give yourself the time and space you need to understand what is going on in your body, and in your heart.

2. Get all the information. It helps bring a new clarity about what you must now give value to.

3. Don't be shy about letting your loved ones know what you need, especially when it is space from them—this is your time.

4. Be honest about how you feel, no matter how unsavory the emotions may feel to you.

5. The process of grief you will experience begins to open your heart and mind to deeper understandings for you; give yourself permission to feel it.

6. Many people who are sick resist feeling grief or don't have the energy for it. However, grief during illness is common and necessary. It is a natural part of the emotional-healing process.

7. Know that after processing the loss you feel, a new identity will begin to emerge if you let it: a new powerful you, a restored spirit.

For the soulmates of the person receiving a terminal diagnosis:

1. Shock can take a while to wear off; pay attention to the subtle signs and signals your loved ones give you about their needs. Sometimes, saying nothing is better than saying the wrong thing, for them. This may be your loss, but it is their life.

2. Direct, honest, and gentle communication is necessary during this time. You may find yourself needing to set aside your feelings to create space for your loved one to grieve their own mortality.

3. Some people are just not good at being around difficult emotions; if that's you, feel free to be honest about it and make yourself useful another way.

4. It is common for a person receiving such a diagnosis to resist its harsh reality for a while. It's not your job to change that unless they deliberately call on you to do so.

5. You, no doubt, are going to have a plethora of emotions of your own. Do your best to process them on your own or with outside help. To

express emotion through your empathy of your beloved is one thing, but to make the moment about your grief is another. Again, take your cues from your friend.

6. Helping someone through an illness is a powerful gift to them. As a caregiver, you need help as well, so don't be shy about getting it.

NAVIGATING A SUICIDE

When someone dies by suicide, those left behind are usually left wondering, "Why?" With more than 40,000[1] suicides a year in the US alone (they are on the rise globally), it is quickly becoming a major health crisis. Suicide is currently recognized by the American Psychiatric Association as a symptom of major depressive disorder or borderline personality disorder and is currently under review to be admitted into the psychiatric diagnostic manual—DSM-5—as suicidal behavior disorder. Doing this may put more focus, money, and research toward the study of suicide, but it won't necessarily answer the real questions that are revealed to loved ones, in the wake of suicide.

While it might feel like suicide is the end, spiritually it is not. We tend to focus on the trauma of the profound physical loss, and the shame and stigma that often eclipse the real burden of a death by suicide—the guilt and lack of understanding of what exactly went wrong. I'd like to focus on the spiritual aspects of the aftermath of suicide for the ones who have killed themselves and the friends and family they have left behind.

In my twenty-five years working professionally as a spiritualist—and simply being empathic to those fundamentally devastated by the spiritual traumas that plague them—I have met, counseled, and provided a medium back to the real world for many who have died by suicide. It has often been awe inspiring how spirit has led certain families and their loved ones (who've trapped themselves in the in-between worlds) to my awareness for assistance.

Their intent wasn't to end up spiritually locked in the ethers, but to release themselves from the pain that relentlessly followed them. In my experience, this pain takes many forms. Psychically, the pain is an uninterrupted wall of apathy with no path out. Emotionally, the pain may feel like a heavy, immovable, wet blanket that can be changed only by death. And, spiritually, this pain can take the form of entities whose only goal is to perpetuate the state of mental chaos the

---

1   (Fehling and Selby 2021)

person finds themselves in, until finally they can take no more.

All these forms of pain are perceived to be immovable by the person who experiences them, and they have no ability to recognize the temporal state of their condition, which inevitably leads to their death by suicide. Sophia, whose story we hear later has this to say on closure:

> *I counsel people to have closure, which has the possibility of prevention in and of itself. I say, if you choose to do this, you must help the people you love and will leave behind by answering their questions, telling them why you want to die. From my experience, it's not giving permission to someone to take their life but offering the cold, hard truth of reality for those they leave behind. The ones I've spoken with (and followed through with later) have ultimately chosen to live to fight another day, as a product of doing so.*

—Sophia M.

DO PEOPLE WHO DIE BY SUICIDE HAVE A CHOICE?

This is the question that often tortures friends and family of those who've died by suicide. It stands true that as uniquely as an individual lives their life, they will claim those same idiosyncrasies in death as well. There is no one single truth for us in death; there are only the righteous choices we are driven to make on the basis of our spiritual patterns, our worldly experiences, and our DNA's responses to those factors.

It is our judgment of those who die in this way that promotes our struggle with being left to answer, sometimes, the unanswerable for ourselves. It is our guilt from not having done enough or been enough to save our loved ones that we grieve the most. Ultimately, this grief teaches us that those who die by suicide were going to do it no matter how we felt, or what we said, or what we did or did not do. A friend relayed a brutal story of a woman who had her husband committed to a mental institution to save him from the massive depression and suicidal thoughts and behaviors from which he suffered—only to have him, days later, break out of the lockdown facility and kill himself.

Sophia, whom I quoted in the previous section, told me the story of losing her partner in this way:

"Dan woke me up in the middle of the night with a gun to his head, saying he couldn't bear living anymore, and although he didn't take his life that night, he assured me of his eventual demise by suicide. He wanted for me to be ready, and I wanted to help him save himself."

Sophia went on to tell me of her husband Dan's first thoughts of suicide at the age of nine and the profound battles he fought to overcome the overwhelming belief he should never have been born into this life. He was battling spiritual trauma that was exacerbated by a childhood gang rape by boys his own age, among other afflictions.

"The fact that he lived past forty was a real testament to his strength and fortitude," she retorted in the middle of our conversation.

Dan would, within three years' time, die by suicide—when Sophia was left with no more questions. In those three years, she never condoned his belief in death as the answer to his plight but sought to understand the deep, searing pain that rattled him daily. It was from this compassion that she found acceptance of his condition and his choice.

Fully listening to someone who has plans to kill themselves, and holding them accountable for the reality their actions hold for others, isn't giving them permission to do it; it is offering them the space and time to be mindful of what they want to do, why they want to do it, and possibly the opportunity to find another path to reconciling their struggle.

Emotional pain is real, but killing oneself to release the spirit from the body doesn't transform that pain. When pain is present at the time of spiritual release from the physical body, it travels with the spirit to another realm—to be processed by that soul without the distractions of a physical form. It by no means is the end of the life of the soul, only the new beginning it needs to find true solace, in their own time.

Often, those who die in emotional pain or spiritual trauma choose to stay in a peripheral world close to those they love for a period of time, to fulfill the spiritual commitments they may have made to them. This allows them to work through the pain they possess, without the distractions or obligations of the physical world. However, this can also be the obstacle to expediently healing the rift in their spirit in one incarnation, and the vehicle to carry it over into the next. In no way does suicide change the pain one feels; it only disempowers them to address it expeditiously.

THE SUICIDE TRANCE

A suicide trance is a loop of running thoughts a person experiencing suicidal thinking and behaviors gets swept up in. They are focused on feelings of unworthiness and beliefs that their death will bring relief to them and those they love: "The world is better without them." This trancelike experience is so powerful it can lead someone to making an irrevocable life-and-death decision.

This dynamic is believed by many health professionals to be chemical in nature, and possibly treated by psychiatric medication, but the spiritual patterns that perpetuate these chemical structures cannot be underestimated. In my experience in working with the demographic of people who've sought psychiatric treatments, the medications often prohibit the processing and healing of the spiritual patterns that promote the suicidal thoughts and behaviors, and have their own sets of side effects that make sustaining a good quality of life a challenge. It might be a temporary Band-Aid, but not a solution for the very real-world trauma that many experience every minute of every day.

Many years ago, I found myself in a suicidal predicament. I was in my early thirties, and although I thought of death often, I knew suicide was not an option for me. I lived almost every day up until this point with undiagnosed depression and anxiety, and profound spiritual and emotional trauma. As a rape survivor, I was too angry to want to die—until I met a soulmate with whom I had a powerful connection. We had a profound spiritual and emotional bond that energetically contained within it the past-life history we shared.

His presence in my life awakened me to a recollection of a past-life memory of being enslaved and impregnated on a Spanish ship in the early 1500s. The vision was of a woman (me), Higuemota, eight months pregnant, on a ship in the middle of the Atlantic. The moon was bright, and I could barely hold down what little food my captors had given me, worsened by the relentless, choppy waters, which had not been still for hours.

The stench in the belly of the ship where I was lying was intolerable. I was aware of a darkness that surrounded me; it encouraged me to find my way above deck and, finally, to relieve my suffering by throwing myself and my unborn baby overboard. It turned out—as my drowned, lifeless body fell toward the bottom of the ocean—that my pain, devastation, and rage were alive as ever.

Reliving my own suicide trance from that previous incarnation, and facing the entities whose job it was to capitalize on the profound apathy I was feeling in this life, propelled me to take important measures to ensure my safety through this dangerous passage of remembering and healing my spiritual trauma.

It is the conundrum of needing to secure safety through psychiatric medication and the desire to heal the original pattern that is the reason we need to forgive our judgment of another's death choices (conscious or unconscious). We may never know the multiple levels of trauma a person is navigating, and the many incarnations it will take them to find the peace and healing they seek.

It is common for those who are prescribed medication for mental illness to go on and off those medications for a myriad of reasons: searching for the combination that brings them the relief they need, going off the medication when they feel better, or disrupting use when the medication causes them to feel "nothing." It's possible that the best use of medication is for buying more time for those motivated to get the help they need to resolve the emotional and spiritual trauma they carry, or to keep them from being a danger to themselves or others.

No matter how you feel about the source of suicidal thoughts and behaviors or their treatment, there is no blanket answer. There are a plethora of spiritual understandings and wisdom that each soul will have to uncover for themselves through grief, ultimately absolving their burdens and leading them out of the darkness where they reside.

POST-TRAUMATIC GROWTH

Posttraumatic growth is a phrase coined for what happens as a person begins to work through the pain of their traumas—all the ways they expand in emotional intelligence, ideological viewpoints, and spiritual understanding. Processing the grief from our pain allows us to grow as human beings and to cultivate the compassion needed to solve some of our solitary and collective mysteries. Grief reconciles our fears and quells our hatred of the things that make us feel powerless. Finally, it shows us the common ground we all share.

One of the statements I've heard from almost every person who's lost someone by suicide (or homicide) is that they, at the beginning, felt safe or comfortable being around only those who've had the same experience. While it may feel genuine, for those of us who've not been touched by any of those specific losses, to say we know how you feel isn't accurate—we don't. The truth is it is often difficult to hide the unconscious bias, judgment, or fear that surrounds such an unfathomable or controversial death.

Part of posttraumatic growth, for everyone, is practicing the compassion and patience to become self-aware, and masterful of our emotions—that is, our capacity to understand what we feel and why, and our ability to reserve words or actions until we have considered the impact they will have on others.

Stephanie's story

Stephanie C. was married to Mark for twelve years, five of them in blissful love. Mark suffered from bipolar depression and spent the last seven years completely checked out of their marriage and in his own world of emotional bondage. He'd tried every medication possible, and nothing worked. The house began to take on a devastating darkness that became intolerable for her and her young son.

When she could no longer endure the murky condition of their home life, Stephanie asked the love of her life to move out (with secret hopes that it would inspire him to find a way to make things better). The last two years of Mark's life accelerated into increasingly chaotic behavior and emotions until finally he died by suicide.

To a person who wants to kill themselves, their pain is so insurmountable it feels like giving themselves psychic surgery without anesthesia: a never-ending loop of pain.

—Stephanie C.

Guilt, for Stephanie, was the biggest hurdle to overcome in response to her husband's death. She sought refuge in a grief group for those who'd lost loved ones from suicide. In time, she eventually came to understand that self-blame was a throughline or common denominator for everyone she met. Knowing that survivor's guilt was a powerful foe for others as well helped her accept what happened, let go of the guilt, and embrace the healing process for her and her son.

NAVIGATING HOMICIDE

Sometimes in life and in grief, we are left with only half the information, and all the trauma of the loss of a loved one and the damaging nature of their death. When a person dies by homicide or an uninvestigated suspicious death, where many of the details don't seem to sync up with what appears to be possible, the loved ones are left with a massive void that begs to be filled with the facts that could bring peace and the daunting task of finding closure all on their own.

Twelve-year-old Harold Jr. was awakened early in the morning from an unexpected knock on the door and news of his father's death. It wasn't until later, while riding in the back of a pickup truck on the way to the family cookout, that he doubled over from what felt like a punch to the gut. The lump in his throat kept the air from moving freely in and out of his lungs, as the news began to wash over him. The officer's words echoed in his head, "Your father, Harold Sr., has been in a fatal car accident." In the wake of this tragedy were only questions.

On May 27, 1967, on a dark New Mexico highway, with only a half moon to light their way, a car with two men, a woman, and her two children gently pulled to the side of the road on their journey toward Smith Lake. That would be the final ride for one of the unwitting passengers. The Navajo Reservation police report given by the female passenger said, "After we got out of the car, it began to roll down the side of the road toward a 15-foot embankment and then crashed into the arroyo. Harold Sr. was still in the car, and he was dead." The report made no sense; Harold Jr. was certain there were missing details.

Several weeks after the accident, Harold overheard his aunt and uncle speaking freely, believing he was fast asleep in the back seat of the car, as they drove. Uncle Johnny had been there that night. Coincidentally, he'd been driving on the opposite side of the freeway when he saw car lights disappearing down the embankment. Driving up on the incident from the opposite direction, he distinctly remembered seeing something never mentioned in the police report.

There was talk of murder and several mystery men who'd been waiting in another vehicle on the side of the road, but a motive for murder was never revealed. At some point, a promise was made to Harold Jr. by his uncle to tell him everything he knew, when he got a little older. Unfortunately, time did not pass quickly enough, and the secrets were never divulged. Harold Jr.'s uncle died without saying another word, and he was left with a lifetime of unanswered questions.

There are many victims in the aftermath of a homicide or mysterious death. Along with the natural rage and confusion one feels from experiencing such events, there is a sense of judgment and shame that often aligns with the controversy of murder or the unknown. It's true: people in their lowest minds are fearful of what they do not understand, repulsed by what they know would devastate them, and downright awful to others in their blissful ignorance.

However, despite such profound conditions, those who are left to grieve must grieve not only the loss of their loved one but other elements as well, such as the details uncovered in an investigation, an inquiry that never happens, a murder trial that ends unjustly—all of these leaving justice never to be found. And finally, adding insult to injury, is the relationship to the public through news channels, social media, and others that can ferret out untruths as well as obfuscate the facts from being discovered. It is this reality that touches the lives of a select few, but when it does, it becomes their life.

Managing the void left behind

On Sunday, May 28, 1967, both Harold Jr. and his father had been ushered into completely new worlds: Harold Sr. was with his ancestors; Harold Jr. had been thrust into a relentless world of unknowing, where facts would be few and far between. For Harold Jr., growing up without a father was the least of his grief. The consistent chatter by older family members and townspeople about what may have happened to his father (but never revealing the truth) caused the greatest anxiety and rage for him.

> *Not knowing what happened is a void that never goes away—the feeling of powerlessness. It's made me mistrustful; I can sense danger on the streets. My whole life, I've suffered from feelings of abandonment and isolation—any time someone I care about leaves the house (even to run errands) and doesn't arrive back in the logical time it should take for them to accomplish what they left to do, I feel anxious. I begin to think of how I would react if they didn't come back or were taken from me abruptly.*

—Harold Jr.

This form of hypervigilance is the number one fear that children formulate and often keep well into adulthood or for a lifetime. It can be the cause of chronic anxiety and panic attacks. Feeling unsafe after a loved one has been murdered can leave the entire family shattered and confused. It is also common for family members to experience fear of retaliation by the murderers, if they are not caught or convicted.

This dynamic creates a phantom effect where one always imagines the unseen perpetrators as still active in their lives and waiting around every corner. It's hard to feel safe in any environment when a life-altering violation has taken place.

Grief and managing the void of time, space, and emotion can be difficult for the victims of violent crime. Grieving requires surrender and release of emotion. But it is the shock and hypervigilance that comes from addressing what is known, or what is unattainable information from the aftermath of a homicide or suspicious death, that can inhibit any form of future relaxation. The important thing to remember is that moving forward even an inch is still moving forward.

Five important ways to move forward

1. Breath work: Practices such as meditation and yoga require a deep awareness and mastery over your breathing. When we are in trauma, we have a tendency for shallow breathing and are often unaware of our breath patterns. This can render us unprepared for an emotional trigger or panic attack. Take a breath in through the nose, deep into the diaphragm, and exhale it to a count of four. Doing this four times can help calm and center you.

2. Going with the flow of grief: Allow yourself to feel the small expressions of grief, such as when a smell reminds you of the person who is gone, but you choke back the tears. To let yourself feel the minor grief responses reduces the buildup of emotional layers and diminishes the need for intense grief responses or breakdowns.

3. Get a hobby that evokes joy: When our minds are active with an activity that we enjoy, we become relaxed and begin to feel more trust of ourselves and our environment. When feelings of grief arise, we are less intimidated at the prospect of experiencing them, and they often pass through more quickly. Also, this meditative time is when we often receive intuitive epiphanies about ourselves and life that give us the inspiration or clarity we need to move forward.

4. Practice mindfulness: Mindfulness is a form of meditation where you, while engaging in other activities, become present to your feelings and can experience them or gain insight into them.

5. Claim forgiveness: Forgiveness is something we choose for ourselves; it is not what we must give to another. When you forgive yourself and others, you are claiming a new commitment to releasing yourself of the thing or person you are forgiving. You are letting go of your attachment to it and opening your heart to the new element of life that will take its place.

Revenge is a fantasy

The rage that engulfs the friends and family of a murdered loved one is formidable and can catch them by surprise. Revenge fantasies are common for victims of violent crime and their close loved ones, and sometimes even helpful, to find a glimmer of power in a completely disempowering situation. However, to follow through with actions of revenge only changes or doubles the burden you carry.

Anthony Ford was a young man who struggled in his life. At twenty-three years old, he'd lived through a lot of experiences and seen many unsavory things. As a teen he'd been drawn into a gang, and for the past few months he'd been moving away from that life. He had been working at a new job, as a mechanic, and was showing up every day on time. He was reconnecting with family members with whom he'd lost touch, and was in a seemingly stable relationship. In a recent visit with his older brother Tony (Antonio), he exclaimed, "Yo, man, things are good. The job's working out and things with Tania, well, they're good."

Tony hadn't seen him this happy or excited about anything in a long time. And at the end of the visit, they shared a long embrace, which, although it was a little uncharacteristic, Tony was deeply grateful to see his little brother inspired for the future—a look he'd rarely seen on him. Tony waved him off as he drove away, and wondered if things were really turning around.

It wasn't more than a few nights later, on a cool December midnight in San Bernardino, California, when everything changed. Anthony and his girlfriend, Tania, were enjoying the company of friends and wanted to relax with a joint or two. They had been arguing about her insistence at being the one to go and buy the weed from the guys on the corner, outside her apartment. They were in a rival gang to the one Anthony was pulling away from.

And when we use the term "gang," it bears mentioning that some of these folks had been Anthony's lifelong friends and acquaintances. They weren't a "gang" to him; they were his friends and confidants. Moving away from a life of crime was easy; it was leaving behind every friend he'd ever known that was difficult. But Anthony really felt that spending a lot of time with the new lady in his life would be the key to it all.

He had gotten a job and was learning new skills. He was doing everything he could to stay away from the people, places, and things in his past that had led him down a bad path, but unbeknown to him, his new girl was making time with one of the guys on the corner.

Finally, getting her way, she went out, bought a couple of dime bags, and came back into the apartment. Anthony was mad. The two had words again, and he left out the back door, to an alley area behind Tania's apartment. He needed to smoke a cigarette and calm down. Suddenly a car rolled up, with a few of the guys from the corner. "What set you from?" they asked

Anthony was no longer in the life and wanted nothing to do with it or them, and he turned to go back inside. But as he walked away, someone in the car shot him seventeen times in the back. Anthony staggered—by the sheer force of will— back into the house, where his friend Shawn saw the bullet holes in his bleeding body and the confusion in his face. Shawn shouted, "Call for Jesus!"—which made no sense to the other panicked people in the apartment. But it did for Anthony. "Jesus" was the last thing he said as he collapsed, and the light left his eyes.

Antonio, or Tony as his friends knew him, was twenty-seven years old when his younger brother Anthony was murdered. By 10 a.m. that morning, the family had gathered at their sister's home and began to process the news. Tony had gone outside to get some air, but as he sat with the reality of his brother's death, the rage began welling up inside him. In fact, anger and fear had been building for days. He didn't like his brother's girlfriend and had a bad feeling about her. He was so mad. In his heart, he knew Tania was to blame in some way, although he wasn't sure how. He felt it to his core.

In those moments, the impressions of revenge began to overwhelm him. His thoughts started to wander into the darkness. In his rageful mind, he silently called on Satan to bring Tania to him so that he could kill her with his own bare hands. In a trance, he began to bang on the backyard fence, where, on the other side, the neighbors had two pit bulls that were becoming increasingly agitated. At 6 foot 2 in height and a solid 200 pounds, Tony was a force to be reckoned with and oblivious, even to his own peril.

His rage was so powerful and all encompassing that the force he used was ripping the fence apart nail by nail; you could hear the cracking wood. The fence was about to give way when a woman tapped him on the shoulder and said, "Hey." It was her; it was Tania. Tony flung her around by her shoulders, backing her up against the enclosure, choking her with both hands, until finally his sister hit him over the head with a trash can and he fell to the ground. He awoke several minutes later, enough time for Anthony's girlfriend to leave the house.

Over the next three weeks, Tony gathered his things and his family and left San Bernardino for good. He was horrified at the rage he felt for the people involved, and the police for not having taken any interest. It seemed their philosophy was to let the "gang problem" resolve itself. He never wanted to see any of them again, and he wanted to be safe—not only from himself but from the unchecked murderers (whom everyone knew). Tony didn't trust himself to stay in town and remain peaceful.

In Anthony's case, there was never a full investigation, charges, or a trial—as often happens when the victims are judged with the blame of their own demise. Not only are the family members left with the trauma of their lost loved one, but also the fear of reprisal or retaliation from a free, known assailant.

At this point, and even for the next few years, Tony was not able to allow the grief emotions that could help him find some solace; however, he took authority over his own feelings by removing himself from the place where the triggers of his brother's murder could torment him, and by bringing his family to safety. From that point, the mental, emotional, and spiritual components of his battle were palpable, and he fought them on every front: he had a good-paying consistent job, he tried multiple medications for his depression and anxiety, and he reinforced his relationship to God by going to church. Even so, he still struggled.

Managing judgment

For many people, our justice system is a judgment system where their lives are dismissed, diminished, and devalued by the ones in authority. Investigations aren't made and resources are withheld because of the personal, social, or racial biases of those we deem in power and in whom we put our trust to take care of everyone.

When managing the judgment of the outside world, the power you have is, first, in not joining them in criticizing who you are. Second, it is in forgiving them for being hateful and ignorant. Third, you must do what you can, how you can, to remedy the circumstance. The only person who can diminish you in any real way is you.

Of course, sometimes the power structure in life isn't fair, and we are forced to make hard decisions to take these unlawful people to account or walk away and put ourselves in a new position. Either way, we are tasked with the job of holding our confidence and not allowing the behavior of others to put us in a position to think less of ourselves. Dignity and respect are something we choose.

UNDERSTANDING YOUR RELATIONSHIP TO CONTROL

When addressing the very real traumas in our lives, and especially in the face of death, we naturally grasp on to anything we can, to feel like we are not losing it all. This unconscious desire to take control of ourselves, others, or our environment is a natural habit that stems from the fight-or-flight mechanism we have, to save ourselves from temporal or permanent harm. Learning to recognize this on a rational level and to ultimately reprogram it is a powerful feat.

The antidote to managing our desire to control the outside world, and the hypervigilance that comes as a byproduct of our trauma, is developing our intuition. Grief and our intuitive self work together to peel away the layers of our fear and ego, and to help us envision something new: a new viewpoint, feeling, belief system, or innovative solution to a problem. I've spoken of this element multiple times over the chapters you have read so far. It is the magical aspect of the interconnectedness of us all—the Universe, the planet, and the people with whom we live.

As we develop our psychic, telepathic, and empathetic channels to become aware of the subtle synchronicities we are always provided with along our path, we can begin to understand the deeper reverberations of the patterns in which we vibrate and how to transmute and transform them with new thoughts, ideas, and behaviors. We do this in two ways.

The first way is to develop an awareness of your intuition by paying attention to the subtle thoughts and leanings when you make a decision. For example, it was the holiday and I'd purchased a small gift for my nephew. I had it sent directly to their home but was disappointed when it arrived a few days before Christmas on my doorstep.

I couldn't send another, since there wasn't time. I also knew I wouldn't have time to get to the post office, either, and had no plans to visit my sister in the immediate new year. So, against a gnawing feeling of hesitancy, I dropped the gift in the gift bag of a client, knowing her child could get some use out of it.

The decision sat with me for a few days because I was certain to have sent it to the correct address—my intuition was telling me it was something more. I would find myself wondering about it, and then I'd remember that my sister and I hadn't exchanged gifts in many holidays and rarely had contact, so I'd put it out of my mind.

On Christmas Eve day, my doorbell rang, and it was my sister and her son, stopping by to bring a gift (something they hadn't done in years). Of course, I was unprepared and graciously accepted the gift. They stayed only a few minutes and then were gone. I had a good laugh after, thinking that things would have worked out nicely if I'd just trusted my feelings rather than giving over to my rationale about my gift-giving pattern with my sister. Because I saw the relationship with her as tenuous, I tried to control the situation rather than trust the messages I was getting.

The second way is to pay attention to the synchronicities of your environment—the subtle signs and events that show up around you leading up to and following an experience. A synchronicity can be anything from overhearing a conversation that is pertinent to what is going on for you, to seeing a specific animal or other creature or thing that has special meaning to you. We can also experience synchronicity by witnessing something in the media, a book, television show, or friend who calls, all with important pertinent information that connects to what is going on in our world.

Surrendering to the intuitive process and your synchronistic relationship to the world helps you gain and manage any wisdom you may need to reconcile your circumstances or events in your life. The more you become aware of it, the more you see how nurturing and helpful the magical realms of the Universe are in helping you get all your needs met. This intrinsic trust of yourself, your environment, and the Divine helps you release your desire for control (and any accompanying habits you may have). It assists you in becoming one with the flow of energy in your life.

A Ritual for Synchronicity and Understanding

Affirmation: I embrace my mortality by loving myself and choosing others deliberately. I hold space for a deepening of my awareness and disallow any fears to take root. I am safe to be vulnerable and open to the Divine.

What you'll need for your ritual:
    one gold jar candle
    one fire source (a lighter or match)
    a black cloth (any size) to place on the sacred altar area
    a piece of paper with your greatest fear about dying written on it
    a piece of Mongolian quartz
    mason jar
    paper and pen
    frankincense for offering
    one medium-sized metal pot to burn herbs (and charcoal if needed)

Herbs you'll need:
    St. John's wort: This herb bathes the spiritual body with golden light as it expels heaviness in the heart and solar plexus areas. This herb is extremely healing and connects you to angelic qualities and information.
    Black pepper: Black pepper is calming, warming, and comforting. It brings much-needed solace and grounding as you begin to explore new and uncharted territory.
    Marigolds: These flowers are a way to connect with the ancestors for support while facing death, endings, and transformations, and signifies calling on understanding and forgiveness. You may ask for support from the ancestors to help you through life.

Begin your ritual by cleaning and clearing an area in the center of your home. Collect all the items for your altar and put them in the cleared space. Place the herbs in the mason jar and hold it in hand while repeating the affirmation (you may also say prayers of your choice for healing). Exhale your breath onto the herbs to release the energies of the affirmation.

Write the affirmation on the paper, fold it over twice, and place it under the candle. Light your candle and let it burn to the socket, or for a few hours a day until it is complete. Once the candle is finished, burn your herbs in the burning pot.

Pay close attention in that week to any signs, symbols, or synchronicities you may come across. Write them down. Also, pay attention to any dreams, daydreams, or visions you may have. Write them down. At the end of the week, go over any themes that came up for you, and contemplate their messages.

DYING: THE RICHEST PATH TO LIFE

We're all going to die. It's one thing to recognize death as a natural part of life and address it in this way, but to be in the dying process with a foreseeable end date is another thing entirely. The journey from the physical life to the world of spirit is an awesome bridge of transcendence, an awakening into the emotional and spiritual dimensions, eventually leaving the body behind.

Just as grieving brings us into a new awareness of ourselves and our surroundings, it illumines for us a new path on which to move forward. It is the same for dying—as we shift awareness from our physical body, all the other spiritual dimensions to which we align open to our view as we are ready. We begin our relationship to dying by connecting to those feelings we had in life that have not been reconciled, and end our heavenly journey by walking home with the ancestors.

You could say that the process of dying is to shift your awareness from the physical body to all that lies beyond the veil of the three-dimensional world, sometimes relieving ourselves of our burdens or wrapping them up to take with us to be processed in another time. There are no hard-and-fast rules. We die oftentimes as we have lived; if there is fear in life, there will be fear in death. If there is joy in life, there will be joy in death. The only thing assured is that time and existence carry on, bringing us new perspectives from the vantage of love—for eternity.

DISCOVERING YOUR MORTALITY

We develop in life through our awareness. Sometimes I am in awe that I made it out of my teens. There were a few years when my friends and I did a lot of drinking and driving. Blessed be that no one, including ourselves, was ever hurt with our shenanigans. There was absolutely no cognizance of dying from our folly. Our consciousness was focused on all we were going through emotionally, and physically there was a feeling of invincibility.

In metaphysics we talk about the dynamic of "where you put your focus is where you see results or change." We can look at others throughout our lives, people who remain ignorant to a component of humanity (human rights, for example), and they seem to be protected from the immediate consequences of their choices regarding that aspect—until the point in time when they gain an awareness of their impact, or a hint of remorse for their actions. It seems that guilt is a major factor in our process of enlightenment, and grief is the drawing factor that brings us the life-changing shift and knowledge we seek.

Every person will enter life with an energetic road map to guide them to the information that best develops their character and fulfills their intentions for this round of existence in the physical world. For there are things that can be done in the physical realm, only to be understood in spirit. To discover your mortality is to begin imagining all that can be accomplished in the spiritual dimensions of life, and to comprehend what it would take to do them. The impermanence of every stage of life, the fragility and power of the human body, and the formidable eternity of the soul—these help us move forward.

WISHING FOR DEATH

Wishing for death is a way the human spirit calls out for freedom from the physical, mental, emotional, and spiritual tyranny it experiences from being incarnate, such as the times in which we feel trapped from a body riddled with illness, a mind locked in thoughts or memories that do not allow reprieve, or a soul imprinted with irrevocable circumstances—whose energy cannot be changed but only transformed through grief. Ultimately, we are tasked with taking authority over every aspect of ourselves, at some point and in some way, to begin to integrate the wisdom that comes from our earthly struggles and to align it with our transcendental angelic selves—all in the spirit of achieving our highest earthly potential.

I would be remiss if I didn't, again, speak about suicide in this chapter. When speaking of suicide, the languaging has become very important over the last few decades. We now say a person "died by suicide" instead of "committed suicide," to recognize that suicide is a disease, and the person could not help themselves. This is fast becoming the norm, because with choice comes blame, and blame for those left behind is a whole other trauma to process.

The reasons why people take their own lives are as varied as the people themselves. In our DNA, our body is wired to save itself at all costs. The fight-or-flight system ensures that we make the effort to grapple with any situation that comes our way, and to do our best to stay alive. But does this mean that everyone who dies by suicide is mentally ill?

As a spiritualist, this is not my view. Not only for the circumstances of, say, a suicide bomber or other martyr, but for those of people who consciously choose death over a fatal illness, or even for those who suffer from chronic depression and are unable to break the cycle of the feelings (or lack of them) promoted by their biological chemistry. There are innumerable stories that have propelled humans to end one human life cycle, only to start another in hopes of a more favorable experience, or to make efforts to bring their soul into balance. These are the hidden aspects of choice that aren't always available for the viewing of others. But they are, in fact, choices that are made all the time. Spiritual contracts being carried out by all involved, with the ultimate hope of cultivating compassion, patience, nonjudgment, and love.

I do believe that all suicide, or afflictions, for that matter, are the result of spiritual trauma. But because science does not yet take into consideration the force of the human spirit or the maladies of the soul, the conversation is often excluded when it comes to the idea of taking one's own life. Spiritual trauma is the energetic pattern from past events that reverberate in the soul of a human, following it over lifetimes, waiting for the chance to be shifted—they are intended to be our teachers of self-awareness. The change we require is what we call "healing," and the pattern itself is a love note from the past event saying, "Please don't forget me. Help me." There is no time limit in which to support a spiritual pattern; it stays in play until it is transformed through grief to another vibration and pattern of forgiveness.

That's why when we conceptualize grief, we often think of it as the mechanism we have to help these patterns of force and desperation move through our mind, body, and spirit as long suffering. It can take lifetimes to process. Grief causes the healing integration and forgiveness we require to reconcile a trauma; it can take an enormous amount of time to process through the entire event to completion. Often, suicide is one of those long-suffering events for everyone involved—those who take their own lives and those who are left behind in the aftermath.

Answering the question "Why has our loved one died by suicide?" calls on grief to bring us the understanding we need to complete the event. Asking the question, but fearing the response, reduces the grief and postpones the spiritual reply until a later time, when the one grieving may be better equipped to manage the knowledge of what happened, the deeper purpose for it, and their reaction to it.

There are many ways that people subtly wish for death in their habits of self-nurturing or coping with their traumas, such as overindulging in anything that puts the body at risk. It is our many levels of veiled awareness that guide us to or from indulgence in any given situation. But it is our intrinsic desire for freedom imprinted on the soul that ordains our constant relationship to death and dying, and that cultivates the inspiration and innovation to continue to live.

THE DIFFERENCES AMONG COPING, GRIEVING, AND COMPLETION

There are three phases of reconciling a trauma: coping, grieving, and completion. Each of these phases isn't guaranteed for everyone. It may take lifetimes for some events to process through to a full understanding and forgiveness for the injury in question. When we are coping with our trauma, we are in shock and finding strategies that allow us to remain on the periphery of our pain, never fully indulging the frantic flow of grief to move through us. When we are grieving, we may be in what feels like a catastrophic flow of emotion that has a life of its own, until the storm has passed and clarity comes. Completion is when we have a total release of attachment to what has taken place, and feel centered in the understanding that has come from the experience. Each phase deepens our wisdom and awareness.

Coping

When we use coping strategies to subsist with our losses, our grief becomes stagnant and can be hurtful to our physical health. Our body will always tell us what we need to do to reconcile our burden, but doing it isn't always our spiritual purpose. Much can be gained from remaining in a pattern of managing our pain, without feeling it. Pain is a motivator in many ways to "rise above" what we believe we can do, to make a difference to ourselves and for others.

When one is in a state of coping, meditation and prayer are the way we connect our highest selves to our lowest vibrations to find the healing space in the middle. Any passage from your holy book, or affirmation of your deepest desires, will help your densest emotions align with your consciousness. Below are three prayers you can work with to embrace your integration of new ideas, leading toward your grief.

Prayer #1: Mother Father God, I embrace your mercy, wisdom, and justice. I am grateful for all you offer and open my heart to your truth.

Prayer #2: I am whole, even, and full on all levels. I choose forgiveness for myself and all others.

Prayer #3: I am safe to feel gratitude for all I have and all the Universe is sending my way. I trust in divine timing.

Grieving

When we grieve, we release and replace every part of our relationship to what we have lost. The change in perspective also leads to a shift in the way we connect to everyone and everything. In the dying process, this shift can be perceived as positive or negative and will reveal the spiritual priorities of the one who is transitioning.

As the body loses power, mindful awareness strengthens, and many questions can be answered or resolved. We may have been searching for the answer to a question in our process of living but recognize—within our process of dying—its lack of real importance to us. In this way, we gently let go of what no longer serves us, or become clear on the ways in which the question itself has provided for our needs. Below is a mindfulness affirmation to connect you with what holds value for you today.

I see all I need to see and forgive everything else. My mind is clear, my heart is open, and I am free to hold on to or let go of all I value.

Completion

When we complete a spiritual trauma, we move through all the circles of grief. Completion means we have traversed and transmuted the pain, shifted the understanding, and let go of our attachment to what happened. It also means that we have grieved the presence of the trauma by forgiving ourselves for the choices we made because of our circumstances, and we have moved on by helping others with their grief, thereby gaining objectivity and resilience from our own. Once we have moved through those elements of perspective, we are free.

However, in some cases it is the act of dying that brings the completion we need to transition in peace. It is the spiritual reunion with the love our soul desires, and for which we are always searching. The place where forgiveness, truth, and creation exist and where our consciousness calls home. Below is a mantra to connect you with the mighty I AM.

*I am free. I am loved. I am filled with the light of all consciousness
and released of all my burdens. All my relations are empowered
by the legacy I leave behind, and are given to the light for sustenance
and protection. I am free to move on.*

RECEIVING A FATAL DIAGNOSIS:
JAN'S STORY

Many years ago, a client came to me after she received a fatal diagnosis of severe multiple sclerosis. Her doctor reported that the lesions on her brain were so advanced that she needed to go home and get her affairs in order, since her condition could not be sustained, and they didn't have many successful treatments at this progression of the disease. She was devastated and wanted to hear my thoughts, hoping that I would tell her that her future was different from what had been described.

As we sat in silence together, the message began to channel through. She needed to make a choice: to live or to die. Certainly, she could go home and get her affairs in order, or she could decide to live and start the treatments that were available. Only she knew which one she wanted. Yes, death was inevitable, but the amount of time she had was up to her and the choice she would make today. The diagnosis told her that personal changes would need to be made with how she was living.

On that day, she recognized she'd lost the privilege of asking, "Will I die?," and now must choose one or the other. From that moment forward she focused on life and the treatments available to her, and only the elements of her life that supported her well-being. Within three months, many doctors were in awe of the new brain scans showing almost all the lesions having disappeared; nobody could explain it. Her day-to-day resilience came back, and she was able to resume normal activities.

It's been over ten years since her diagnosis, and she has now married and started a new life. While there have been many ups and downs, good days and bad days, no doubt her choice to live fully the life she had remaining paved the way for her to do so.

The moral to this story isn't "Be positive and cure yourself"; it is that our soul knows what our greatest destiny is, and we are empowered in it. We are entitled to embrace death by choosing life so fully that our fate is activated and we are not afraid.

YOUR LAST WILL AND TESTAMENT

The only time to write your last will and testament is when you are of able body and sound mind, and, of course, in those times we are always busy doing other things. If you have any bank accounts, assets, or items of value, no matter your age, it's imperative you write up a last will and testament and have it notarized. If you don't and you die, your loved ones must go to probate court to manage your final affairs. This isn't always the case, but when there are multiple family members who will become heirs to your estate, and there is no official record of your desires, that's where it will end up.

The only real way to avoid this situation is to make sure that every bit of personal property and whom it goes to is explicitly detailed in a last will and testament, and to let all family members know your wishes before you die. However, this often doesn't happen when people are young. Even when they've accumulated valuable items and assets, they think, "Nothing's going to happen to me." Consider sitting down right now and evaluating what assets or property you have and whether you have assigned them beneficiaries. Consider these things:

- Bank accounts
- Crypto and alternative currencies
- Gold/Silver
- House
- Car
- Investments
- Life insurance
- Jewelry
- Antiques or other valuable items
- Artwork
- Cash

Handling the estate in the state of grief

When it comes to end-of-life expectations, people can get funny about money. A person's character in life becomes exacerbated when they are in grief. Being funny, wise, selfish, paranoid, distrustful, fearful, joyful, grateful, angry, mean, or self-centered—all these things are not softened by grief. If family members struggle to compromise while things are neutral, they will most likely be even less tolerant after a loss.

I have seen folks steal items from an estate to sell without telling anyone or create secret plots to recover funds not left to them. For this reason, it is imperative to address each asset or item as you accumulate it—doing it after the fact can be tedious for those left behind.

If you find yourself in a tenuous situation around money or property with loved ones, consider the value of your relationship to them first. Many connections are severed, sometimes permanently, over issues around dividing an estate. If you love them, do your best to be kind and thoughtful, and compromise where you can. Some divisive situations are better left for the courts to decide, but that often can leave someone in a financial bind. The bills of the estate, such as mortgages and car payments, must continue to get paid.

When a family is grieving, there can easily be miscommunications. Sit down with a third party, an attorney or neutral friend, and communicate about your needs and wants regarding the estate. If there is no last will and testament, figure out what the deal breakers are for you first, and then negotiate the rest. Always keep at the forefront of your mind and heart that the decedent would not want conflict over all they've left behind.

Planning your end-of-life celebration

Along with the last will and testament are your end-of-life wishes. Have you assigned a medical proxy (someone to make medical decisions if you are unable)? How and where you want to be buried? Do you want to be cremated? Do you want to have a memorial or funeral? Should it be a religious ceremony? Should there be a party? What can the people who survive you do to best honor your life? You honor those you leave behind the most when you take the time to convey these wishes to paper or a legal document. Take this opportunity to write down a few of your final requests right now.

A Ritual for Transformation

Affirmation: To be free is an understanding of life and death. I activate this freedom in my soul and embrace the wisdom it brings.

What you'll need for your ritual:

> one black jar candle
>
> one fire source (a lighter or match)
>
> a silver- or metallic-colored cloth (any size) to place on the sacred altar area
>
> one piece of tourmaline (black, pink, or watermelon)
>
> mason jar
>
> paper and pen
>
> sandalwood incense for offering
>
> one medium-sized metal pot to burn herbs (and charcoal if needed)

Herbs you'll need:

Kava kava: Is a wonderful supportive root that helps with transformations in all areas of life. It also helps you find and attract supportive people and communities that will help support your journey of transformation and letting go.

Mushrooms (dried or fresh from the supermarket): A reminder that from death and decay comes new life, new potentials, and new magick. Mushrooms remind us that there is always newness and new life after death and destruction.

Pomegranate: Symbolizes the underworld, death, and transformation. It is also a giver of life and helps us achieve and understand the true meaning of transformation (what parts of us need to be let go) and to fully integrate a new reality.

Begin your ritual by cleaning and clearing an area in the center of your home. Collect all the items for your altar and put them in the cleared space. Place the herbs in the mason jar and hold it in hand while repeating the affirmation (you may also say prayers of your choice for healing). Exhale your breath onto the herbs to release the energies of the affirmation.

Every night or early morning for seven days, at the same time each day, light your candle and contemplate what freedom means for you, and what elements of your life feel restricted and why. Take time to write your thoughts and impressions as you remember them. Each day, add the new paper filled with your journaling to your altar. Once the candle is finished, burn your herbs and journal pages in the burning pot.

Pay close attention in that week to any signs, symbols, or synchronicities you may come across that bring you further information about freedom. Write them down. Also, pay attention to any dreams, daydreams, or visions you may have. Write them down. At the end of the week, go over any themes that came up for you, and contemplate their messages.

Performing this ritual may inspire a grief response, and that's okay. Allow yourself to feel anything that comes up. The release and rejuvenation you seek will come in many ways over time. Give yourself permission to go with the flow.

RELATIONSHIPS: YOUR GREATEST TEACHER

The key to addressing any loss in life is to first have overcome your own loss of innocence and self-pride—reconciling who you are and grieving the truths about yourself is the foundation of enduring and processing all other loss. Without grief to strengthen you, you are vulnerable to the illusions and opinions of others, including your own self-critique. Your stability comes from knowing who you are and accepting it on all levels. The emotional, psychological, and spiritual integration that takes place during developmental phases in life is brought on and completed with grief.

The personal connections we have with others contribute the most in-depth education we ever receive about ourselves. We cultivate this relationship, first through how we perceive our parents and their presence, then through the ebb and flow of acquaintances, friendships, and lovers throughout life. Additionally, through our relationships to the natural world, animals, and the Creator. All these relations promote and provoke certain aspects of our personality and spiritual makeup to reveal who we are and the goals we have set forth for ourselves in life.

The way we are able to connect with a parent (or caregiver) from birth, and their presence or lack thereof, will establish in us our initial pattern of relating that is to come. It divulges the spiritual blueprint ingrained in our soul—specifically, the mental, emotional, spiritual, and physical ways and means of how we will develop, and on what aspects of life we will put our focus. Our ability to emotionally attach and trust another human is understood from very early on in life. While we can manage any condition of relationship we find ourselves in, it is grief that becomes the change maker in these partnerships. To embrace the ritual of grief early in life, without sullying its reputation with shame or weakness, will be the greatest gift you can give yourself and others.

Relationships in our late teens and twenties, especially marriages, are powerful teachers. They come at a time when we haven't necessarily taken authority for ourselves and often draw a partner to take that power and control for us. And when, in later years, we begin to feel confident enough to take control for ourselves over our likes and dislikes, the partnership we are in can begin to feel like a competitor to our personal authority. It is these power struggles we experience (often while engaged in relationship) that are the way we are working through our inner conflicts, revealing all the different aspects of our soul, heart, mind, and body. Finally, they will show us who we want to become. Ultimately, the more we are at peace with ourselves, the more peace we find in our unions.

Grief, then, is a set of transitional emotions that help our heart and brain release outdated feelings, beliefs, and patterns, and the relationships they nurture. It opens new possibilities of self-mastery and connections. All along our life path, it is the relationships we encounter and the grief they inspire that mold us into the beautiful human beings we are destined to be. Take a quick inventory of some of the relationships you've encountered thus far and the impact they've had on you. Proceed with the exercise below and allow your intuition and stream of consciousness to guide your answers. As you scale the list, write the first thoughts that come to your mind, without editing or analyzing them first.

> **Exercise:** Write down the first person that comes to mind under each relationship on the list below, then write the most potent memory you have about your connection to them. Be brutally honest about the memory and its details, even if it brings up strong emotions.
>
> Mother
>
> Father
>
> Sister/brother
>
> Aunt/uncle
>
> Cousins
>
> Best friend
>
> Intimate partner
>
> Coach/teacher
>
> Spiritual leader
>
> Animal/pet

The purpose of the exercise is to recount any powerful memories and the grief they may still hold.

RELATIONSHIPS: MIRRORS TO YOUR SOUL

The concept of mirroring in relationships is popular today and goes as follows: the people whom you attract and engage in any form of a relationship (even a momentary crossing of paths) mirror you on some level—mentally, emotionally, or spiritually—and through getting to know them or reflecting on the situation, you learn about yourself in deeper ways. Mirroring doesn't imply sameness; you may not be the exact reflection as the people you encounter, but you may be experiencing the same issues or dynamics in life or handling them similarly. These synchronistic messages from the Universe can reveal your potential if you are willing to receive the message.

Mirroring is a viewpoint that allows us to become objective about ourselves. However, depending on how much self-awareness has been developed, mirroring can also be observed through our judgments and opinions of others. When our emotions are strong, it is an indication that our unconscious self is seeking to disclose an aspect to us that has remained hidden until now. It begins to express itself sometimes through dreams and visions, then strong judgments of others, and then finally through a subtle grief process. Through grief, the information bubbles up to the surface of our awareness to be acknowledged, reflected on, and then integrated, on the basis of what we need at the time.

How to "let things go"

When you hear people use the phrase "just let it go," what they are speaking of is grief. The only way around the idea of "letting go" is to go through the grief of letting go. But, somehow, in our culture of positivity we have nearly erased the reality of the process it takes to move forward mentally, emotionally, spiritually, and then physically on something as simple as changing your mind or shifting your behavior in any circumstance. Grief and mourning are a part of any change we make, no matter how subtle or overt, and we are entitled to embrace it.

Grief keeps the flow of life moving—the best way to let things go is by using grief to help us embrace this flow of energy and movement. The grief process can look different, depending on whether you are grieving or mourning. The anger, lamenting, and then crying—part of your big-emotion phase—are deeply valuable to shift your brain and body into a new relationship to what is now gone. The mind or soul must transition through new thoughts, ideas, and the creation of new habits. Here is a whimsical way of beginning this process.

Habit-shifting exercise:
Every day, for fourteen days straight, take a pot from your kitchen and move it to a new room in your home. Day 1: the bedroom. Day 2: the living room. Day 3: the bathroom, and so on and so forth. You may include any outside area, your vehicle, or your office. Once the pot has visited each room, start revisiting each of them until you've done this for fourteen days.

How this works:
Change is difficult, and very often we resist the feelings of grief because of the illusion of permanence the transition holds for us. Moving a pot around your house allows you to make a simple, silly change every day, effortlessly. Don't be surprised if you become emotional or in deep resistance to moving the pot, since any response you have is a natural release to the real transition you are in. At some point, through grief, every transition we experience will be reviewed through this simplistic lens.

THE ANATOMY OF A RELATIONSHIP

Every relationship, no matter with whom or with what—or how intimate—has a connection: whether it be on the peripheral psychic levels only detectable by an ultra-awareness, or a palpable physical attraction. We even have spiritual connections to passersby and acquaintances. This subtle energetic connection creates the matrix of people, places, and things that we are attracted to, and who will rise up in our environment as we navigate everyday life. When we see life through the eyes of another, we are reawakened to the "awe" of life. To be open in this way lends us to more curiosity, collaboration, humility, and altruism.

We have these partnerships not only with people, but animals, the spirits in nature, the cosmos, and the elements of wind, water, fire, and earth—essentially, everything. An individual's awareness of such relationship varies and can be cultivated by choice, but the connection is inherent in each of us and is an entitlement to living on planet Earth. It is the process of grief that will bring us the awareness needed to communicate with the subtle vibrations of our environment, and the process of mourning that will help us to navigate the transitions intrinsic to those partnerships.

It is easy to pigeon-hole grief into a big, dark world of sorrow that visits only upon the heels of death, but that could not be further from the truth. Grief is the salvation we call upon to bring us the mercy, understanding, and wisdom we seek when we are struggling and perplexed by an encounter or situation. Many years ago, every time I was saddled with a confusing situation—some form of rejection or intense connection that seemed to steal my focus (at least that's how it felt)—it would throw me into a wave of agony and tears. This pattern showed me the process of how my deep-seated need to understand and break free from these energetic ties kept me in bondage, and it called on the flood of emotions that would do just that.

After crying for a period of time, the needed information and ideas would pass through my mind, helping me understand the connection and what I needed to shift in my thinking and behavior to change the dynamic to best serve my highest good. Once I became accustomed to the process, I stopped resisting the emotional grief and would have visions during these episodes. A woman, an ancestor of my soul lineage, would appear to me consistently; when I saw her, I would understand the alchemy of the situation, people, and environment in which I was surrounded.

Once grief has revealed a ray of light found in between our shadows, the vision and viewpoints we've harbored begin to transform into new, usable energy for rebuilding our attitudes, thoughts, and feelings, which will lead us forward into more beautiful and synchronistic bonds with the world we live in.

We are not solely defined by the sum of our experiences but are transported through grief and mourning to a new level of liberation. Imagine waking up every day and saying to yourself:

> *Today will reveal a new way of being I have yet to discover in myself and my world.*

Picture the magnificent power you exude by opening your heart to this golden matrix of synchronicity—an authority no one can diminish in you, in any way. Revel in the tears of truth that clear the path on which your wisdom will travel, with your words and actions close behind.

CULTIVATING STRONG PLATONIC OR ROMANTIC RELATIONSHIPS

Within each transition listed below, there is a refined process of grief that we will pilot. Some are an easy, smooth ride, and others not so much. Emotions experienced in this more refined grief are sorrow, confusion, gratitude, anticipation, anxiety, uncertainty, and openness—to name a few. Learning the language of this delicate communication with your environment, others, and yourself is what we call synchronicity. We all are messengers to one another, and our awareness strengthens to this relationship as it is necessary or because we have called on its meaning.

As you move through the descriptions of the multiple stages of a relationship (platonic or romantic), not only contemplate and receive a new understanding of your human partnerships but reflect on the subtlety of your communications with the natural world and the creatures in it, your environment, and the Divine.

Meeting: When you meet (to become conscious of) anything for the first time, you bring it into your awareness and see the reflections in the liked or disliked aspects of yourself. This inner reflection, no matter how pleasant or unpleasant, must be revered, since it is your higher self beckoning your attention in a new way. This new information offers you the opportunity for change through grief.

Courtship: Getting to know one another is the initial exchange of energy in which you engage. Pay close attention to your demeanor or temperament in these encounters. Your emotions (state of relaxation or anxiety) are powerful indicators of the patterns you have in common, or the current resonance you share in the moment. Feelings of joy, sorrow, or disappointment are but a few of the ways your grief will be expressed in this transition.

The first disappointment: This is your first awareness of the unconscious expectations you have of yourself, and possibly a recognition of what changes will need to be made by you to find peace or happiness in this partnership. Grief is what will cultivate this heightened awareness.

The first fight: The power struggle we have with others is always about the power struggle we have with ourselves. Take note of your feelings of conflict and what you are resistant to letting go of or receiving into your heart, and where feelings of sorrow may point to this mental or emotional transition.

The how and when of moving forward: In any relationship, there is a point in time when you decide to move forward and invest more time in the connection or opt out of it. This point in time, and your awareness of it, will determine how you feel about yourself and how you are empowered in the relationship. If you are unaware of this moment and the decision you make, you will move ahead feeling victimized and disempowered in the union. If you consciously make the choice to continue in the partnership, you will be more likely to be accountable for your feelings and actions and to participate in a genuine and holistic fashion. Grief in this transition can be the elements of resistance to a new way of being or sorrow in letting go of your old way of being, inviting in a new pattern to include your friend.

Commitment: When a person commits to their relationship (with a person or something else), they are training their focus on that relationship and taking it on as a consideration in their decision-making process. We grieve and mourn every commitment we make or release.

Intimacy: Our sexual and spiritual union with a partner is a powerful choice we make, and will impact every part of our connection to ourselves, regardless of one's awareness of that impact. We naturally share information with our partners through psychic, telepathic, and empathic vibrations that bring us closer. Each of these vibrations resonates with different forms of personal information we communicate. Grief can be shared between partners in this way.

Psychic channels: They transmit higher information such as dreams, visions, and ideals—information without an emotional quality. Sometimes we can share our psychic information with partners across time and space, and how we may become aware of this sharing is through grief and our more subtle emotions and thoughts.

Telepathy: This is the way we communicate thoughts to one another without using words. Grief can be shared telepathically as well.

Empathy: This is a vibrational channel through which we transfer our emotions to our partner, including grief, depression, anxiety, or passion. People do not have to share sexual intimacy to share information on energetic levels, but it is often through a sexual relationship that we become aware of all the subliminal knowledge we share.

Value systems: It is through our shared values that we begin to understand the subtle vibrations through which we communicate with one another—the common ground we share on all levels, including the lowest common denominator. These value systems aren't just hopes and ideals but, more importantly, the fears and frustrations of unfortunate or traumatic experiences. These vibrationally dense values arise in the space between two people immediately, and often grief is triggered by the weight of their presence. These are values such as pain, anguish, fear, and distrust . . . to name a few.

I had a boyfriend named Alan for about eight months. He had just moved from NYC, and everything seemed to be right on point. He had a great job, he was cute, he made me laugh . . . but he was funny about money, and I was broke at the time. He took me to a music shop and started piling CDs into a basket, all the music he wanted to share with me. He then offered to purchase anything I might want for myself. At the time, there had been one song I'd wanted to learn, and I quickly found a CD that contained it. I placed it into his basket. When we arrived at the counter to pay, out of the thirty CDs he was purchasing, he plucked from the basket the one I'd chosen and said, "You should buy this for yourself." I didn't know what to say. Imagine how humiliated I was: I knew that my overdrawn account couldn't withstand the ten-dollar price. I said, "No—that's okay," and ran from the store before the tears struck with barely any warning.

He and I shared the same values of independence around money; however, I had a deep resonating fear of bait and switch when it came to negotiations, and that energy clearly matched equally in him. The fact that we didn't know each other well only made our communications that more awkward. The emotional shock and awe I experienced that day really made me consider what lay beneath. Of course, the relationship didn't last too much longer, but grieving the experience transformed how I am able to communicate about financial matters today.

Compatibility: The longevity of any relationship hinges on the compatibility of the partners. And within the "get to know you" process, there is an intellectual and sometimes emotional grieving that happens when two people or group members have different likes, dislikes, and values. Your grief informs the transition to accept the person or group as they are, not as you'd like them to be.

Cohabitation: Moving in together, whether it be for a business or personal relationship, is a potent transition. It is certainly a merging of the habits as two physical worlds collide, but if the partners are new to one another, it will also be an integration of beliefs and values. Grief plays a major role in these transitions. This is a major turning point that becomes an indicator of how long the partnership will last, on the basis of the ability of the partners to negotiate and grieve their differences.

Creating a family: Childrearing is an experience fraught with grief, as any parent knows. Like any partnership, watching a child grow and reveal who they are over time is a powerful lesson in patience, love, acceptance, and grief. It is natural for the parent to want their children to have what they did not, or a child to fight for their independence. And, of course, all the decisions a couple makes about how, when, and where they will raise their family, and the energetic patterns it puts in place for their development, are crucial. It all boils down to how willing or able the partners are to completely process the grief that releases them of fear, judgment, or resentment, and opens their hearts to one another, the real needs of each child, and the Universe that will guide the process.

Reconnecting in the relationship: Every person changes over time on the basis of their habits, environment, condition, and experiences—and so it goes that the relationship will change as well. This can cause emotional, mental, spiritual, or physical rifts in the connection as it was, and require a process of rebalancing the relationship through grief.

We all have witnessed living in the time of enormous political unrest, personal strife, Earth changes, and a pandemic—what comes with those are people awakening to the cognizance of their lowest common denominator: fear. This fear is the fight-or-flight response that arises from deep within us, to keep us safe. This dynamic of change paired with fear becomes many things to humans who spiritually struggle: elitist, exclusive, self-righteous, fanatically religious, delusional about skin color and other human traits, righteous about body control, judgmental of sexual orientation, or confusion around gender understanding.

Imagine waking up in a thirty-year marriage to a partner who, in what seems like overnight, is now emboldened in victimized and racist views—what would you do? Of course, there were subtle signs and symptoms that were easy to dismiss. Based on a society that was determined to systematically ignore as much as possible, those notions were kept at bay—until they weren't. Now, as the universal Truths of equality, inclusion, and connection begin to gain massive momentum on the planet, you must now reconcile a powerful discord within yourself or your relationship.

The natural cycle that flows from fight-or-flight is depression. How aggressively you flow in your fearful thinking or actions will be the momentum to which you will plummet into depression. While the fight-or-flight cycle is geared toward increasing your physical power and emotional awareness in the moment—it does not cultivate wisdom. The depressive cycle does that. When you are depressed, you slow down to take the opportunity to reflect. If you allow yourself to do so, you will grieve. This emotional expression draws to you the clarity you need to coalesce the information you've gathered and to compare your truth to that of the Universe. Grief is the path to the Truth you seek in any situation.

Ending the relationship: Life is a series of beginnings and endings; we tend not to teach or acknowledge this too much in our culture since it is often perceived as negative and unpleasurable. But endings are often completions in the making that spiritually awaken us to a truth and the good grief that clears the way for glorious forward movement. Consider that an end in a partnership isn't "the" end, but only an end to an outdated form of relating that no longer serves either of you.

CULTIVATING A STRONG CONNECTION TO THE NATURAL WORLD

As I've mentioned before, grief is the key to our vigilance in the many dimensions of our world. Subtle or overt, our feelings communicate how we address the natural world and how much we trust it to provide our needs. This trust is not determined by our experiences; it is practiced through our daily choices. This relationship of trust in nature is intrinsic to us, and deeply valuable all the time, but often is pursued only during times of grief. The more you are connected to nature, the more clarity you will have about human nature.

Cultivating your awareness exercise:
There are many ways to reawaken your connection to the cosmos, the planet, and all her inhabitants—to reinvigorate the natural trust you have in them.

To begin with, take a quick inventory of the following dynamics and feelings, comparing on a scale of 1 to 10.

1. I trust myself _____

2. I feel relaxed _____

3. I feel safe _____

4. I enjoy solitude _____

5. I desire companionship _____

6. I feel fear _____

7. I feel angry _____

8. I feel hopeful _____

9. I see a positive future for myself _____

10. I want to connect with others _____

Now, for the purposes of this exercise, choose one of the following: a natural element (earth, wind, water, fire), a planet, an animal, or a plant being. Take fifteen minutes a day to find out everything you possibly can about your subject for one week.

Next, take five minutes a day for the following week, to begin a connection with your subject in meditation. (This means close your eyes and imagine the subject of your inquiry and see what pictures or thoughts come to mind.)

Take another week to begin a dialogue with your subject. In your meditation, ten minutes a day, begin a conversation with your subject. Start with a positive greeting and allow the natural exchange that comes next. Always say thank you and express your gratitude for your subject's presence and connection.

Once the exercise is done, retake the inventory of dynamics and feelings that you took before you began this exploration. Compare how you felt before the exercise and how you feel after.

WHAT IS A KARMIC RELATIONSHIP?

The idea of karma in a relationship refers to the patterns of emotions, attitudes, and behaviors that inform how one participates in their relations. It also points to the unreconciled triggers from spiritual and emotional trauma that an individual may be moved to process within the pairing. We all are drawn to one another through the conscious and unconscious resonance we share.

When we come together in a partnership, each individual has a lock or a key that attracts its personal match. These components may be temporal, an opportunity to learn something new about ourselves or transition a belief, emotion, or attitude that no longer serves us, or they may be ingrained and permanent, a part of one's true character, leaving one to accept themselves on a deeper level. Whichever it is, when we meet these soulmates and engage in these karmic relationships, we are fulfilling a soul contract that will use grief to help resolve the elements that are generating discord and to reveal a growth opportunity or alternative path.

The types of human karmic relationships we can come across in life are often defined by harsh experiences where power struggles are evident, such as a dominant/submissive interaction or a victim/perpetrator dynamic. They can also exist in partnerships that will create the greatest change on a personal, professional, or collective level, such as marriages, long-term entanglements, familial relationships, or authority figures and their subordinates. These can be destructive or inspirational in nature, but even the injurious forces will carve out a new way of life for all involved, ultimately leading to a path of forgiveness and compassion.

Yvonne L. had struggled throughout her life to find the love and affection she deserved. Born to a mother who died of cancer by Yvonne L.'s fourth birthday, and a father who had no idea what to do for his children but to provide as much as he could (all the while being swallowed alive by his losses and the addictions that followed him in life), Yvonne L. went to private schools but never fully felt the acceptance of the authority figures in her life. So when it came to relationships, the men she chose were more than willing to bully and bait her to do their bidding.

Ultimately, this led Yvonne L. into a sixteen-year relationship with an addicted sociopathic partner who bullied her with violence and baited her with minuscule moments of affection as a ruse to get his basic needs met. In the life of this relationship, the beatings and humiliations were many, and the police were called more than two dozen times for assistance. Although they were legally married and divorced twice, they never created a home together (all the while, he had a permanent residence with his mother, or whomever else he could find to provide for him in any way). If Yvonne L. said no to a request or there were no resources to feed her husband's addiction, he would seek it out in any number of the relationships he kept in the queue. He would sometimes be gone for months at a time. Yvonne L., herself, was repulsed by drugs and began to find her salvation in her religion.

Although the facts are difficult to fathom, and it might be a little too easy to judge another for a circumstance we cannot imagine for ourselves, it is the many layers of spiritual and emotional trauma that can render a person to appear in shock and motionless amid a violent environment. This stationary appearance is what it looks like for the abused to spiritually process their condition and cultivate the strength they need to leave the relationship and save themselves. Like Yvonne L., people who suffer these circumstances are further isolated from those who can help, because in our culture they are shamed by the very people who claim to have their best interests at heart. Many call it tough love, but often there is a tendency to criticize and judge, in lieu of the mindful ear and honest compassionate help they seek.

More often than not, the victims of intimate-partner abuse are kept in a constant state of fear by the abuser and are isolated from any onlookers who could recognize the patterns of their mistreatment. This condition inhibits feelings of safety and the grief process that brings the spiritual wisdom and strength they will need to extricate themselves from this relationship. In this situation, grieving will come in layers and change in intensity over time—amplifying as they are safer to feel. It is the reason entire networks are set up to intervene and help the abused escape the circumstances set forth in this dynamic.

The greatest outcome of this particular karmic relationship was the cultivation of Yvonne L.'s indomitable spirit. Her relentless drive to break out of the spiritual and emotional patterns that left her vulnerable to others and hardened to herself helped her finally break off all contact with this man. Through the consistent shedding of grief, Yvonne L. has finally awakened to the opportunity for a life that includes love, acceptance, and the expression of her personal power. However, unlike Yvonne L., there are many who do not survive this type of relationship.

HOW DESTRUCTIVE RELATIONSHIP PATTERNS IMPACT YOU TODAY

Spiritually speaking, a destructive relationship pattern is meant to break down the rational parts of the personality and to connect one with the subtle vibrations of how we communicate, how the Universe functions, and to align them with their higher selves. Ask anyone who has suffered abuse and they will tell you they could sense the vibration of the anger and could tell from the microexpressions (the subtle shifts in a person's face) of their abuser that a beating was forthcoming, or maybe it was a telepathic message sent from a look in their eye. People communicate on subtle levels all the time, and some people are good at keeping their true intentions at bay. Sometimes, to such a degree, it takes special training to sense the lies they are telling.

There is a spiritual idiom that postulates that "everything happens for a reason." What this means is that we gain wisdom training from every experience we have— especially the tumultuous ones. What it does not mean is that it was good, that one should be happy to learn the lesson, that one deserved it, or that it was their fault. Every event that happens in life, we grieve. And the one level of energy that holds together all the others is our spiritual self, higher self, soul—whatever you'd like to call it. Its function is to access for us the wisdom in everything we experience. Our spirit holds every detail of every moment of our life and lives past. It is the information contained in the spiritual patterns we carry with us to become our teachers about ourselves.

It is because of this sense of purpose in all things that we experience feelings of fault, guilt, blame, and shame. These emotions indicate to us what information, habits, or patterns we hold that connect us to the experiences we have—the ones we share a resonance with. It is why when we have grieved mentally and emotionally and recovered physically that we begin the work of understanding the patterns we've engaged that intersect with experiences and events in our lives.

There is an Old English word: *wyrd*. It is representative of the vastness of our personal universe and the multiple opportunities we have access to, on the basis of our vibrational pull at any one time. It is different from the concept of destiny or fate, since it shows us where we have power and can make choices to determine our own direction, if we are willing to do the work of grief to reveal these unconscious patterns and conscious behaviors that pull things to us from the well of wyrd.

GRIEVING A VIOLENT CRIME

Violence is so prevalent in our world today that we almost treat it as common. But if you're the person suffering from a rape or assault, it is a powerful thing to process, not only the assault itself but the profound feelings of powerlessness, rage, and distrust that come after. The lack of safety you experience everywhere, along with the hypervigilance that comes with monitoring your environment and the people around you—wondering if your assailant or another is sitting at the table next to you—is simply exhausting.

Your relationship to friends, family, and the outside world changes dramatically, and it can often become hard to sustain love relationships, because when it comes to sexual assault, people in your life sometimes wonder, "What did you do to make that happen to you?," even if they never say it out loud.

Jean was born for great things, to hear God tell it. On special days you might see her outside playing in her favorite pink tutu, her long, dark, wavy hair blowing in the breeze, and the deepest dark eyes you'd ever seen—still filled with the light of wonderment. As she grew older, she began to daydream and fantasize about a *Star Trek* utopia where the real facts of her life wouldn't have reign over her experiences. Her father had bailed in her early childhood, and her mother was of fragile integrity and was still reeling from the many abuses she'd suffered that left her deeply resentful, in pain, and self-absorbed—these were not the ideal conditions in which to nurture a young son and daughter, but only a testament to Jean's relentless will, faith, and vision. After her parents' divorce, Jean moved with her mother and brother to the Southwest, where there were many days they went without.

To help her find solace in the many confusions in her life, she cleaved to the church. But after being molested by a youth pastor, she delved deeper into her longing to live in her intergalactic fantasy world. She was forced to leave the church and find her faith another way. Over the years of her adolescence, Jean's mom was consistent in bringing multiple men into the household. After taking a job at a "massage parlor," she befriended the owner and brought him home with her on multiple occasions, leaving him in the house alone with her teenage daughter. A fifteen-year-old Jean remembers exiting the shower one morning and finding him in the bathroom, waiting for her.

Even so, as a family they muddled along. All the while, Jean recognized, somewhere deep inside, her connection to something bigger would eventually bring the safety she'd always longed for. She understood she would walk this path alone, with no Mom or Dad to bring her up. But this was never more evident than when she was seventeen years old; arriving home from a party around 11 p.m., she was startled by a grown man hiding in her closet.

Somehow, he'd gained access to the house without alarming her mother and brother, asleep in their rooms. He told Jean that if she screamed, his friend, waiting outside the window, would come in and kill her family—he seemed to be familiar with them and their home. He then proceeded to brutally rape and terrorize her for the next six hours.

Jean never told anyone about being molested or all the times she'd been sexually accosted by men. She was so terrified by this event that it took her weeks to tell her mother and then the police. Then it was back to life as usual. No one was ever caught. Jean, however, moved forward in life with a new layer of terror and fear she would spend the rest of her years tending to. Jean's most traumatic injury was the one to her psyche: the constant hypervigilance that comes as a result of enduring terrorism and violence.

The role of grief within this circumstance was like making a roast in a Crockpot. The epiphanies that arose through Jean's grief came slowly over time, since her devastation and sorrow were kept on a low heat. The soul is an amazing cache of every bit of information we cross paths with. It takes in and remembers every small detail, even when it appears our brains do not, waiting to reveal these details to the conscious mind at the appropriate time and place.

This information, combined with the soul's spiritual directive (destiny), is what we call karma—the spiritual contracts we make with ourselves prior to incarnation that assist us with our human development and growth. This in no way implies blame or fault to the victim, only a path out of the power struggle that ensues after the assault has taken place. Jean's conflict or spiritual pattern to be resolved here is betrayal, and her resolution to that conflict is independence—guilt, grief, faith, and trust are the vehicles through which she will find peace.

When you are grieving a violent crime perpetrated against you, there are many losses to grieve:

- Power
- Dignity

- Safety

- Peace

- Physical harm

- The unknown

- Trust

- Friendship

- Connection

- Control

- Loyalty

Your first step is to simplify your life. Clean and clear your home of any unneeded items. Cleaning can help you take command of at least one aspect of your existence. This ritual allows you the space to grieve all the things that feel immovable to you, and can lead you beyond the rage and anger left after the assault.

It will become the gateway to your grief. Let your closest connections know that you have a long road ahead of you, and what you are going through is not about them. They can support you by respecting your boundaries and letting you tell them what you need when you need it. Keep the lines of communication open, because while this event is yours to process, you do not have to be alone to do it.

Inevitably, you will address the list of dynamics above as you feel comfortable to do so, but remember you will be experiencing a whole host of big emotions, and patience may not be one of them. You will need to call on patience in between your bouts with the other emotions. Consider these breaks to be little respites during your emotional journey. Do your best to accept that—for now—your world has changed dramatically, and this change can allow for new awareness and light as you explore the darkness.

HEALING FROM SPIRITUAL TRAUMA
WHERE IT BEGAN

It is in the healing of spiritual trauma (the energetic imprints or patterns we have) where magic comes in. Everyone is a magician, a witch, or a unicorn. We are made up of a magical spirit that is omnipotent and powerful if we will call on that aspect of ourselves and wield the Universe around us. To choose our magical selves requires an expert-level ability to be accountable for every aspect of what we think, do, feel, and speak. When that's in place, we are ready to understand and embrace our true source of spiritual power and connection to our higher self and the Divine.

Magic is the etheric energy that connects all things, and when we practice our spirituality through a ritual or religion, we access this aspect of ourselves. When we understand the magical realms, we amplify our self-awareness and our awareness of others and our environment. We begin to witness the vibrational patterns that connect us all to one another, and we are better able to address any situation in which we engage because we have become witness to the nature of the vibration that created it.

I have always been a magical person and was born with the ability to visualize ideas—create them or destroy them. In my early childhood, I spent my days using my creative energy and vision skills making dollhouses and sewing clothes for the dolls in them. I would dream up a design and make a pattern to construct the outfit I wanted to make. However, nighttime was less fun. I would have nightmares and supernatural visitations from scary creatures. My earliest memory of one of these visitations was when I was in my crib and able to stand. I saw a dark shadow from across the room, and I didn't make a peep.

I eventually came to understand that the recurring nightmares I would have often in my childhood were past-life memories of experiences where I had no power. Memories of being sex-trafficked, enslaved, and drug-addicted. Every night I would cry myself to sleep or wake up crying. If I wasn't crying, I was praying to myself and the Creator to help me understand, resolve, and heal these devastating images, and all the spirits that came with them. There was no one to tell, since these topics sparked enormous fear in others, or I'd be labeled mentally ill or insane.

There was never a time I felt out of control, or powerless to change my circumstances, even if I did not yet know how. Written in my spirit was a guide to healing that I had faith to follow. However, the fear at times was unbearable. There wasn't much relief in those years other than my grief and my creative rituals to bring me solace, but it was between those two driving forces in my life that I found the healing integration I knew was there for me—and magic. I found magic: it was everywhere, in everything and everyone, when I would choose to see it.

It was magic that showed me the path to finding the origins of my grief and to complete them once and for all. Magic was the parallel dimensions I discovered where I was reliving my past spiritual trauma daily. Magic was the feelings of hope and inspiration that kept me in the game when I wanted to tap out. Magic was my vehicle to understanding the Creator and the creation and everything in between.

No doubt you've heard by now that our inner world creates our outer world. To say it another way, your vibration, or the pattern of your thoughts, attitudes, and actions, is what creates your reality. That's because, unlike what past scientific theories assumed, the space around us is not empty. It is full of a living intelligence, which is like a conduit that carries our mental and emotional frequencies out into the field of possibility. Our external circumstances don't just happen; we connect to them. Like oscillations of a shrill sound, the choices we make are heard and given form.

In the early 1900s Carl Jung conceptualized a form of meditation to access and bring to light information from your hidden realms. If you are out there suffering from an unexplained trauma, try this exercise and see what information comes up for you.

Active imagination

Get a paper and pen or use a computer and settle yourself into a comfortable, quiet place. It's best if you are alone in the process.

Active imagination is a dialogue between you and an unknown pattern, dream, thought, energy, entity, or memory that is causing discord. It is your opportunity to access the nature of what it is (the vibrational resonance you share), where and when it originated (in any time and space), what you gained from its presence (most likely you already know the pain it caused), and why you are experiencing it.

To begin your *active imagination,* close your eyes and take four very deep breaths, breathing in through the nose and out through the mouth. Once you are relaxed, visualize a park bench anchored by two very large trees. Visualize yourself walking to the bench and taking a seat. Now "see" the object of your inquiry taking a seat on the other side of the bench. Remember that no matter what you see, you are safe and well taken care of.

Now, ask any questions you like. Write them down along with any answers you receive. Free-form write. Don't worry about spelling or punctuation or meaning; just write. Always, at the end of your active imagination, express your gratitude for whatever shows up. Then visualize getting up from the bench, by yourself, and walking to the street and back to the chair where you are sitting right now. Take another four deep breaths and bring yourself back to present time.

Here are some questions to break the ice between you and your unknown:

1. Who are you?

2. What can I call you?

3. Where do you come from?

4. How did we connect?

5. What is the energy or emotion we have in common?

6. Why are you here?

7. What do you need to resolve?

8. What can you teach me?

Once you've completed your active imagination, and you have had some time to process the information, you no doubt have been opened to some of the deeper understanding of why you are the way you are. Accessing these other worlds of spirit can promote and soothe your grief and offer you a new perspective on which to build the rest of your life. To recognize and transform the origins of these spiritual patterns will change how you feel and approach the habits you'll want to change as you integrate this new information.

A Ritual for Reconnection and Awe

Affirmation: I see the world (or replace with specific person or idea) with fresh eyes and new inspiration, easily letting go of old beliefs, experiences, and circumstances. My world is exactly as I need it to be.

What you'll need for your ritual:
>   three jar candles: pink, green, and blue
>
>   a fire source (a lighter or match)
>
>   any colored cloth (any size) to place on the sacred altar area
>
>   a small bouquet of peonies
>
>   golden kunzite
>
>   mason jar
>
>   paper and pen
>
>   nag champa incense for offering (burn at the altar before starting the ritual)
>
>   one medium-sized metal pot to burn herbs (and charcoal if needed)

Herbs you'll need:
Arnica: A strong healing herb that helps bring resolution to all traumatic injuries: physical, mental, emotional, and spiritual. Arnica helps heal injured parts and paves the way to greater understanding.

Willow: A healer with ancestral energy. Often our traumas are part of a larger ancestral pattern, and willow connects you to the ancestral healing field through the water element—an agent of connection. Good for emotional pain and grief stored in the heart.

Angelica: This is a beautifully uplifting and protective root. It has high vibrational, angelic energies to help heal trauma of any form and encourages one to reconnect with the parts of oneself that feel separate.

Begin your ritual by cleaning and clearing an area in the center of your home. Collect all the items for your altar and put them in the cleared space. Place the herbs in the mason jar and hold it in hand while repeating the affirmation (you may also say prayers of your choice for healing). Exhale your breath onto the herbs to release the energies of the affirmation. Now, light a stick of nag champa.

An exercise in awakening to awe

This ritual is going to be a little field trip. Chose any natural place that inspires awe in you, be it a body of water, a large tree, a mountain, or forest, and plan to go for a visit. Preferably, you want to choose one that is easily accessible (or not). Like you did in the other ritual, *active imagination*, you are going to this awe-inspiring place to have a conversation with its spirit. Take as many deep breaths as you need to relax and connect with the spirit of the place, then ask to receive its story and message for you. Take along some corn to leave as an offering of gratitude and respect.

Once you arrive back home, light the candle and burn your herbs in the burning pot. Then, take a few moments to write about your experience. Remember what your body felt like being in that place. Breathe in the scents and aromas of the atmosphere. Feel the warmth or cool of your experience, reliving every bit. Remember what your heart felt being in its company. Were you at peace? Inspired? Afraid? Joyful? Write about these things and reconnect to the experience on all levels of your mind, body, and spirit.

This exercise allows you to connect to the larger world around you and to open your heart so that any grief you have can be shared with this outer world and released from you. Pay close attention during the week to any signs, symbols, or synchronicities you may come across that bring you further information about other things that make you feel joy. Write them down. Also, pay attention to any dreams, daydreams, or visions you may have. Write them down. At the end of the week, go over any themes that came up for you, and contemplate their messages.

ELEVEN

TRAUMATIC INJURY AND ILLNESS:
FINDING THE UNBROKEN LINK

On a spiritual level, every experience we have seeks to connect us to a hidden part of ourselves. In the metaphysical world we call this "shadow work." Your shadow is the soul information that awakens as you grow and develop as a human being. It gradually opens our hearts, minds, and bodies through the movement of our life-force energy—kundalini, ki, or chi, as it is called—which travels up and down our spine and eventually all throughout our endocrine system and body.

We may also experience an awakening via a traumatic event that causes an immediate shift in consciousness, such as an injury, illness, or accident. During which, your chi connects to your energy centers (chakras) and auric field (energy bodies) to allow for the transmission of new information and growth. With every one of these experiences, the spiritual blueprint contained in the soul is revealed, and the individual connects more deeply with themselves. Grief always accompanies these awakenings and will surely be a part of the recovery of any traumatic injury, illness, or unexpected accident.

It is not always our soul's intention to live longer, be well, or find peace living in a body. Our bodies are wired to save us from peril, not necessarily our soul. The spirit that dwells within each of us seeks to elevate, expand, and include every part of ourselves and eventually others, and to do this we must be challenged to face our fears, accept ourselves, and find the resilience and forgiveness it takes to start over. This is the glory that trauma brings: empowerment.

On the day I wrote this, I awoke from a dream in a subdued panic. In the dream, someone was slowly plunging a knife into my gut and holding me down in such a way it was difficult to move. I also felt weakened by the shock that the person hurting me was a friend. I had loved them, and they were betraying me in the worst way, by taking my life. I lay there, in the dream, feeling powerless until a voice said, "Fight!"

My body was having a rough time moving, but my mind became stronger and stronger until my body began to progress toward healing. My frenemy seemed to disappear, and I was now focused on stopping the bleeding of the wound. I was physically aware of the pain in my waking mind, while still in the dream. I kept my focus trained on seeing the light heal the wound from the inside out, until it was done. I then shifted dimensions to the awareness of another "part of me," possibly from another lifetime, a person who had died in a similar manner, a sword stabbing and betrayal of a friend. In that experience, I was unable to overcome those wounds and died in that state of powerlessness. I called on the light to heal him too.

In reflection, it articulated a deeper understanding of the spiritual, mental, and emotional gains we compel with every experience we have and decision we make. There is no spiritual blame for any condition we might find ourselves in; however, the human mind interprets finding power in a powerless place as blame. "You did this. It's your fault." This is what we may subconsciously say to ourselves, while contending with the betrayal we feel from the wounds we carry in our body, our mind, our history, and our soul—all "friends" we must overcome by any means necessary.

Grief is the dynamic through which we make a foe a friend again. In illness and injury, our pain and suffering are the light bringers we call on to elevate us to our next level of understanding, joy, and empowerment. This is not the viewpoint of a friend or family member who is caring for us in such a tragedy, but our vantage, alone. Ultimately, it is only we who are empowered to make the right decisions that will bring the sought-after and necessary result of our wellness or demise. All things are possible, but only one thing will take place—and only you know deep in your heart what it is. Grief will show you your one true path through any dark land you come across.

UNDERSTANDING ILLNESS, RECOVERY, SPIRITUALITY, AND DESTINY

The body is a physical representation of our spiritual energy. Our spirit contains certain directives: thoughts, beliefs, and memories that our soul would like to work with. Some we will accept and adopt, some we will learn to manage, and others we will do away with and replace with new ones that better serve our growth. The first step to understanding why we have encountered the condition we are in is to grieve its presence. We must embrace our illness or injury and all that comes with it: what happened, why it happened, and the result.

Guilt

Guilt is often a precursor to grieving illness or injury. The reason for this is not fault or blame in any way. It is the result of a spiritual directive we are imprinted with on a soul level; the directive is this: as humans, we learn by being accountable for every aspect of our being. The process of expanding our cognizant understanding to consciousness and all that lies deep in our unconscious selves is the mystery we are tasked with exploring over our lifetime. Every event, whether destined (that which our spiritual patterns unconsciously attract) or consciously chosen, is intended to help us with our spiritual objective.

The emotion we call guilt is a spiritual directive itself. When we feel it, we connect with the pain in our heart or stomach that indicates to us the ways in which we are not taking care of ourselves (heart) or others (stomach). Our guilt reveals the information we need further understanding of, to reconcile what we feel guilty about. Guilt is a form of energetic attachment to a person, place, thing, or event that we hold on to to access more information. As we gain more understanding of the facts, the wisdom that is uncovered is about the value and meaning to us of what the guilt represents.

Spiritually speaking, the concepts of fault and guilt are not the same. Fault we attribute to the repercussions that occur from an action we've taken. Guilt is the acknowledgment of how we contributed, in any way, to the event or experience we or others have had. From a spiritual vantage point, in any one experience or event, there are too many details that offer support to the inevitability of an incident.

This is a spiritual dynamic we are only beginning to explore in our consciousness and through our justice system. Take, for example, lawsuits that seek to hold pharmaceutical companies accountable for drugs or other substances that have adverse effects on those they come in contact with, parents who are being charged for the crimes their children commit, or the government's struggle in making only meager reparations to the many generations of Black and Brown people in America whose lives and lands were stolen by way of colonialism. (They do not fully recognize the brutality of those who came before us, for fear it may leave them legally vulnerable—leaving only a few of the courageous to admit fault for their ancestral contribution.)

There are no hard-and-fast remedies for the suffering we experience, especially for those tragedies for which the blame seems obvious, because, ultimately, every accident, injury, or illness has a thousand hands that formed it over time and space. It is for this reason that we are spiritually imprinted with impetus toward self-blame and accountability. We seek the empowerment we need to find healing, recovery, and acceptance.

Denial: The grief that injury and illness can bring

The grief that injury and illness bring is often subtle and comes in stages. Of course, each person will grieve differently. But I think that how to articulate it more specifically is that when we receive a critical diagnosis or receive a critical injury, every part of us goes into some form of shock, except our spirit. Our mind, heart, and body move into a stasis on some level to connect with our spirit, to receive the directive of what to do next. It is common to withhold emotion until some form of rational clarity becomes apparent. This is what many may call denial, but I don't think it's helpful to understand it this way. Again, denial is another inflammatory word that implies shame and fault as it regards grief.

Denial is actually a state of shock that shifts our awareness to accessing from the soul what our true intention is for the experience. It is in this process that we make inquiries to our higher selves to understand where our position of power is in this instance. What is the conflict within us we seek to reconcile, and how do we move forward in resolution? Again, this is something that only we can know, and the process to get there does not always look conscious. However, remaining in this state of "shock" while we connect with ourselves allows for us to disengage from the needs of everyone else around us while we are in crisis; it gives us the space we need to recognize the path that is appropriate to take. Several years ago, my dear friend Hayli was diagnosed with cancer of the kidney and describes this state perfectly.

It's important for me to first mention how I ignored changes and warning signs coming from my body that were apparent for quite some time. Having always been active and overall healthy, I feel that many women like myself don't listen to and tune into their bodies unless pain is present. Although cancer can be asymptomatic . . . ultimately, I had to come to terms with the signs that had been there.

Very early on there was a lump under my left rib cage, which I brushed off as a weird muscle or something pushed out of place after years of different abdominal exercises. That discovery was to remain there for a long time with no change, and the cramping in my legs I attributed to exercising in the heat. Funny how the mind works. Setting all these subtle symptoms and changes aside without a worry. Weeks before my diagnosis, I had asked my teenage daughter to feel the "lump." She expressed her worry and asked that I promise to have it looked at. Something that would be in the back of my mind moving forward.

Sometime later, I headed to the emergency room in the middle of the night due to a urinary tract infection, knowing that I had to host a party the next day. All I could think about was getting some antibiotics to ease the burning and frequent urination. While there, at the end of my conversation with the doctor, my daughter's request came to mind. Definitely treating it as an afterthought, I asked if she wouldn't mind taking a look at the "lump." After having me lie down and feeling the area, I'll never forget the look on her face as she asked how long it had been there. I actually felt embarrassed to tell her, knowing innately it had been way too long. Years was my reply. I remember the change in her demeanor and how she chose her words very carefully. "It's definitely something that concerns me. We must get an MRI immediately." And her answers to my questions: "It is a growth of some sort. Too early to tell what exactly it could be."

Time seems to slow down when you're faced with something pivotal, seriously life changing. Cancer. Tumor. Emergency surgery. Is there someone I'd like to call? I seem to remember only certain words. From that moment on, I was on autopilot.

I was separated at the time. My first instinct was to call my husband, but I called my oldest son instead. I couldn't reach him, since he was away at college. Then my sister. Within twenty-four hours I was surrounded by family and going in for emergency surgery. I remember praying and a feeling of calmness. A defense mechanism to be sure. I took comfort in the fact that I led a healthy lifestyle and was thankful for the turn of events. Not to mention that the head of nephrology for Texas Health Hospitals was taking my case. I was supported and surrounded like never in my life . . . the strength it provided me was immeasurable. It was everything.

The night in the emergency room was the last time I allowed any more feelings of doubt that everything would be okay. It was a conscious decision. The first one of many in my life.

Conversations with doctors are very clear in my mind, being jokingly called a unicorn. I was the young, healthy woman with the disease often saved for those who'd given themselves less care. However, the doctors seemed to explain it away because of the other incidents of cancer in my family. Everything happened so quickly, for which I'm thankful for to this day.

The tumor was quite large, and they had to remove the kidney. It was determined to be renal cell carcinoma. Measuring 17 cm, it had grown to a fist-sized tumor on my left kidney, protruding from under my rib cage. It was given the dubious distinction of a 4 out of 4 on the "Furman" scale, a medical

*scale used to classify tumors by size and malignancy. The description provid-
ed in my medical records was frightening.*

*My first meeting with my oncologist was preceded with conversations
between the two acquainted doctors about the rarity of the situation. As it
turns out, most cancerous renal tumors metastasize at 7 cm; the tumor they
removed was over twice that size, and my margins were clear. Gratitude and
feelings of being supported were in the forefront of my mind. Something I would
never take for granted. Chemo and radiation are not options with renal cancer;
usually, oral medications are used. I was not going to need any follow-up
treatments. I was watched very closely for five years, after which I was "out of
the woods," so to speak. It's coming up on ten years, and my life has changed
dramatically. My well-being and health are a constant consideration.*

*I've struggled whether or not to classify myself as a survivor, having not
been through chemo or radiation like my mother or my sister. After years of
reflection, I have concluded that yes, I'm a survivor. Even though my experience was addressed quickly, I believe that my mindset moving forward and
making conscious decisions to become an active participant in listening to,
taking care of, and honoring my body is valuable beyond measure.*
—Hayli E.

The other phases of grief we experience, beyond the state of shock, may take
years to present and process through to completion. The mind and body will
immediately rise to the occasion and handle the crisis to fulfill what the soul in-
tends, while the heart waits silently in the wings, ready to open itself to all the
understanding inspired by the illness when the crisis is over—in life and in death.
Our consciousness will make a choice that our mind may not be aware of, until
the emergency is over.

The trauma of catastrophe

In Kentucky, the aftermath of many powerful F3 tornadoes capable of producing
winds as strong as 206 mph left many people with traumatic physical, psychological, and emotional injuries. One woman suffered with nightmares in the days
after being buried under thousands of pounds of rubble. She reported, in the
following days and weeks after her rescue, that upon closing her eyes she would
envision being buried again, the memory jerking her awake and rendering her
unable to sleep. This type of posttraumatic response is normal after such a tragedy.

People are resilient. Each aspect of ourselves is equipped to provide the information we need to help us transmute and transform any event into usable energy for our wellness—through grief. The mind records memories and details of our experiences, our heart records the emotions we feel, and our soul records every inner and outer detail of an event. This includes the other people involved and their words, feelings, and actions. It includes a replay of every bit of the environment and its smells, sounds, and temperature, and any other defining element. All this information serves as an alarm bell that rises up in our consciousness to help us not repeat similar events that are dangerous and to keep us safe.

The repetitive nightmares or flashbacks we have after a traumatic event occur to help us recognize the process or pattern of events that took place before the trauma (to prevent it from occurring again in the future). We reinvigorate memories of what happened during the wounding to help us process the emotions we have from the experience. And, when we are ready, we will process all the events that took place after our trauma occurred, through the three circles of grief.

Any one of these phases of grief can be systematically pushed aside by the psyche until a person is ready to process the memory and emotions from their encounter. These memories may reveal themselves months or years down the line, either when the individual is in a safe place to process or through triggers unearthed by similar dynamics that a person may collide with in their daily life. And, depending on the level of catastrophe, the soul may just keep this memory hidden until there are lifetimes of space in between the occurrence and its recollection. Either way, at some point, we all will process and grieve our traumas.

The destiny in this case isn't the fact that the event happened; it is the eventual healing that will occur because of it. As I've mentioned before in earlier chapters, the soul incarnates with the spiritual patterns that attract certain experiences and the inner knowing a person uses to resolve the patterns in question.

Exercise to handle trauma flashbacks or dreams
When you awaken from a dream or have a traumatic flashback:

First: Take deep, slow breaths until you begin to feel calm and grounded.

Second: Use your imagination to go back into the dream or memory by choice. Visualize yourself being back in the scary circumstance. Pay attention to the fact that you are safe.

Third: Visualize yourself changing the situation, such as by speaking a command and seeing it being followed, or simply seeing the circumstances shift to no longer cause an affliction for you, and then see yourself walking out of it happy, safe, and healthy. To integrate the mind, emotions, body, and spirit, you must realign yourself with your whole healthy self. You may have to create this visualization many times, but ultimately it will take you on a path of grief that will allow this spiritual fusion to take place.

If you sustained physical injuries, spend time daily imagining what it looks like for your wounds to heal, your bones to reform and rebuild themselves, and your central nervous system to readjust to feeling calm and centered. Every time you begin one of these heal- ing visualizations, practice your breath work before and after (four deep breaths, breathing in through the nose and exhaling out through the mouth).

Illness and trauma are never your fault

It cannot be said enough: your circumstance or condition is never your fault. However, that does not mean you have no power or control over it. The self-help genre of books gets a bad rap when it comes to helping those in dire straits. "Liv- ing your best life" does not usually translate to surviving cancer, overcoming a violent crime, or learning to walk on one leg. In fact, the people working within these circumstances often feel like the "do it yourself" healing community mini- mizes or diminishes the profundity of the task before them.

Although every book has its message and certainly finds its community of readers, many self-help options don't want to indulge in the raw, dark places we must go to find peace within our trauma. Nor do they travel back in time and space to resolve the origin of what causes our deepest rift—the spiritual pain we carry with us, intended to reveal our greatest power. So, if you find yourself be- coming enraged as you stroll through the self-help aisle, you may need a perspec- tive that can help you dig through the deepest layers of your soul.

This type of healing is called spiritual integration, soul retrieval, or the pre- viously mentioned shadow work. It encompasses every aspect of our beings and requires a complete and total commitment to its reconciliation. It may not nec- essarily bring us the "best life" we'd imagined, but it will inevitably bring us the peaceful and balanced life we didn't know we could have. I was having a conver- sation with a friend the other day, and the topic of her autoimmune disease came up. No sooner had I asked her a question than she responded with "I am so tired of people blaming me for being sick!"

I could feel the rage, anger, and frustration coming through the speaker on the phone.

I took a deep breath and asked, "Have I blamed you for your illness?"

"No," she replied, "but you were going to."

"I was?"

Now we both sat in awkward silence, awaiting her response. "I'm sorry," she uttered.

"No need to apologize. I get it. You can be as sick as you want to be. I would never want to take that away from you, and I do not judge you for it." Again, another awkward silence.

Finally, I asked, "Is it possible that you judge yourself?"

"Yes," she said, "I suppose I do."

I have never, as an Empath, called the profound physical burden that processing spiritual and emotional energy brings a "disease." I have contended with the symptoms that many with autoimmune ailments experience: restless nights, sleepful days, chronic colds and sinus infections, body aches, and joint pains. I have instead had a hyperawareness to what the systems of my body are doing, so that I may give them what they need to remain in balance. In general, I never sought Western medical care for these things, since I was unwilling to medicate myself in any way for them, nor did I feel that receiving a diagnosis would be helpful in any way. Instead, I have used alternative and integrative medicine to stay well.

The concept of being at fault for our condition is a way our psyche interprets how we may be empowered to influence our circumstances and make changes to find improvements. I came into this life with the spiritual directive that all I would face was within my power to remedy, and thus far it has brought success—not comfort all the time, but success. The most important takeaway here is that each of us has our own spiritual directive that will see us through any experience. It will divulge our spiritual intent and show us what we will gain from the revelations at hand, helping us see how the directive will be fulfilled. In sickness or health, in life or death, all are sacred.

Understanding what recovery means for you

Trauma has a special way of revealing the soul. It brings to the surface anything previously embedded in the spirit so deeply that it takes the shock and awe of tragedy to unearth it. Through a powerful event, some of the soul-knowledge is awakened in a person's consciousness, and other elements will arrive on the tails of grief.

Recovery is the sacred integration of those pieces of ourselves proclaimed through our trauma, and is connected, one to the other, by the multiple mental, emotional, physical, and spiritual phases of grieving. When one of these profound events takes place, everyone involved will have their own process of mourning the circumstances. It is often those closest who must tolerate the initial wave of shock. As spoken of before, sometimes this can be viewed by others as denial.

When we are unable to process certain information, our psyche can compart-mentalize the knowledge, while we reconcile other aspects of ourselves needed to integrate what has caused the stupefaction. Denial would imply a cognizant awareness on behalf of the person in shock, which is most often not the case.

Sometimes, the only way a person can manage daily life is to set aside the trauma so they may take care of the tasks with priority. Within a family dynamic, when the adults are doing their best to keep the fragile balance of daily life moving or caring for the one in recovery, they also are multitasking their grief. This leaves the children in the environment vulnerable to the emotions in the space. Often there is at least one person (no matter their age) in a household who will process the emotional grief for the whole group.

The ones who are unable to process the emotionalism of the situation will inevitably experience it in another time and space, when they are safe to do so—this is what we recognize as posttraumatic stress disorder (PTSD). Here are some indicators of PTSD that may occur after one has experienced a traumatic injury, accident, or illness. Their presence lets you know that you are ready to emotionally grieve what happened.

1. **Reliving the trauma:** consistent flashbacks or recurring nightmares

2. **Anxiety:** a constant feeling of foreboding, stomachache, or worry

3. **Avoidance:** resisting talking about the circumstances to others, or anything associated with the event

4. **Reduced emotional connection:** a subtle or obvious reduction of time and energy spent with others, and movement into isolation

5. **Hypervigilance and arousal:** exaggerated reactions in everyday situations that can include startling easily; hyperawareness to one's environment; taking precautions to prevent more tragedy; hyperawareness of sniffles, sneezes, or other common symptoms; anger at risk-taking behaviors of other family or friends; being irritable; and being unable to sleep

Children will reveal their PTSD in other ways:

1. bed-wetting

2. nightmares

3. crying over anything

4. refusing or being unable to speak

5. hyper-attachment

Experiencing heightened anxiety during recovery is natural. When you embrace your feelings of worry, it helps make them manageable. Recognize that grief always follows the presence of feelings of apprehension, and allow the natural flow of emotion that will bring you relief. Here are some methods to try when you find yourself becoming anxious:

1. Mindful breathing: Take slow, deep breaths; inhale at the count of four and exhale at the count of four.

2. Be present: Focus on the world around you. Notice physical objects in the present moment instead of mentally reliving the traumatic event or the fear of it happening again.

3. Mudras: Hand yoga practiced while deep breathing can bring enormous relief, positive focus, and grief.

4. Seek help: Grieving through recovery is a powerful experience, and it is always important to have support, whether it be a group of people with similar experience, a good friend to confide in, or a therapist or counselor—no one is meant to go through it alone.

It is important to recognize that recovery means something different in every situation. Some people are healing physically, while others are healing mentally, emotionally, or spiritually. These different forms of healing require different outcomes: some people will find a spiritual directive that brings full physical recovery, while others may never regain the use of a limb or continue life in their current body. But for all, there is ensured a conscious connection between them and their higher selves. It is the awareness of this aspect of their consciousness that holds the secret of their recovery and path through the burden they carry.

Chronic illness

When you live with a chronic illness, there are different levels of grief to address. Initially, you must contend with your physical body and all the changes that may have taken place, along with any ways you have lost function. Those who suffer from chronic illnesses often suffer from some form of depression as well. And finally, being chronically ill means there are doctors, hospitals, medications, pharmacies, insurance, and constant worry about resources. All these elements must be grieved. The old you (the person you were prior to your illness) must be left behind to embrace and empower the new you, and your new circumstances.

Radical acceptance is a term I use to embrace what feels unembraceable. People spend an enormous amount of time resisting what is inevitable for them; radical acceptance is the opportunity to surrender to a new flow of ideas, beginning with owning the current reality. Only when you do that is a new path revealed on how to endure and thrive in the new way. Chronic illness is an opportunity to draw in your energy and forces from the outside world and use them to support, manage, or heal you from the inside out.

Learning to communicate with yourself differently is the key. Every day we participate in self-talk, and many times we have no awareness of what we are saying to ourselves. We may be playing over in our heads the opinions, thoughts, or beliefs of others around us and parroting them as if they are our own. Your first phase of healing integration is to become aware of your self-talk by journaling once a day. Start by listing the five people closest to you, then write down what you have heard them say about you, or what their actions toward you may have implied to you about yourself. Once you are in the flow of writing about others, you will begin to become aware of your own self-talk or chronic thoughts of disempowerment you may be experiencing.

Grieving every element of your chronic experience of illness is a natural and necessary way to find a place of empowerment to heal your life—to find peace with the circumstances or conditions you find yourself in leaves you free to discover the path forward.

Grieving and accepting your circumstances

Acceptance means to find power in your situation, to gain understanding on a deeper level as to what empowerment your circumstances will bring. There is always some form of revelation that comes with trauma if you will acknowledge it. This empowerment is your key to transmuting or transforming the situation and then transitioning from its current condition. Life is about mastering this process—always being in a state of acceptance and empowered to make choices.

Margaret had been living an emotionally singular life despite her lengthy relationship, and she didn't even know it. She didn't see it that way. She only felt the awkwardness and isolation it was beginning to inspire in her. At the time of the accident, she was twenty-seven years old and had gone to dinner with some friends of her husband's. She was a passenger in a car filled with colleagues of her mate—people with whom she was only mildly acquainted—driving down Melrose

Avenue. Her husband had been out of town at a conference, and she was left to take his place at a work function. Melrose Avenue was busy that night, quite a few cars on the road. They were stopped at a light when they were hit from behind, and the man who hit them was clocked at driving 50 mph.

The car ricocheted into a few other vehicles before rolling to a complete stop at the side of the road, as they heard sirens begin to sound. There happened to be a cop across the street who saw everything.

Suddenly the woman in the front seat turned around and said to Margaret, "Do. Not. Move. I heard your neck break."

From that moment on, she lay still, paralyzed in fear, as her new reality began to settle in. While she had thus far overcome any obstacle that was thrown at her, this was one she could not fully comprehend. She remained there, as motionless as possible, waiting for help to come. Within minutes the ambulance arrived and took her to the hospital. No one else seemed to be as hurt as she was, so they were able to call her husband, who responded with his characteristic nonchalance: "Oh, she'll be all right; I'll be home in a few days."

Although her neck was not broken, it was deeply injured. Doctors said she needed to stay as sedentary as possible so that she would not injure herself further. When we are healthy, the neck has a natural curve to it. But for Margaret the accident straightened her neck and compacted all the bones. It put her in constant pain with continuous spasms. She needed round-the-clock care until she could begin to rehabilitate and acclimate to her injuries. Unfortunately, her doctor said her circumstances did not warrant remaining in the hospital.

Margaret was discharged in the care of one of her husband's colleagues from the accident—her husband was unwilling to break his plans to come home to be with his wife. It was an awkward situation all around, try as she may to make the best of it—the embarrassment, agony, and vulnerability wound into a tight rope of despair for her to drag along into her future.

The grief for me came when I recognized the sense of emotional vulnerability I felt being incapacitated. The accident made me aware of my feeling of being isolated and alone, despite being married for almost a decade.

—Margaret F.

No matter the revelation, once acceptance has come, the subtle flow of grief can pass through, cleansing the heart and mind as it does. Peace and empowerment become inevitable once we see the immediate possibilities in front of us. We can choose a direction and begin our forward movement regardless of our condition.

It is this bit of freedom that begets more with each choice we make. Acceptance is a form of facing any fear we have, and utilizing that fear to propel us onward, progressing and advancing on the path set forth for us in a powerful way.

THE SPOILS OF WAR

Hundreds of thousands of soldiers and first responders all over the world are left with traumatic injuries (physical, mental, and emotional) from the service they provide. But most are left without the complete support needed, including mental health services, nonreligious spiritual counseling, or rehabilitation support. In addition, this soul group has been conditioned to withstand the perils of their jobs. This confluence of conditions does little to allow for the process of grief.

Certain beliefs or thought patterns literally act as an obstacle to the deeper wisdom and knowledge that grief seeks to bring, leaving an enormous gap between injury and healing. This puts many who suffer from PTSD at an emotional disadvantage to achieve the healing they need. Some of the beliefs that support survival in wartime or street-level conditions inhibit relaxation and trust in the healing process of everyday life. An emotional retraining must take place if a soldier or first responder is to find peace as a civilian.

Michael F., who has served for decades as a first responder, beginning his career in the fire department and currently working as a paramedic in emergency medicine, has learned that how he perceives a person or situation determines his fluidity in detaching from them after the medical crisis has passed. One of the most powerful elements of grieving traumatic injury for the first responder is learning to let go of your opinions about why someone ends up in the conditions they do, which can keep you attached to them, their case, and what happened after they left you. This is an example of the body's fight-or-flight system and the extreme hypervigilance cultivated by people in the crisis industry, and their need to process grief.

When you're in the medical field, you sign up for seeing things you could never have imagined dealing with in your life. You need a support system. You can't keep your experiences in; you must talk to the people who work with you.

At the beginning, I would find myself wondering about whether someone we brought into the ER survived or not, or how they ended up in my ambulance. When I first started in the fire department, we received a call to assist a set of infant twins—one was not breathing—and we were unable to revive him. Those parents lost one child and had to figure out how to continue taking care of the one left. I couldn't let that go. I myself had an infant child at the time and, after that call, found it nearly impossible to sleep at night without checking on him every few hours.

Eventually, I had to learn to let go and to address my fears and the ways my work carried over to my life—I learned not to judge others, no matter their condition. I stopped following up on people I'd treated . . . when you see 150–200 people a day, it's impossible to keep them all in your mind.

—Michael F.

If you are a person currently serving as a first responder or in the armed services, it is imperative that you consider the natural role that grief must play in your life, and commit to finding a time and space to express it and supporting your colleagues to do the same. Expressing your sorrow at the things you see daily, a bit at a time, will keep your anxiety at bay and allow for you to be more emotionally present on the job. Finally, practicing nonjudgment for yourself and others is necessary and a powerful tool to find balance between your work and home life.

EMPOWERING YOURSELF FOR HEALING

What does it mean to empower yourself to heal? Healing is an integration of sorts. It is all the information regarding a way of being, a situation, or an event coming together, so that there is no separation or gaps in our spiritual, mental, emotional, or physical relationship to it. Helping others has the nature of water: it drips and runs until it wears down what contains it, to rejoin the whole or to gain freedom. Rivers and streams eventually make their way to the ocean. A dripping faucet will always become a full leak if left to its nature, untouched.

Grief, too, is like water. As an Empath, I am in the crisis business; many of the clients I work with find me after something difficult has come up in their lives. Doing this work has required me to do my own healing on every level: mentally, emotionally, spiritually, and physically. My constant grief connected all the stories of my soul and allowed for me to process them and let go, one at a time, to ultimately arrive at my integrated consciousness.

Once you have integrated, you begin a new level of fusion. The first healing integration helps release you of your burden and frees you from the concept of victimization and suffering. You begin to use all that you have in a concentrated and effective way, but there are always new understandings to gain. One is not done with life when their burden is gone, but is left with freely choosing what they are skilled to do, not obligated on the basis of the spiritual patterns they may no longer carry.

Empowering yourself to heal is giving yourself permission to find out everything there is to know about you and your spiritual, mental, emotional, and physical self. It is analyzing any self-pity you have, to reveal what you must learn to do on your own. It is surrendering your feelings of isolation from a world you believe is against you and making your suffering unbearable. This frees you from your own self-criticism. Remember, you are like water. Even the largest mountains can be worn down in places to let the water pass. All situations have a remedy to their obstacle if you will stay focused on it by empowering yourself to heal.

Trivializing trauma

When people speak of the "lessons learned" in life experiences, there seems to be a glossy, positive haze that feels feigned—which, frankly, is quite irritating when you are confronting a powerful, life-altering event. In our culture, people are accustomed to being repulsed by the cold, hard truth. They would rather hear you say, "Fine," in response to their salutation "How are you?" than to be saddled into an uncomfortable conversation of reality.

Unfortunately, this is why those who experience traumatic injury or illness would prefer to stay silent until they are certain that the person or people to whom they reveal their pain completely understand. They cannot or do not want to help others process the shock and suffering they are experiencing from their condition.

As a witness, it is important not to trivialize the experience of someone in crisis because we are unable or unwilling to grasp their depth of suffering. It is best to be present and listen, or to be honest that you are unable to do either, than to diminish another's experience because it is uncomfortable. Using euphemisms about their reality, or positive platitudes about their recovery (such as "Lesson learned!"), is not helpful or supportive. It only further isolates the one who is having to relearn their entire life and grieve the one they left behind.

Make no mistake about it: witnessing your loved one's suffering is profound and difficult for you as well, but it is imperative that you find a way to process your own grief without help from them. A traumatic injury will take everything a person has to process, recover, and transform their life into the new way of being caused by the trauma.

Helping the whole family grieve

In any family dynamic, when there is a traumatic injury or illness, it affects everyone. And if you are the injured party, you may not be able to help anyone but yourself. That's just a fact. However, more often than not, those around you may take on what happened to you and make it about them. It is important to understand and engender compassion for everyone learning to adapt to the changes these new circumstances require. Whatever role you are playing within this dynamic as a caregiver, family member, or the one enduring the traumatic event, consider these elements of grieving in a family.

The one suffering illness: Their burden is to grieve the feeling of betrayal (by their body) or guilt (the illusion that they somehow caused their own suffering). No one else can do that for them, nor does it leave them available to help others processing this same grief. They must also grieve the pain and symptoms they experience, and all that comes with it (doctors, testing, medications, side effects, insurance, and resources). Additionally, they must grieve the fact that they cannot do it by themselves, and let go of the once-autonomous life they may have lived.

Ultimately, a person who has suffered a traumatic injury or illness must choose to participate in life if they are to move forward in any form of rehabilitation. Recovery doesn't always mean you resume the capability you once had; it means only that you fully embrace the capability you do have, and make the most of it on all levels. Remember: you do not have to do it by yourself.

The grief of immediate family members: Immediate family members must grieve the loss of participation by the one who is sick. They must grieve and adapt to a life that does not include all the things the person can no longer do for them, and adapt to getting it done themselves. They must also grieve the fear they feel about an uncertain future for them and the one who suffers. They must also grieve the possibility of a new responsibility of caregiving.

Outer-circle friends and family: Everyone in this circumstance must learn how to process and be accountable to manage their own feelings and fears, especially the outer circle of friends and family. This is the group of people who can have the most impact on helping a family seeking to recover from a traumatic injury or illness, should they choose to do so.

Accepting care from others

This is where pride comes in: learning to accept help from others. True self-pride is the confidence to include others in your struggle. Your journey, no matter what it is, was never intended to be taken alone; hence the spiritual patterns you reverberate into the world, drawing the people, places, and things to which you relate, live, and celebrate life.

To consciously, by your choice, allow people (be it a loved one or caregiver) to walk with you on your journey is also a part of theirs. You have something for them that they cannot get anywhere else but to help and be witness to your life. Surrendering to having a witness to your suffering is powerful medicine for everyone involved.

A Ritual for Grace

Affirmation: I call on grace to guide my words and actions. I am overwhelmed with the peace and compassion I have for myself and others.

What you'll need for your ritual:
>   one pink jar candle
>   a fire source (a lighter or match)
>   a multicolored cloth (any size) to place on the sacred altar area
>   one item that represents your goal
>   one piece of rose quartz
>   mason jar
>   paper and pen
>   myrrh incense for offering
>   one medium-sized metal pot to burn herbs (and charcoal if needed)

Herbs you'll need:
Echinacea: Helps one to pinpoint the shadow aspect in our ethereal body so that true healing can occur. It helps with locating the true cause of chronic illness in the emotional and spiritual sphere.

Daisies: These cheery flowers help ease the mind, body, and spirit into true healing. They calm the emotions and help shed the traumatic layers of the ethereal body.

Borage: Helps cultivate the faith and courage to see through chronic illness. It instills upliftment when feeling discouraged.

Begin your ritual by cleaning and clearing an area in the center of your home. Collect all the items for your altar and put them in the cleared space. Place the herbs in the mason jar and hold it in hand while repeating the affirmation (you may also say prayers of your choice for healing). Exhale your breath onto the herbs to release the energies of the affirmation.

Every night or early morning for seven days, at the same time each day, light your candle and contemplate the item representing your goal and what it means to you. What elements of your life feel restricted around that goal, and why? If possible, take time to write your thoughts and impressions as you remember them. Each day, add the new paper filled with your journaling to your altar. Once the candle is finished, burn your herbs in the burning pot.

Pay close attention in that week to any signs, symbols, or synchronicities you may come across that bring you further information about grace. Write them down. Also, pay attention to any dreams, daydreams, or visions you may have. Write them down. At the end of the week, go over any themes that came up for you, and contemplate their messages.

Performing this ritual may inspire a grief response, and that's okay. Allow yourself to feel anything that comes up. The release and rejuvenation you seek will come in many ways over time. Give yourself permission to go with the flow.

TRANSPERSONAL GRIEF: SHARING THE BURDEN

Grief can sometimes feel like it has a life of its own. On a soul level, your grief is purposeful and deliberate—spiritually crafted to liberate you from energies that no longer serve you. The dynamic of *transpersonal grief* can be prompted by the connection we have with others and the elements of life we have in common. Such things as how much we have, how we feel, experiences we share, and the beliefs we hold—all these notions put us in alignment with one another, even when we've never met.

In the spiritual world, we call it "agreement." We energetically and spiritually "agree" with each other when we share vibrational common ground—we call this dynamic empathy, and it allows for transpersonal grief: the sharing of emotional burden.

Simply put, transpersonal grief is when we feel the grief of another person or group of people who are in trauma. When the attacks on the United States took place on 9/11, the world grieved. Not only for what America was going through, but for the illusions it dismantled of our invincibility, and the emotions, for those who were experiencing the event, were unable to feel. We spoke earlier about when a person experiences a trauma; their mind and body can shut down the energy centers that allow for the flow of emotion through their physical framework until they feel safe to express feelings. The waiting period can be hours, days, months, or years until the person is out of shock and able to allow the rush of emotional energy to move through their body.

Until this time, the person's grief sits in their energy field (aura) and is available for an ultrasensitive person to energetically connect with it, take it, and express it. Now imagine this process in the collective—an entire group, town, or country in grief but unable to express it. This energy lies in wait until a person or group can process it.

WHAT IS COLLECTIVE GRIEF?

There are many ways we can experience collective grief, but they boil down to our karmic and soulmate groups. These are the groups of souls with whom we share mutual energetic bonds and spiritual goals. A collective can be members of our family, a car club we form, people who share culture or ethnicity, our neighbors, folks with whom we share political views, or other organizing factors such as being a first responder or teacher. All these groups share a similar vibration, and when trauma befalls one in the group, it is easily transferred to the entire group for processing.

Of course, the nature of the collective grief must be a dynamic that can connect and affect all of us, even if we do not experience it in the same way as others in our collective. Things such as illness and disease, the fear of losing our personal rights, war-torn communities, death of a public figure (or what they represent), or a natural disaster, to name a few. These are all opportunities to experience grief and for an individual to share the burden of the collective.

For those who resist the act of grief, their relief is little and hard won. There are themes that echo throughout the practice of grief: they are accountability, expansion, compassion, truth, and evolution (those who don't grieve don't evolve); it is the linchpin to our advancement. When we grieve, we love harder, accomplish more, think and feel more deeply, and consider others in our choices; these are the elements of a successful society.

The transformation of a Vietnamese tragedy

Many years ago in California, several hundred thousand Vietnamese Americans were thrust into the collective grief of the trauma that had brought many of them to the United States: the fall of Saigon in 1975. In the late 1990s, a man named Truong Van Tran displayed the Viet Cong flag and poster of Ho Chi Minh (Vietnamese dictator) in his store in Westminster—home of more than 200,000 Vietnamese Americans there and around Southern California (it was the largest Vietnamese community outside Ho Chi Minh City at the time). This display of solidarity with Ho Chi Minh reopened a painful wound for the hundreds of thousands of Vietnamese whom he caused to flee their homeland.

For over a month, Vietnamese communities all over the United States were propelled into a visible grief, previously unexpressed for several decades. They were now living in America, with jobs, homes, and families—and most of all, safety. The community was able to grieve aspects of their trauma collectively, many of whose families had been exiled from the only country they had ever known.

As an Empath and having strong ties to this community, and being no stranger to grief triggers myself, I processed the emotion right along with them. Although their story was not my own, the pain was the same and flowed from me for days on end. I remember, at the time, spirit showing me how one person could inspire such a profound release of torment, carried by so many. Energetically, over those coming days and weeks, I witnessed it as a dense cloud of emotion, dissipating by the day, until it was gone.

When one experiences the grief of a collective, it is allowing them to dig more deeply into their own spiritual coffers, and to release the imprints of emotion they may carry from another time and space, while at the same time helping to lighten another's load.

Does everyone experience transpersonal grief?

By design, transpersonal grief is a developmental tool for empathy. Not everyone will experience it, and when they do, it will flow in waves for certain events or mass traumas and then be done. It's like jury duty: you are called to service, and if the case is a fit, you process the collective emotion until it's complete and you are released from the obligation. You may never serve on another jury, or you may get called to serve repeatedly, all on the basis of your own spiritual needs and the layers of emotion you brought with you to process in this incarnation.

9/11 and its impact on the world

If you ask just about anyone, they know where they were on September 11, 2001, the day multiple attacks, perpetrated by terrorists, took place on American soil, killing 2,996 people. On that day, Holly was on her way from the Poconos to New York City with her husband for a business meeting, when, just as they entered the freeway, he realized he'd forgotten the identification he needed to enter the downtown building where they were headed. Luckily, they'd gotten an early start and had plenty of time before the eleven o'clock consultation. So, uneventfully, they turned back home to retrieve it.

It was a pristine, beautiful morning with clear skies as far as you could see, and the rich scent of fall leaves filled the brisk air. They were about fifteen minutes from the house when both their cell phones began to ring incessantly. Neither Holly nor her husband intended to take the calls, since they were enjoying the serenity of the drive, but the rings kept coming until finally, back at home, the caller urged—turn on your television. As the news unfolded, they witnessed the second plane hitting the twin tower and its defiant collapse into rubble. For the next three days they sat in front of the television, in shock about what was happening.

Nighttime would come, and both would be awakened from horrific dreams—the world was on fire. A gnawing memory began to rise up in Holly's mind. Two years prior, her friend Reese had had a vision. He saw Manhattan burning, walls of fire, gray ash falling, and smoke everywhere. It was a nightmare coming true.

A few weeks after the attack, people were encouraged to go into the city to support the businesses. Driving on Highway 80 through Jersey, there's a point where you could see the World Trade Center twin towers; it's how you know you're getting close to New York City. Holly was driving that day, and just as they turned the bend, curving right into view of the city landmark, Holly's hands began to shake and silent tears streamed from her eyes. The collective traffic began to slow at this juncture; there was only smoke rising from where the towers had stood.

After dinner at a restaurant in the West 70s, the overwhelming reality of the human losses was apparent. Everywhere were flyers: "Have you seen my brother?" "Have you seen my daughter?" "Have you seen my husband?" Thousands were now missing, many were dead, and it would take months to uncover the personal stories of each person who had perished.

Long-term grief

Some life events carry such an impact that the grief you experience comes in waves throughout a lifetime; we will be grieving 9/11 for generations to come. When groups of people experience a common ground such as 9/11, we call them a soul group.

This soul group will process all the different levels of the events from 9/11 from their own individual perspectives. Here is a sampling of perspectives where members of this soul group will begin their grief process:

1. The people on the ground in the different locations where the multiple attacks took place

2. Those who watched from afar

3. Those who died

4. Those who learn about the events from media or history

5. Those who supported, planned, and caused the attacks

6. The children and family members of those who suffered, in any way, because of the attacks

7. Those who cleaned up the aftermath

8. All the unforeseen traumas that came because of the attacks

When an event takes place, there are many factors that guide how we can grieve. My father died when I was eleven years old. I was prepubescent and hadn't fully created an emotional bond with him like young girls do once they've hit puberty. This level of development was the guiding factor in how I related to my father's death, by keeping me somewhat emotionally detached about his absence.

My grief wasn't necessarily about his lack of presence, since there wasn't an enormous physical presence when he was alive. My grief was about the dispersal of the family dynamic, my mother's grief, the lack of connection with my sisters and their eventual departure from the household, and my overwhelming sense of isolation from not being a "regular" kid.

It wasn't until decades later that I would grieve the impact losing my father had on my perspective of many things, including my relationships with men, a man's role in the family, and my father's relationships with others I witnessed as a child. (Dad was a regional celebrity and deeply valued by the public. As it turned out, he put more energy into his philanthropy than he did his family.) There were many new understandings about my father and what I had truly lost. As I grew and developed as a person and viewed life with an adult awareness, these new discoveries revealed new layers to the grief I felt.

Every stage of development that occurs in our lives creates a newly layered perception of loss and grief. The amount of time we spend with what we've lost is also a contributor. All these factors will dictate our relationship to grieving a major event. As our understanding and value of that connection to what we lost grows and changes with us, there will be a new level of grief. To illustrate what I mean, I'll use my relationship to the death of my father and how it changed over time.

Developmental stages that form our viewpoint

Childhood: Zero to twelve years of age

The stability my father provided was not evident to me at this early age, since he didn't have a huge role in my emotional or spiritual sense of safety from which I suffered a deep lack during these years, something I wouldn't be able to process and grieve until decades later.

Teens: Twelve to eighteen years of age

My teenage development without my father would garner a strong solidarity with women, a burgeoning independence and leadership quality, and my relationship to money and resources as I began my work life at the age of thirteen. This fierce independence would shape all my relationships as an adult; ultimately, I needed to learn how to compromise with others if I was going to be a successful adult. Over time, I would grieve the appearance of a loss of independence it took to forge these new adult relationships.

Early adult: Eighteen to twenty-five years of age

My late teens and early twenties would reveal my complete absence of knowledge in how to relate to men in a new way outside the patterns in my spirit. My spiritual trauma supported an enormous grief related to past-life abuses, and my current life supported an absence of structure that men traditionally provide. Although I am a part of a new generation of women who were born emotionally free of the restrictions our culture had dictated between the genders, eventually I needed to grieve the lack of structure in my life because of it, in addition to grieving the fear my spiritual trauma promoted.

Childbearing years, twenty-five to forty years of age

For me, having children was never in the forefront of my mind. Healing my mind, body, and spirit from trauma was the only focus for many years—until it was too late to have children. The childbearing years promote multiple levels of grief for one who cannot or does not want to bear children. A woman's DNA and hormonal directives perpetuate the desire to procreate and therefore put one in conflict with herself, on a deeper level. Ultimately, it was only the many levels of grieving that allowed me to reconcile this need to procreate written in my DNA, with the more valuable spiritual and emotional need to heal first. Through grief, I found peace in not choosing to have children.

Professional success, twenty-five-plus years of age

Adjusting to the professional climate of the culture in which you live is a powerful experience, especially when you are in a marginalized demographic. I was never able to sustain a job where I didn't have some form of autonomy. I worked in the food industry, the cosmetic industry, and the entertainment industry, all of which prepared me to eventually create a business of my own in the mind, body, spirit marketplace. Going out on my own without the backbone of a larger company was terrifying and necessary, and ultimately I needed to grieve my fear of not having enough resources to live. This grief transformed me over many years at different levels of thinking, feeling, perceiving, and decision-making.

Marriage

The dynamic of marriage in our culture and the expectations or judgments put on everyone to fulfill them are powerful things to overcome, especially when you are female. I grew up with the underlying judgment that if you weren't married you weren't "good enough" to be married—that somehow marriage was a right of passage for extraordinary people. Where these images came from, I am not exactly sure; it was never something I was told directly, but seemed to be the messaging from society in general on the basis of the value that seemed to be placed on marriage. Eventually, I needed to grieve this illusion to completely embrace myself in the world.

Fifty-plus years of age

This period of life is unique. The changes that happen in the mind, body, and spirit during these years are powerful and must be addressed with patience, reverence, and respect. One must learn to grieve their independence once more at some point. In addition, we all will need grief to help us reconcile our emotional and spiritual feelings of youth with the changes of our aging bodies. Statistics say that people aged sixty to seventy accomplish the most out of any other decade in their life. I will let you know.

MANAGING YOUR EMPATHY

First, defining empathy is paramount to understanding the vast implications of this broad concept. There are three types of empathy: cognitive, emotional, and compassionate. Cognitive empathy is your ability to fully imagine what it is like to experience something as another person experiences it. Emotional empathy is taking on and sharing in the emotions of another. Compassionate empathy is one's ability to be inspired into action on behalf of another, on the basis of your empathetic connection. An Empath will do all three. Most people will experience one or two of the three forms of empathy, but everyone at some point will connect with others empathetically, on the basis of their own life and spiritual experiences.

Empathy is the conduit through which we communicate information we may not have cultivated a language to accurately or fully convey our feelings or experiences. It is not uncommon for a person opening to their empathic channels for the first time to judge or feel repulsed by the intensity of the feelings they have. For example, when someone is angry, depressed, or heartbroken and you feel their emotion—it's normal to respond in dismay: "You're so negative." Or, when posed with the difficulty of another's profound grief over an occurrence, people naturally respond, "I can't even imagine what you're going through," often because they are deeply uncomfortable in that moment as they imagine what you are going through.

The secret to empathy: we never take on any emotion we don't already feel on some conscious or unconscious level. The empathy we feel from another reveals only what we may have been hiding from ourselves. This is the reason for any feelings of resistance or repulsion we may encounter. Oftentimes, witnessing our deeper emotions can be difficult or awe inspiring, but most likely not routine.

When it comes to managing your relationship to the outside world, you must be impeccable with your inside world. Certainly, this is easier said than done. To be flawless in your relationship to yourself means to acknowledge every part of who you are on all levels, and to become accountable for them. You must accept and embrace yourself in your current condition and change what no longer serves you. Our empathy for others is the way we grieve for ourselves, and it causes the healing integration for which we are prepared.

When transpersonal empathy takes over, during a collective crisis or connection with a friend or loved one, it may reveal things about you that you hadn't acknowledged to yourself. The experience can be quite confronting. The only way around it is to make the effort to investigate the "whys" of your life.

Take a few moments to answer the questions below in ten words or fewer (requiring precision helps narrow down the information and pinpoint what's important).

1. Name three events in your life that still provoke emotion.

2. Name one event that you avoid thinking about.

3. Why do you avoid thinking about this event?

4. What is the worst thing that can happen if you allow the emotions you feel about this event?

5. If you could, how would you change the event in question?

Do you see any emotions you might want to explore in depth, or patterns you may want to challenge? To give yourself permission to fully grieve and then challenge your habits is what it takes to cultivate the self-acceptance you must have to move forward.

HOW TO NAVIGATE TRAGIC ANNIVERSARIES

Every part of our being remembers a tragedy. Our body shudders with aches and pains upon waking up on the anniversary of a trauma (other physical ailments such as cardiac events, pneumonia, colds, flu, and inflammation are also common). Our hearts feel heavy, and tears flow around the holidays or on the birthday of a deceased loved one. We are triggered on anniversaries of all kinds by spiritual, mental, physical, and emotional memories of a loss, especially when we experience similarities in our current-day activities.

Blue skies

Joseph's trigger? Summer days and cloudless blue skies. It was a beautiful, clear, end-of-summer Tuesday as Joseph was making his first cup of coffee in his East 14th Street apartment in New York City—when the first plane hit. Now, every blue, cloudless sky reminds him of 9/11. A physical deep sadness comes over him on days that should bring the most freedom and joy.

On many fair-weathered days, Joseph flashes back to NYC newscaster Roma Torre on the television screen, with the image of the twin towers smoking. Joseph witnessed the second plane hitting the remaining tower as it was happening on the screen in front of him—he screamed in terror and sat down in shock as the reality rolled over him. Soon, people started filtering up 3rd Avenue covered in white dust. Tanks and other heavily armored cars began to fill 14th and surrounding streets.

"The month before, I'd been down there reflecting on the setup and layout of everything. And now it's all gone."

At the time, he remembers feeling that his grief was so big, he couldn't imagine processing it.

"It was pure horror. So much confusion in those days. . . . But people really came together in a way that wasn't usual: the kindness, and allowances for their different ways of expression."

I asked Joseph if he thought beautiful sunny days would ever get their luster back. He responded emphatically:

"No. Part of me doesn't want it to change, so I can still remember what everyone lost on that day. The dread memorializes the loss and pain, and to let go of that feels like a betrayal to all that was taken from us on 9/11."

—Joseph P.

We humans are wired to hold on to pain and trauma so that we don't repeat choices that caused the pain, or so we become present to the patterns that lead to traumatizing experiences. The only drawback is that we begin to make associations with elements that would otherwise create good feelings. As an Empath, I have learned that when we do the grieving work connected to a loss, eventually letting go of the pain is a conscious choice that many do not make, to remember the consciousness that created the trauma in the first place.

If we are ever to move beyond our painful experiences, we must commit ourselves to becoming present to the patterns and circumstances we can control, and surrender to being open minded about those we cannot. It is important to begin to pay attention to seasons, days of the week, times of day, and temperatures as details that can trigger grief responses.

Four things you can do to manage your trauma anniversaries

1. Prepare: Take a few moments to sit with a yearly calendar in front of you and write down the details of the traumas you've experienced on their corresponding days or months. Write these items out for each one: the time of year, the weather you remember, the day of the week, the time of day, and any other memorable details. Armed with this information, you can plan a staycation or other relaxing activity to offer you solitude or companionship on or around the anniversary. Your goal is to manage your stress, give yourself space to grieve, and ultimately change your relationship with these memorial days to one of consciousness rather than unconscious reaction.

2. Remember: The anniversary week of a powerful loss is a perfect time to build a memorial altar to commemorate the person, place, or thing you've lost. You can place on your altar letters (current or past) to communicate your feelings, pictures, memorabilia, or favored items such as food, drinks, or candy. Other altar staples include a candle (the element of fire helps with grief), a glass of water (it takes in any harsh energy, then you can dump it in a plant or outside when your altar is complete), and a small bowl of oats, corn, tobacco, or cedar as an offering of gratitude. When you keep a memorial altar in a place of prominence in your home, it helps align everyone in the house with positive empowerment to support them in their grief.

3. Connect: Anytime we make a deliberate effort to connect with ourselves and our grief—but especially around anniversaries, birthdays, and holidays—our erratic emotions begin to subside and our attachment to what we've lost evolves into wisdom in the new relationship we have formed to what is gone. The emotionalism of a grief anniversary is temporary, but the self-knowledge we gain is forever.

4. Support: The most important thing to do around a grief anniversary is to communicate your feelings and needs to others. The value in garnering the support or space you need from others is powerful, but being clear on your boundaries is necessary. When in grief, sometimes there isn't room for the opinions or feelings of others, and there is nothing wrong with that. It's crucial that your friends and loved ones understand to the extent you have room for conversation, listening, or social activities. Don't be afraid to let them know how you're feeling and that you have less energy to offer right now. Also, this conversation is a great time to ask for what you need from them in support.

POSTGRIEF CALM

After any intense shedding of emotion, colors seem more vivid, your normal sight is conjoined with your inner sight and becomes clear, and the world seems even and hopeful. This is the opportunity for innovation to take hold and to create something new and wonderful. When your heart is open, everywhere you look there are masterpieces in and of nature, and beings of all sorts. It is here that you own the power of a quiet vision: the ability to see through time and space the consequences of your actions, the impact they have on you and others, and your soul's true intent for a well-spent life.

This is the honey in the deepest recesses of the comb, where the queen herself lives. The honesty in this place is an open door to your exorcised heart. A place that is at least one conflict less than it was and has more open space to understand the errors of its ways—and it's vibrating to make change.

The vision that is accessed from the postgrief calm, especially when connected through transpersonal grief, is enriched with the insight of higher vibrations. The resolutions to any problem are found in this place, along with the acceptance needed to forge ahead in power and wisdom. All this good comes from a rainstorm of tears and waves of laughter that allow you to see the beauty in anything. (And just so you don't get it twisted: sometimes, finally getting out of bed for a shower is the beautiful outcome you've been waiting for.)

THE GHOSTS LEFT BEHIND IN TRAGEDY

There is a reason ghosts exist. Not only the metaphorical ghosts, such as a memory that haunts you from times past, but a literal, otherworldly entity or energy that remains with the land, a building, or a person when tragedy strikes. Ghosts exist because the energy left unreconciled from a catastrophe must, at some point, be transformed through grief and understanding. The souls who pass to another dimension without processing their shock, fear, or grief will take it with them until they reincarnate again. The land and buildings left from past war or genocide will carry the weight of that burden for generations to come, unless the people living on it (or in it) help balance the scales by changing the patterns, beliefs, or ideals that led to the devastation in the first place.

Hauntings

People are haunted by memories of events or spiritual imprints from past lifetimes for which they have not grieved. They can also be a part of a soul group that is culturally working to process the violence and other atrocities committed against their ancestors. The human soul incarnates with some specific objectives: certain things to accomplish in this lifetime. The imprints of trauma or fear the spirit brings are the obstacles to be overcome by the person—to unlock the hope, inspiration, or innovation needed to achieve their goals. A person can follow the bread crumbs lined up by their empathy; it's a road map of their service to others and themselves.

Spiritual entities are beings in other dimensions: discarnate souls, emotional energy that's been left to collect in a locale, or beings from other planets—all who vibrate at different levels and can connect with people who match their energy. For example, an angry person will attract other anger in the space or entities that oscillate at that level. It is the release of grief that allows for the dense energy to be transmuted by the person experiencing the grief; this shift will create an awareness of any outside energy that may be contributing to the experience of the griever, such as an entity or discarnate spirit.

For years, dating back to early childhood, I would wake up in a panic from dreams of burlap sacks of apples. As I would awaken, I would see these large bags of apples everywhere around my bed. It was as if they were real, and the dream carried over into my waking life. I did not understand what could generate such fear about apples, but it could take hours to relieve my panic. As I got older, this dream subsided and other terror-stricken nightmares took its place.

It wasn't until I had the experience of reliving the moment of my past-life death by lynching that the terror of the apples was revealed. In the mid-1800s I had lived as a freed slave on a plantation whose main crop was apples. I was lynched as a retaliation by white youth against the plantation owner for being progressive and forward thinking for the times. I remembered and relived my soul leaving my hanging body. I'd been haunted by this spiritual memory from birth, and now I could grieve my loss. I wept and wailed for weeks, with only respites to work for an hour or two at a time.

It was then that I was able to witness with some objectivity the spirits I carried with me from that lifetime and others. The spirit of my husband, who was also murdered with me in that life, had been a lifelong spiritual companion in this one. Now, through this experience, he was free to move forward. I felt him leave and watched as he entered the light. As it turns out, it wasn't "till death do us part." Grief allowed us our reconciliation and freedom from living in the memory of our demise. It was then, for the first time, I experienced being white; or at least, I could recognize how others saw me within their cultural understanding of being "white."

When a person experiences a traumatic event, it is through their strong emotions such as guilt, shame, resentment, disappointment, rage, or fear that they can energetically "call on" entities from other dimensions, or discarnate souls who "match" the vibration. They naturally do this to receive help, protection, or solace. I know this must sound scary to those who don't hold these beliefs or who are being exposed to this information for the first time, so let me try to put you at ease. A person becomes haunted by their own agreement on some level, conscious or unconscious; they have all the power in the situation, and the visitation upon them is temporal.

Of course, it is also important to understand that regardless of whether an entity has brought comfort or more strife, they have brought companionship and connection and have cultivated a relationship with you for some time. This relationship will need to be dismantled, as any relationship that is breaking apart does. It is normal to feel deep sorrow and loss for any spiritual connection when they leave, even negative entities. I have had hundreds of conversations with clients who were reticent to let go of an entity for fear of the void they leave behind. Grief helps to call on new light and love to fill the space.

Taking back your power

Feeling powerful emotions can hold enormous fear for many. Ultimately, as humans, it is our own personal power we shrink from by disguising it through our lens of victimization. Emotionally speaking, it is easier to give our power away to others than to be accountable for wielding it with deliberate intention and compassion. Human beings hold the power in our physical world; other entities can influence only our emotions, our mentality, and the spiritual dimensions we all share, and can have power only when it is surrendered.

An entity's purpose on Earth is to influence people who are struggling with their own confusion, and to encourage or force them to take a stand. They will also create havoc in the world so humans are forced to make peace within themselves and commit to the choices that make things better for everyone. Of course, there are beautiful positive beings (angels, extra-terrestrials, and spirit guides) who protect and love us through our lives as well. Every person has their own group of spiritual entities that are here to be of service to them. They will always love and guide you according to your divine will. I have not focused on them in this section, because it is necessary to work through what we fear, first.

Who or what becomes haunted?

Buildings are haunted mostly by people who are haunted, but can also retain the ectoplasm (lower vibrational spiritual energy) of positive or negative events. Places where murders have happened may leave their victims spiritually stranded in the energetic field of the space, until they can transform their own vibration or be delivered by a connection with someone who has empathy or compassion for them. The space will also attract energy or discarnate spirits from other areas and can become a collective force of the vibration they have in common.

If you've wondered why certain people have the awareness of these hauntings, it's because they have an empathetic connection (emotional) or telepathic connection (mental) or spiritual connection (matching spiritual imprints) and can therefore "read" the energy in the place. Coincidentally, they also have the power to transform the energy of the building and to transmute it in themselves. They may do this through their willingness to grieve and through telling the stories the building holds in its energetic fields. Through this process of storytelling, they can release any discarnate spirits left behind. We all need to be seen and heard, and spirits are no different.

Land is haunted for the same reasons buildings are haunted—for what has taken place upon them. A parcel of land can retain the thousands-of-years-old cataclysmic natural events such as hurricanes, tsunamis, earthquakes, fires, floods, volcanic eruptions, tornadoes, and asteroid strikes. These events tend to be cleansers for the areas where they occur.

If there is loss of human life in the event, that new energy of trauma will "repossess" the land to create a spiritual memorial for all who will visit. This dynamic is the reason why certain places and people tend to be retraumatized since they have become collectors of the energy they retain, negative or positive.

When you release the fear from your vision of "haunting," it is easier to understand that there is a natural process of life and death. Each element of life, presence, death, and remembrance uncovers the sacred texts of the divine through human consciousness. Within our collective grief, spirit reveals the ancient knowledge of survival, pleasure, transition, and love, all through which we build or reduce our lives and create the foundations for others to do so as well. It is a profound challenge, responsibility, and legacy for which we've been given stewardship.

ANCESTRAL GRIEF

Grief is the processing of pain to gain wisdom and understanding of the dynamics at hand. When a generation of people are not equipped with the spiritual design, emotional intelligence, or impetus to grieve for the traumas created by themselves or their ancestors, that grief is kicked down the spiritual road for future generations to process. A deeper understanding of karma (also referred to as spiritual patterning) is valuable here. Karma is not punishment or reward, but the impact of actions over time and space. The idea of blame is not helpful, since we tend to want to blame a person or group of people as the cause of major tragedies, but in fact, everyone in some way contributes to the circumstances in their environment.

I'm sure you've heard it said that "you can be a part of the solution, or you become a part of the problem." Every individual will play a role in the cultural trauma they experience. They will create it, perpetuate it, refuse it, articulate it, understand it, grieve it, or change it, or any combination thereof.

It is the job of our human mind to break things down into bits, which are then communicated through our thoughts and eventually our words. However, it is this process that often disconnects us from our heart center and place of understanding (with the guise of efficiency). The illusion is that rational thought is more valuable than heartful emotion or compassion. Indeed, it is not. It is only a slice of the whole story, and when used as evidence of righteousness or selfish gain, it can be dangerous.

Every person follows their own truth until they arrive at the spiritual truth we all have in common, which excludes no one. This is how humans expand and integrate with the Divine intelligence. We connect through our energy centers, working through the different vibrational obstacles until we grieve what we once believed to be true, and replace that belief with a new one that includes more, cycling up until all our energy centers are connected to each other and the Divine.

The mind's need to seek understanding through separation causes a misconception of our spiritual goal of integration and has left us confused about many truths:

Truth 1: There are many races of beings, but only one human race in which all Earthlings are included.

Truth 2: Each culture and geographical area where humans live contributes information about the collective human design.

Truth 3: People will incarnate over the millennia in different bodies, different eras, diverse cultures, and different traditions, with unique societal norms, all as wisdom teachers of how the world works.

Truth 4: Each life will be tasked with understanding human nature, integrating our spiritual bodies with our physical bodies, and leveling up our consciousness to recognize our unity.

It is through these four spiritual Truths that our ancestral and cultural trauma plays out. There is no "superior" people, color, or race of beings, only unique expressions of the Divine imbibing in the Universe and the multiplicity of dimensions within.

Changing the story over time

Science is just beginning to find evidence that human life on planet Earth has been here much longer than previously thought. With every new scientific notion there is a spiritual one that has preceded it. There will always be a discrepancy between scientific understanding and spiritual understanding; science represents what people are ready to know, and spiritual understanding represents the Divine Truth. Both are valuable and personify one's journey of awareness. To understand the magnitude of human potential and impact, we must follow the path of a soul through the thousands of stories it will tell. An individual life consciousness grows in experience and understanding through each incarnation.

A soul can experience being Black, Brown, White, or Asian—and being Indigenous to each of the continental first nation's tribes. A soul can have experienced being rich or poor, rational or insane, consciously aware or unconsciously reactive. They can experience living in many countries and cultures and speaking multiple languages. They can experience slavery from both sides: the perpetrator and the victim. They can participate in all the 4,000-plus recognized world religions, or they can be agnostic or atheist. They can be a lover and a fighter, male and female, and gender fluid, transgender, and any place on the continuum of sexual orientation. They can be born with one or many souls in tow or decide to tap out midstream to offer another soul the use of their body (called a walk-in). A soul can spend lifetimes contributing to what ails society until they change their mind and become a part of the solution.

From a spiritual perspective, all these roles are sacred. It is impossible to be right until you have been wrong (wrong being the actions that cause chaos and negative outcomes). We will know compassion only from learning the vast space in between us. Every religion offers us precepts to live by, but our true expansion comes from being accountable for embracing the duality of life, and taking responsibility for every choice we make, despite those agreed-upon principles. With every incarnation our story changes over time, and through our grief of times past, we begin to know ourselves, open our hearts to others, and awaken within us the divinity that connects us all.

Generational grief

It is no secret that the experiences of our parents and their parents (and so on) create a natural blueprint for how we, as their descendants, will live our lives should we choose to accept this pattern. If you do not know what came before, you are at a loss for the information you need to choose a new path forward. Generational grief presents in two diverse ways: how families work through major tragedies such as war or collective trauma and process their grief through multiple generations, and the spiritual, mental, emotional, and physical DNA limitations of each generation. Not every group will have an ability to conceptualize the root causes of their ailments or be able to find the remedies that promote their healing.

Colonialism is a perfect dynamic to use as an example of what I mean. Colonizers (anywhere on the globe) acted in the interest of their own needs and as their nearsighted altruism dictated, to remedy and build the world they lived in. However, from their basic (selfish) understanding and limited information of the times, they had no space to consider the cost of their actions to other tribes, their cultures, their needs and ideals, and the impact to the planet.

Can we say that many of the colonizers were sociopaths with ideas of grandeur and delusional expectations? Certainly, many were in fact criminals, and others with their good intentions sought to create a better world but did not respond when those in power began their reign of criminal behavior.

Did every single person who promoted or followed along with the colonization understand or care about the impact this forward movement would have for everyone? No.

Was manipulation and violence the only way to achieve forward movement at the time? Yes. (In the context that it is what happened, and if there had been another way, then that would have happened.)

Are they all responsible? Yes.

Have they all reincarnated in multiple distinct roles in the same dynamic to receive a deeper understanding, today? Most likely.

From a spiritual perspective the question here is not about right or wrong, good or evil, black or white, victim or perpetrator, or any other dualist pairing you can come up with; it is only about the impact and consequences of the choices we make. The ideology of doing something "wrong" points only to the severity of the impact on the majority of the people. The ideology of doing something "right" points to the ease or efficiency of doing something with the largest positive impact for the fewest.

Certainly, the concept of righteousness became bastardized over the centuries as the Industrial Revolution began to take hold all over the globe. We began to witness the lack of fluidity in pushing forward in erecting great buildings, roads, and infrastructure, all the while establishing big business and government. Along the way, ignoring or obfuscating the impact on the people and planet, or fighting to overcome that impact through marketing, lies, and manipulation to everyone, including ourselves. If every individual alive on the planet today could go back in time to the life in which they made a choice that compromised the well-being of the collective and themselves, the world would be a different place.

Unfortunately, there can be no do-overs, so this imaginative thinking leads us to the closest possibility we have to reconciliation: Transformative Grief. The truth is if we could have done better, we would have done better. Now we can do it differently. We have too much information to continue to make choices that devastate each other and Mother Earth. Transpersonal grief is the mechanism that will help us become honest about accepting the conditions of today and paving a common perspective that serves everyone instead of only a few. It is up to each generation going forward to assist with the collective ideology and world culture of inclusion that will pave the way for our survival.

CULTURAL TRAUMA

It has been proven that there is only one human race, so why then do we feel the need to continue the illusion that the color of our skin defines our race? This commonly made assumption exists in our psyche and our language; even so, we all bleed red. It only perpetuates the illusion of difference and separation, and even superiority.

All people are human on this planet (unless, of course, you are an extraterrestrial passing for human), and our uniqueness is born of our culture's traditions, which are based on the location where the first nations from which we descend lived in the beginning. Over the millennia and through time and travel, we adapted to new locations and changed our habits (some cultures straying further than others). This is the collective "birth" story for us all.

With the elements of every different culture, religion, or spiritual belief that has evolved, we learned to survive and live with Mother Earth and the other beings in our environment. Although, at the end of every major transitional cycle, humans have not made the cut. We shall see what we do next. Culture is the defining and distinctive expression of humanity, not race. With every collective planetary shift humans live through, so do the traumas of those who came before us. They will lay the groundwork for the future atrocities that will build, shape, and transform the world we live in, the humans we become, and the survival of all the other beings that live here.

Racism

Not a house in the country ain't packed to the rafters with some dead Negro's grief.

—Baby Suggs, in Toni Morrison's *Beloved*[1]

In the United States of America, racism is the most long-standing cultural trauma that we have experienced, and it affects every person in this country today. Either we are knowingly perpetrating it, unknowingly perpetrating it, consciously reevaluating our bias, or a victim of it. In 2020, more than half the entire population of the US was white (non-Hispanic), approximately sixty million more than all other ethnicities combined.[2] People who live in this country have much to reconcile, and grieving is the key.

You may feel affronted by my statements above. You might say to yourself, "I do not participate in racism; this does not affect me." But the truth is, every person participates in one of these ways: creating it, perpetuating it, refusing it, articulating it, understanding it, grieving it, or changing it—consciously or unconsciously, we do. The only way to get to the empathy that reveals the grief is to pick a category and get to work. You see, the founding fathers of our country believed they were doing the right thing by coming here; they believed they had the right to come into an already inhabited land and make it their own by any means necessary—we cannot undo that. Who knows what life each of us was living at that time, right?

Our goal here is not to place blame; it's not helpful. Our goal is to recognize the deliberate or unconscious bias that the system we all share perpetuates, and to be accountable for our placement or vibration in it. Every person in this country contributes something to the whole; that is a powerful responsibility. In the past, there have been many who remained on the sidelines, pushing down their feelings or ignoring the experiences of others, but today it is all out in the open. Believe it or not, that's progress. You cannot process your grief or amend how you think, feel, or live until you accept that you share a past and a future with everyone here—and until you become accountable for your current, everyday way of thinking and behavior.

One of the disservices we have done to the healing process in this country is that we've put a price tag on it. There are still native tribes in the state of Pennsylvania that have not been recognized by the federal government, despite the census showing more than 4 percent of the total population as Native American and

---

1 (Morrison 2007)
2 (Population, n.d.)

Alaskan Natives living in the state[3]—and the reason is money. People are less likely to acknowledge uncomfortable truths if they believe they will be held accountable financially. Victims need the truth acknowledged to move forward, and when they cannot get it, they use the justice system to seek that accountability. But what do you do when the justice system is biased?

Indeed, this is a complicated, never-ending condition with many moving parts, in which we all are tasked with the obligation to begin somewhere. Why not yourself? You are the only person you can control right now. Start with your own inventory on racism. Acknowledge or admit to your role and contribution to it (knowingly perpetrating it, unknowingly promoting it, consciously reevaluating your bias, or being a victim of it). Yes, this is opening a wound that is painful, but it's just you: right here, right now. No one is asking you to be vulnerable to others, just yourself. Breathe.

1. What is my relationship to racism?
2. How do I contribute to the racist system I live in?
3. How do I feel about Black, Brown, White, or Asian people?
4. What do I know about the experiences of Black, Brown, White, or Asian people?
5. Are there events or situations that have led me to the conclusions I have come to?
6. Where do I hold this bias in my physical body, and toward whom?
7. How does having bias make me feel?
8. Is my bias my fault?

That last question is an important one. The truth is that everyone today has grown up in a racist system that holds many entitlements when you are white. Our parents, their parents, their parents' parents, and so on and so forth have grown up in this conditioning from whatever vantage point. Inevitably, you have received some form of conditioning in our educational system; schoolbooks; library books; governing laws, rules, and regulations; social systems; organizations; or the penal system, to name just a few of the threads of learning that show a white bias in our country. This conditioning has diminished you into a state of conflict with yourself. If you bought the hype, you are unconsciously at odds with the

---

3 (United States Census Bureau, n.d.)

Universe, and if you did not, you're at odds within yourself and society (being angry is being at odds with yourself).

Now, certainly, the over four hundred years of American history is not your fault (or your own non-American personal and ancestral history), but it is yours to recognize the painful truths, grieve them, and commit to making the changes you can, the ones within your power to make, and keep moving forward. Grief is about keeping the flow of truth moving, relentlessly, until the personal and societal changes occur . . . and then keep going.

. . .

As we reckon with the truths about race that have emerged since the nation began to pay serious attention, this truth must be remembered: when black folk are not taken seriously, when we are routinely disbelieved, dismissed, or ridiculed for our effort to bear witness to our truths, it only increases the trauma we feel and increases our woeful vulnerability.

—Michael Eric Dyson, *Long Time Coming: Reckoning with Race in America*[4]

. . .

The art of listening

Victims of social bias (whether it be racism, gender, or sexual orientation) do not need or want your pity; they want to be heard and believed. They, like everyone else, want to be recognized equally: equal rights and equal power. Ultimately, however, power is not something that others give you; it is something that you give yourself. You must cultivate your power by becoming self-aware, setting boundaries, communicating your truth, educating yourself about others and the system we live in.

I, myself, struggled with being a sexy, sexual female who was constantly barraged with unwanted male attention. In a puritanical society, if you are sexual, then you're a "whore." Inflammatory language, for sure, but it is the archetypal response. (Even my grammar-correcting program does not like it; it was flagged as offensive, but they had no other suggestions—that sums it up perfectly.) The system we live in is biased in so many hidden and obvious ways.

When I was twenty-three I lived in NYC; I remember this one day as if it were yesterday. I spent the entire day running errands, going on a job interview, and stopping at a coffee shop—I arrived home in the late afternoon. I was grief strick-

---

4   (Dyson 2020)

en and exhausted. I must have interfaced with at least thirty people that day, some I knew but most I did not, and every single one of them made a comment about my breasts. Every. Single. One.

I thought to myself, What is that? It was not plain misogyny, since many women whom I encountered made nonsexual commentary as well. It could not have been what I was wearing; my clothes were not revealing. And I know other people have breasts; they are not new. Why am I questioning what I was wearing? It was their unwanted behavior. These were the thoughts running in my head.

I was angry, frustrated, confused, defeated, and then enraged. I had no language to describe or concept to understand the entitlement that people felt to notice me in a sexual way and then to bring it to my attention. Having been a rape survivor, it was like a thousand paper cuts on my already burned skin. Each one, individually, I could speak to or laugh off—but in their entirety, the pain was excruciating.

That day was a real turning point for me. It was spirit's way of showing me opportunities to stand up for myself and set boundaries, and from that point on, that is what I learned to do. I did not want to blame others for responding to me, but it was my job to reroute their focus or turn them away. It was my job to show them how to respect me, not respond in anger and perpetuate the negative feelings.

A few years back, I went into my local copy store to pick up some professional headshots I had copied. There were two young men working there, and they were laughing as I walked in. The one with whom I was most familiar came over and said his friend wanted to know if I was a porn star. I responded back:

"Now why would he think that? Hey, you, come over here for a minute. My name is Tracee; what's yours? Now, why would you think I was a porn star, and why would you think it was any of your business?"

"I don't know."

"How about this. If I were a porn star and I wanted you to know it, trust that I'd tell you. Anything other than that, why don't you keep your thoughts to yourself?"

"Okay, I am sorry," he responded.

In truth, at that point in my life, I was no longer frustrated, mad, offended, or surprised by his behavior, which I am sure allowed me to address it in a peaceful way. I also found that because I had grieved the idea of people sexualizing me, it "felt" less important for me to bring it to his attention, but that did not mean I should not address it.

To listen to someone is like feeling their heartbeat in your hands. A sacred sharing of honor. When you do this, spiritually, you both connect and become empowered, even when listening is difficult because what you are hearing is uncomfortable. The discomfort you feel is your grief showing you where your disempowerment lives in your body. We experience discomfort only when we have not been truthful with ourselves, and the grief is still hiding. Listening to others shows us that we too have stories to tell.

The art of inquiry

The best way to address any form of bias is getting to know the people who are the object of your bias. Taking an interest in someone's personal experience or pain creates a bridge to understanding and a common ground you can share. It is true that many of the burdens we carry are deeply rooted in the fundamental teachings we may have received, but as adults, our beliefs, ideologies, and education are our responsibility. Just because someone wants their belief to be Truth does not mean it is.

Take your education upon yourself. Read books and articles about topics that are different from your own experiences. Choose movies, television, and music that differ from your norm. And then have conversations with people different from yourself. Your goal is not to discuss racism or social bias; it is to meet everyone on the common ground you share and get to know them for the unique humans they are. Have conversations about family, friends, and interests. Ask open-ended questions. Be with others as you would like them to be with you.

Opening your world in this way will stir the grief you have inside about how you may have excluded others in your life on the basis of fear or bias. The reckoning comes with knowledge, receptivity, and empowerment; you alone are the agent of change in your life. Make no mistake about it; every time someone experiences not being included in a group, situation, or conversation because of something they cannot change about themselves, it becomes a spiritual and emotional burden they carry, possibly never feeling safe enough in life to grieve it.

GRIEVING THE SYSTEM YOU LIVE IN

Before you can change the system in which you live, you must strengthen yourself. You must grieve the way things are: the fact you have been lied to by the authorities and historians in your life, the ingrained bias against Black and Brown people, the unconscious misogyny in which even women participate, and the enormous fear-based beliefs people engage in. All these things are true; some statistically, some spiritually, but all are true. Accepting these conditions as a starting point is paramount to preparing yourself to fight the powers that be to achieve justice for all. If you grew up in the USA, you have said it a million times: "with liberty and justice for all." The Pledge of Allegiance we repeated must now be made true by each of us becoming self-actualized first.

Grieving and accepting the unfair circumstances around you allows you the space to prepare your vulnerabilities, actualize patience, cultivate verbal and actional responses, and engage your compassion. In Buddhism, one of the most popular beings in their iconography is Quan Yin, a representation of ruthless compassion. The expression of ruthless compassion is the teacher for these times of social and political unrest. The people we elect to office can really only be an expression of our deepest collective fears of authority. Of course, some will veer away from that low expectation and rise above or below it; some will show true leadership and good example, while others will become elected criminals. No conspiracy here, just honesty. Once we can comprehend that our system is a representation of our collective hopes and fears, we can become the people we want to represent us.

Again, grieving and mourning in this context are allowing the rage you feel to flow through your body with painful emotion, transforming the brain and clearing the heart for the changes to come. The system we live in is perpetuated by all of us living here, and we have the power to be different in it. We must be peaceful and relentless in our convictions, ruthlessly compassionate toward all people and Earth who sustain us. Eventually, all masks of solidarity will give way to the Truth underneath; it is with this vibration of acceptance we will find connection and unity in some way.

Politics and the loss of identity and idealism

Politics is a public hashing of ideals by those we elect to office. Spiritually speaking, the politicians we hire can only possibly represent the lowest common denominator of the collective; in other words, the people who represent the middle-ground vibration of beliefs, ideals, and possibilities of any community. For example, if you live in a community where, say, 65 percent of the people who live in it struggle with food insecurity, you are more likely to elect an idealist whose job it is to change the hearts and minds of the people in the group, or a money grubber who capitalizes on the lack in the community they are empowered to help.

Now, that is not to say there aren't good politicians, but it is the energetic reason; the ones who could be most effective may not be able to tolerate the biased political system long enough to make a difference. Therefore, changing the political system begins with each of us, individually, coming to terms with ourselves and changing what no longer serves us in our lives. And most of all, grieving our way to believing that we can change the most desperate of our challenges. The more the collective changes, the more its needs will change, and those who are empowered to govern those changes will be transformed as well.

Changing the system you live in

As an Empath, I have been vulnerable to the experiences and energies of others and the collective. As a young adult, I soon recognized that all I had gone through (the life of isolation and solitude I lived as a child, the death of my father before puberty, a well-meaning but prone-to-few-words mother, no college, and life in the Big Apple starting at eighteen) was all for my benefit. Had my circumstances been any but those, it would have put me in even-deeper conflict with myself and my surrounding, than I was already. My father, while well meaning and deeply spiritual (something we shared), was white and grew up in the 1950s; his unconscious bias and polite misogyny alone would have triggered the enormous rage my spirit contained.

Each of us carries soul information that informs who we are, our starting viewpoint, and the obstacles and solutions that will awaken in us as the world and we progress. Globally, over the course of history, groups of people have been murdered for being who they were or for practicing a certain religion, by colonizers seeking to expand into surrounding lands and sometimes for pure hate.

These people who died in such tyranny—without the benefit of grief, understanding, or forgiveness—must find them somehow (over the millennia, this most likely includes all of us). It is not a wonder that groups of people all over the globe have literally "awoken" to hatred, violent fear, and delusional righteousness in what seems like overnight. The mass-marketing tactics of "say it over and over and it's true" at play in corporate and political messaging only exacerbate and challenge our spiritual and emotional integrity.

No matter; as individuals we are still responsible for what we receive and accept as truth, and we are accountable for the actions we take and the impact they have on others. It is these patterns that create our karma over time (karma is the reaction to actions taken). This is the main teaching that empathy has to offer. One must learn to override the sway of the collective and to stand in one's own integrity and knowledge of what is right or wrong, and be able to challenge and govern oneself, first.

Divine intelligence will be the teacher of Truths such as equality, love, compassion, and freedom—not humans. We can enact them only for ourselves. As we do, it is certain to cause a mass "awakening" of heartfulness, confidence, peacefulness, and the unwillingness to be moved by dictators and bullies. Assuredly, we will get there—one changed heart at a time.

THE JOURNEY OF FORGIVENESS

Grief promotes forgiveness, or forgiveness promotes grief—two directions towards the heart of the matter. When the heart "breaks," it expands and generates chemicals that allow for deeper understanding of the dynamics at play. Forgiveness is the process of becoming neutral again after a trauma has taken place, a returning to the zero point a wiser person. When we forgive, we do not necessarily forget; we detach from the focus we have offered our tragedy, choosing transformation and clarity to take the place of the pain we've harbored. This can be the journey of a lifetime.

Humans over the centuries appear to have forgotten the most-abominable tribulations of our times, but the spirit always knows. On a soul level, our guilt will always express itself through emotions such as hatred (deep-layered attachment to something), bitterness, resentment, fear, or shame. All these emotions alert us to the presence of unprocessed spiritual trauma and grief, which must be transmuted before forgiveness can be realized.

Forgiveness is something that we feel; saying it is so is only the beginning of the journey. When we say, "I forgive you," we are committing to the process of recognizing the attachment we engage to our pain and to the events that caused it. Forgiveness requires that we seek whatever understanding we need of what happened and why, and ultimately, that we forgive ourselves and all others involved. Especially in cultural traumas, where there are no clean hands.

Sometimes forgiveness begins with the collective heart before it trickles down into the individuals who compose the whole. The final layer of forgiveness you will cultivate is the need for spiritual accountability, with which we all are imprinted. The aspect of our humanity that must forgive itself for the lives we have lived, the mayhem we have caused, the times we could have spoken up but did not, and the sheer participation in viewpoints or relationships that caused pain for us and others. All the choices made that created the spiritual patterns we must now overcome to claim peace.

No matter where you begin with your relationship to forgiveness, the blessings are significant and bountiful—worthy of the challenging work that will bring them. For you will traverse every deep, dark crevice of your psyche and spirit, searching for the unspoken mystery of who you are, on every level. Masterfully uncovering details hidden away for lifetimes until the revelation is upon you for the healing of your heart, family, community, gender, ethnicity, and species, and any other collective to which you belong. This is the true purpose of a life well lived.

A Ritual for Vision

Affirmation: I am free to see the world through the eyes of others. I open my heart to compassion for every being.

What you'll need for your ritual:
    three jar candles: white, purple, and blue
    a fire source (a lighter or match)
    a paper or cloth with a picture of the cosmos to place on the
        sacred altar area
    one piece of moldavite
    mason jar
    cheesecloth or gauze
    paper and pen
    juniper or piñon incense for offering
    one medium-sized metal pot to burn herbs (and charcoal if needed)

Herbs you'll need:
Sunflower: Is for a fresh new beginning and for guidance, vision, and the solar energy to transform grief. Sunflowers follow the sun and shower the ethereal body with life-giving solar energies. Helps loosen stuck energy in the solar plexus.

Bergamot: Calls on a new start and has an uplifting fragrance (herb or essential oil). A great herb to use when one is not sure where to go or what to do.

Solomon's Seal Root: Provides ancient wisdom, clarity, and knowledge from the past to help one with guidance and direction in life.

Beeswax: Full of vibrancy, vitality, and magick, beeswax can help one maintain a vision for oneself. Hold a small amount of beeswax (or beeswax candle) in hand as you meditate and petition for a vision of transformation, new self-realization, and other goals. Let it burn and know that the prayer is sent to the Universe.

Optional:

Clary Sage essential oil: Helps clear the mind and opens the psychic senses for visions, mental clarity, and clear mind and body, so that the mind/body are aligned.

Directions for using essential oil: You may dab one drop of oil on pulse points (make sure to do a small patch test for sensitivity). Or add three drops into a cleansing bath before the burning ritual. You may also inhale from the bottle as you go through the ritual.

Begin your ritual by cleaning and clearing an area in the center of your home. Collect all the items for your altar and put them in the cleared space. Place the herbs in the mason jar and hold it in hand while repeating the affirmation (you may also say prayers of your choice for healing). Exhale your breath onto the herbs to release the energies of the affirmation.

Prepare your cleansing bath. Run hot water in the bathtub or, if you don't have one, bring a pot of water to boil. Take the mason jar and dump the herbs and flowers onto a piece of cheesecloth or gauze and make a sachet, tying it off at the top so the mixture won't spill into the drain. Add your sachet to the bath or boiling pot and let simmer for five minutes. Write your vision question on a piece of paper:

What is the gift I have to contribute to my community, right now?

Place the paper under the purple candle on your altar and light the wick.

Get in the bath or get a bucket and create a foot soak by pouring the contents of the pot in the bucket, and let the water cool until it reaches a comfortable temperature for your feet. Sit, taking deep breaths until you relax. Close your eyes. Focus on the gift you have to contribute to your community, right now. Pay attention to the thoughts, feelings, pictures, and sensations that come into your awareness. Stay in the bath or foot soak as long as you'd like.

Once your soak is complete, sit with a paper and pen or computer and write the revelations that came to mind in as much detail as you can imagine. Allow any additional information to channel through, and continue to write until it feels complete. When you are ready, on this day or another, read what you have written and begin to make a plan to use your special gift to contribute to your community.

Pay close attention during the week to any signs, symbols, or synchro-nicities you may come across that bring you further information about your gift and how to express it. Write them down. Also, pay attention to any dreams, daydreams, or visions you may have. Write them down. At the end of the week, go over any themes that came up for you, and contemplate their messages.

Performing this ritual may inspire a grief response, and that's okay. Allow yourself to feel anything that comes up. The release and rejuvenation you seek will come in many ways over time. Give yourself permission to go with the flow.

LIVING A GRIEF-FILLED LIFE BRINGS JOY

Transformative Grief is the embodiment of the profound collision of heaven and Earth through humanity—alchemizing and empowering us by divulging the truth on every level. As we shed our illusions about grief and sorrow as being detrimental to our health or being more powerful than we are, we will open to the beauty of accessing our strength from the deepest recesses of our mind, body, and spirit through grief.

Beginning on the day of our birth, we have each been seeded with spiritual information that will be revealed by grief throughout our lives. It is our willingness to process daily these subtle ebbs and flows of emotion that guarantees the removal of energy that is unnecessary for us to harbor, and to disclose what is valuable for us moving forward.

Give yourself the gift of magic that grief brings.

Every day, be mindful of the rise and fall of your emotions and the insights that appear. No matter large or small, these blissful moments of truth and the devastating plunges into darkness will always give way to a lighter, metamorphosed you. Only you can make the choice for yourself to open your heart to a living compassion and love of yourself, others, and the world around you.

10,000 Blessings to You,

Tracee Dunblazier, Los Angeles, 2022

BIBLIOGRAPHY

Buist, E. *This Party Is Dead: Grief, Joy, and Spilled Rum at the World's Death Festivals*. London: Unbound, 2021.

Cobain, B. *When Nothing Matters Anymore*. Golden Valley, MN: Free Spirit, 2007.

Diangelo, R. *Nice Racism: How Progressive White People Perpetuate Racial Harm*. Boston: Beacon, 2021.

Dougy Center. *After a Murder: A Workbook for Grieving Kids*. Portland, OR: Dougy Center: The National Center for Grieving Children & Families, n.d.

Dougy Center. *After a Suicide Death: An Activity Book for Grieving Kids*. Portland, OR: Dougy Center: The National Center for Grieving Children & Families, n.d.

Dougy Center. *35 Ways to Help a Grieving Child*. Portland, OR: Dougy Center: The National Center for Grieving Children & Families, 2010.

Dougy Center. *When Death Impacts Your School: A Guide for School Administrators*. Portland, OR: Dougy Center: The National Center for Grieving Children & Families, 2003.

Dunblazier, T. *Conquer Your Karmic Relationships: Heal Spiritual Trauma to Open Your Heart and Restore Your Soul*. Baton Rouge, LA: GoTracee, 2020.

Dunblazier, T. *Heal Your Soul History: Activate the True Power of Your Shadow*. Baton Rouge, LA: GoTracee, 2017.

Dunblazier, T. *Master Your Inner World: Embrace Your Power with Joy*. Baton Rouge, LA: GoTracee, 2016.

Dyson, M. E. *Long Time Coming: Reckoning with Race in America*. New York: St. Martin's, 2020.

Fehling, K. B., and E. A. Selby. "Suicide in DSM-5: Current Evidence for the Proposed Suicide Behavior Disorder and Other Possible Improvements." *Frontiers in Psychiatry*, February 4, 2021. https://www.frontiersin.org/articles/10.3389/fpsyt.2020.499980/full

Kübler-Ross, E. *On Death and Dying*. New York: Macmillan, 1970.

Kumar, S. M. *Grieving Mindfully: A Compassionate and Spiritual Guide to Coping with Loss*. Oakland, CA: New Harbinger, 2005.

Morrison, T. *Beloved*. New York: Knopf Doubleday, 2007.

"Population." Retrieved from USA Facts. https://usafacts.org/data/topics/people-society/population-and-demographics/population-data/population/.

Psychology Today Staff. "How the Brain Develops." *Psychology Today*, n.d. https://www.psychologytoday.com/us/basics/neuroscience/how-the-brain-develops.

Rand, H. *Everything You Wanted to Know about the Afterlife: But Were Afraid to Ask*. New York: Atria Paperback, an imprint of Simon & Schuster, 2020.

Salaam, Y. *Better Not Bitter: Living on Purpose in the Pursuit of Racial Justice*. New York: Grand Central, 2021.

Tansley, T. *For Women Who Grieve: Embracing Life after the Death of Your Partner*. Toronto: Crossing Press, 1995.

Trungpa, C. *Smile at Fear: Awakening the True Heart of Bravery*. Boulder, CO: Shambhala, 2009.

Tzu, L. *Lao Tzu Quotes*. BrainyQuote, https://www.brainyquote.com/authors/lao-tzu-quotes.

United States Census Bureau. (n.d.). Census.gov. Retrieved from Quick Facts: Pennsylvania, https://www.census.gov/quickfacts/fact/table/PA/RHI325219#RHI325219.

Ursinus, L. *The Body Clock in Traditional Chinese Medicine: Understanding Our Energy Cycles for Health and Healing*. Rochester, VT: Earth Dancer, an imprint of Inner Traditions, 2021.

Villoldo, A., and A. O'Neil. *The Shaman's Book of Living and Dying: Tools for Healing Body, Mind, and Spirit*. Newburyport, MA: Hampton Roads, 2021.

Walsh-Burke, K. *Grief and Loss: Theories and Skills for Helping Professionals*. Boston: Pearson Education, 2006.

Weeks, O. D., and C. Johnson, eds. *When All the Friends Have Gone: A Guide for Aftercare Providers*. New York: Baywood, 2001.

Weller, F. *The Wild Edge of Sorrow: Rituals of Renewal and the Sacred Work of Grief*. Berkeley, CA: North Atlantic Books, 2015.

Wolfelt, A. D. *The Understanding Your Grief Support Group Guide: Starting and Leading a Bereavement Support Group*. Fort Collins, CO: Companion Press, an imprint of the Center for Loss and Life Transition, 2004.